What We Talk about When We Talk about Creative Writing

NEW WRITING VIEWPOINTS

Series Editor: Graeme Harper, *Oakland University, Rochester, USA*
Associate Editor: Dianne Donnelly, *University of South Florida, USA*

The overall aim of this series is to publish books which will ultimately inform teaching and research, but whose primary focus is on the analysis of creative writing practice and theory. There will also be books which deal directly with aspects of creative writing knowledge, with issues of genre, form and style, with the nature and experience of creativity, and with the learning of creative writing. They will all have in common a concern with excellence in application and in understanding, with creative writing practitioners and their work, and with informed analysis of creative writing as process as well as completed artefact.

Full details of all the books in this series and of all our other publications can be found on http://www.multilingual-matters.com, or by writing to Multilingual Matters, St Nicholas House, 31–34 High Street, Bristol BS1 2AW, UK.

NEW WRITING VIEWPOINTS: 14

What We Talk about When We Talk about Creative Writing

Edited by
Anna Leahy

MULTILINGUAL MATTERS
Bristol • Buffalo • Toronto

Library of Congress Cataloging in Publication Data
Names: Leahy, Anna - editor.
Title: What We talk about When We Talk about Creative Writing/Edited by Anna Leahy.
Description: Bristol; Buffalo: Multilingual Matters, [2016] | Series: New Writing
  Viewpoints: 14 | Includes bibliographical references.
Identifiers: LCCN 2016011329| ISBN 9781783096015 (hbk : alk. paper) | ISBN
  9781783096008 (pbk : alk. paper) | ISBN 9781783096046 (kindle)
Subjects: LCSH: Creative writing (Higher education)—Study and teaching. | English
  language—Rhetoric--Study and teaching (Higher) | Authorship—Study and teaching
  (Higher) | Writing centers.
Classification: LCC PE1404 .W4555 2016 | DDC 808/.0420711--dc23 LC record available
  at https://lccn.loc.gov/2016011329

British Library Cataloguing in Publication Data
A catalogue entry for this book is available from the British Library.

ISBN-13: 978-1-78309-601-5 (hbk)
ISBN-13: 978-1-78309-600-8 (pbk)

Multilingual Matters
UK: St Nicholas House, 31–34 High Street, Bristol BS1 2AW, UK.
USA: UTP, 2250 Military Road, Tonawanda, NY 14150, USA.
Canada: UTP, 5201 Dufferin Street, North York, Ontario M3H 5T8, Canada.

Website: www.multilingual-matters.com
Twitter: Multi_Ling_Mat
Facebook: https://www.facebook.com/multilingualmatters
Blog: www.channelviewpublications.wordpress.com

The policy of Multilingual Matters/Channel View Publications is to use papers that are
natural, renewable and recyclable products, made from wood grown in sustainable forests. In the manufacturing process of our books, and to further support our policy, preference is given to printers that have FSC and PEFC Chain of Custody certification. The FSC
and/or PEFC logos will appear on those books where full certification has been granted
to the printer concerned.

Typeset by Nova Techset Private Limited, Bengaluru & Chennai, India.
Printed and bound in Great Britain by Short Run Press Ltd.

Contents

Acknowledgments

Some chapters previously appeared elsewhere, sometimes under different titles and/or in different versions. Together, the contributors updated all previously published work included in this new collection. The authors are grateful to those editors who invested in our work along the way.

Fiction Writers Review: 'Where Are We Going Next in Creative Writing Pedagogy'

Mid-American Review: 'Good Counsel: Creative Writing, the Imagination, and Teaching'

Brevity: excerpt from 'Writerly Reading in the Creative Writing Course'

New Writing: 'Text(ure), Modeling, Collage: Creative Writing and Arts Pedagogy'

The Huffington Post: 'Creative Writing (Re)Defined'

Bookslut: 'The First Book'

Hippo Reads: excerpt from 'Political, Practical and Philosophical Considerations for the Future'

I am grateful for the opportunity to work with the contributors of this collection; their collaborative spirit made this project work. Special thanks to Stephanie Vanderslice, who is there when I need feedback on a piece of scholarly writing or commiseration over how to balance the demands of our careers. I am also grateful for Anna Roderick, Sarah Williams, Florence McClelland and the many others at Multilingual Matters who shepherded this project to completion; their patience and guidance made this a better book.

Thanks to those at Chapman University who've fostered my creative and scholarly career and to Dorland Mountain Arts Colony, where none of this book was written, but where I wrote essays and poems during residencies so that I could focus on this scholarly project for the rest of this past year, along with teaching and administration. Thanks to my family – my sister, my aunt, and especially Doug, my collaborator for more than 25 years – for their care.

Foreword

New Writing Viewpoints: Ten Years Onward

I have been the Series Editor of New Writing Viewpoints for just over 10 years now, from the launch of the series. But the fact that the series exists, and has grown and blossomed over these past 10 years has very little to do with me but rather is because of two key factors.

Firstly, New Writing Viewpoints exists and has flourished because Multilingual Matters (MLM) took a risk in launching a book series for a discipline that, while in many ways well established in certain parts of the world and in a certain manner, was beginning to grow internationally in new and interesting ways. Those plain words 'new' and 'interesting' are used to suggest by their open-endedness that not one thing but many things were going on, defined by different national educational histories and by individual contributions to the research and study of creative writing, of varying reach and influence. The credit for the launch and subsequent growth of the series thus goes in this first instance, unadornedly, to the Grover family, whose publishing success the MLM publishing house has been, to Anna Roderick, the Commissioning Editor, who continues to have an eye for a good idea and a creative sense that deserves full acknowledgement, and to the small but lively team at MLM, from Production to Marketing, who got professionally behind a decidedly quirky notion, given their expertise back then was really in some cognate but certainly different disciplines. Like an Earthling family who had decided to adopt a Martian baby, MLM set about immediately making the atmosphere hospitable, and because of that effort, and the team's encouragement, the New Writing Viewpoints series grew and began to flourish.

Secondly, New Writing Viewpoints was supported and has been successful because, not much more than 10 years back, the discipline of creative writing in universities and colleges around the world began to seek to put more of a material shape to discussions and debates that had gained some momentum over the 10 years previous. Whether in Great Britain or Australia, whether because of a questioning of longer established notions about the discipline's shape in the USA, whether through the lens of the study of English literature or language in countries where English is not the first language, or whether because the critical study of literary texts from beyond or after the acts of literary creation began to some to seem disempowering, 10 years ago the discipline of creative writing had found a distinctive international momentum and was seeking a venue for the publication of research discoveries, the exploration of ideas and the opening up of debates that could lead the way forward for future knowledge.

That assuredly all sounds quite grand, but the origins of the New Writing Viewpoints series were essentially humble. Noticing something interesting was happening at the then still young journal, *New Writing: the International for the Practice and Theory of Creative Writing* (which MLM had similarly agreed to launch, not that many years before) the thought of how some of those interesting articles might look in a longer, book form began to take shape at MLM.

Even she might have forgotten the moment, but I still very much recall the email conversation initiated by Anna Roderick about the possibility of a book series. I remember thinking, and I have not revealed this to Anna previously, something along the lines of 'is she saying what I think she's saying?' I remember thinking too that this was exactly what the discipline needed, and if we could progress such a thing the results would likely be difficult to measure in the first instance and difficult to ignore if we were able to somehow continue long enough to have an impact. Those hopes aside, and Anna will perhaps remember this well enough, the plan was merely to 'let's see how things go'.

The first time I felt that some real progress was being made was when I heard someone quote from a New Writing Viewpoints book at a conference. I believe it was from Carl Vandermeulen's chapter, 'The Double Bind and Stumbling Blocks: A Case Study as an Argument for Authority-Conscious Pedagogy' published in Anna Leahy's *Power and Identity in the Creative Writing Classroom* (2005). Carl later submitted a book manuscript for the series, which was subsequently published as *Negotiating the Personal in Creative Writing* (2011). But that first feeling of progress was around 2007 and at that point the 'series' really only consisted of three books.

It was in 2010 that things began to gain some additional traction, both in terms of reception of books already in the series and in terms of the range of works then being proposed. Dianne Donnelly's *Does the Writing Workshop Still Work?* was published that year. Dianne has joined me in 2015 as Associate Editor of New Writing Viewpoints, and I am absolutely thrilled to have her working with me; but in 2010 we didn't know each other all that well and

I admit it wasn't until I was writing a Foreword for *Does the Writing Workshop Still Work?* that I began to recognize that there was a considerable quality of discussion happening among her contributors to that book. It made me pause for thought. A number of the contributors were people I knew, some well; some were names that I would come to know all the more in the years ahead, people such as Patrick Bizzaro, Tim Mayers, Philip Gross, Willy Maley, Stephanie Vanderslice, Katharine Haake and Joseph Moxley, among others. That they were not all from the same part of the world also seemed to me to be consequential.

By the second decade of the new century, New Writing Viewpoints had indeed published books by authors and editors from the United Kingdom, the United States and Australia, and chapters in those books from authors in Canada, China, Pakistan, New Zealand, Singapore, Ireland and more. But the range of publications had also become much more than merely geographic. That range was also an intellectual and creative range. Some of the writers had emerged from new developments in the doctoral study of creative writing in Great Britain and Australia, some writers came from the USA, either having backgrounds in creative writing MFA programmes or in composition and rhetoric, or in a combination of both, some of the authors had experiences mostly in literature departments, some had expertise in linguistics or in the teaching of English as a Second Language or in education, some were associated with work in the broader creative arts.

In essence these were people from around the world who were shaping the newest discussions, the most investigative debates, the occasionally spirited challenges to the status quo, whether through the practice of creative writing and its critical examination (that is, through what is most often called practice-led research in creative writing) or through varieties of critical examination that either were entirely original or that drew from cognate disciplines and were molding such academic epistemologies to a new and exciting purpose. Not all were thinking the same way, that's for sure, but they were certainly thinking, and researching, thinking and researching in a discipline that was burgeoning here in the early 21st century, the discipline of creative writing.

Further, many of the contributors to New Writing Viewpoints have not only been publishing thoughts about creative writing practices, theories and pedagogies, but actually introducing these into their universities and colleges, trying new ways of teaching as well as exploring topics in their research that have opened up avenues of understanding and indeed shown potential for further research and discovery. Such has been the case in recent work by Nigel McLoughlin, Sara Burnett, Jeri Kroll, Liz Cashdan and Moy McCrory, Jen Webb, Asma Mansoor, Nigel Krauth, Fan Dai, Michael Theune and Bob Broad, Gail Pittaway, Kevin Brophy and Elizabeth MacFarland,

Katharine Coles, or previous work by Tom C. Hunley, Gregory Fraser, David Starkey, Jake Adam York, Mary Ann Cain. . . . The list goes on.

Ten years have passed more quickly than any of us might have imagined possible! In 2015 New Writing Viewpoints published four books: *Towards a Poetics of Creative Writing*, by Dominique Hecq; *Creative Composition: Inspiration and Techniques for Writing Instruction*, edited by Danita Berg and Lori A. May; *Creative Writing and Education*, on which I would not dare to comment; as well *Second Language Creative Writers: Identities and Writing Processes* by Yan Zhao. That single year number exceeds the number of books published in the series between the series launch in 2005 and 2009. But it is of course not simply the increase in the number of books being published that matters, it is that breadth and depth of investigation, the extent of creative writing research, the exploration of ideas, the descriptions of practices and pedagogies, the work being done to advance our understanding.

I am thrilled we are now publishing *What We Talk about When We Talk about Creative Writing*, edited by Anna Leahy, to mark the 10th Anniversary of the New Writing Viewpoints series, which indeed began with Anna's 2005 collection, *Power and Identity in the Creative Writing Classroom*. Anna and her contributors show in their reference 'conversations' that they equally realize that in a 10 year celebration of the entire New Writing Viewpoints series, one book stands in relation to many, both directly and indirectly, and is published to point to the ideas and suggestions of those who are not included here as well as those who have been. It thankfully cannot be otherwise, because New Writing Viewpoints has not sought to publish only one vision, one set of ideals, one collection of authors. Nor has the editing of the series been a matter of finding only those folks who agree with us. There is a kind of editing that apparently works that way, ours is not that kind.

In the years ahead New Writing Viewpoints will continue to believe in the advancement of knowledge in our human practices of writing creatively, in the understanding of these practices, and in the critical investigation of how creative writing happens, what it means, what its actions result in creating, and how creative writing might be researched and taught. If there is anything I wish on a personal level for the series it is that it never loses its sense, so neatly described by Anna Roderick at the series foundation, its sense so well encapsulated in the expression 'let's see how things go'. That openness, that willingness to observe, to explore with no definite sense of what the results might be, to act on a feeling that there is more to know, more to do, more we might discover, is at the heart of New Writing Viewpoints.

Graeme Harper
31 December 2015

Part 1
Introduction

1 Telling Time, Making Use, Turning Together: Conversations in Creative Writing

Anna Leahy

For my part, I have found that interviewing people, exchanging views with peers and friends, and arguing at editorial meetings have been crucial to learning.
Fareed Zakaria (2015: 77)

A roundtable panel at the Associated Writing Programs Conference (now the Association of Writers and Writing Programs (AWP)), led to the edited collection *Power and Identity in the Creative Writing Classroom: The Authority Project* in which several contributors wrote about the theoretical and practical matters of teaching creative writing at college and graduate levels.

That book was a foundation for new growth in creative writing scholarship that has made our discipline stronger and more vibrant. Ten years ago, *Power and Identity in the Creative Writing Classroom* (Leahy, 2005) launched the New Writing Viewpoints series, a bold and welcome move by Multilingual Matters that rode a wave of interest and discussion about creative writing, teaching and higher education. Other publishers, citing a rule of thumb that edited collections don't sell as well as single-author books, dismissed the manuscript because of its strength: a variety of perspectives and voices. Although my intention for that book was, as Stephanie Vanderslice writes in its afterword, to stake 'a vital claim for creative writing's place on the American academic landscape' (2005: 214), the book and series has spurred the emergence of what many scholars now call creative writing studies. The risk we all took 10 years ago paid off. Although that book and this new one have a clear American focus, they are both part of national and global discussions and changes in creative writing and higher education.

This new book takes the concept of an edited collection to its extreme, pushing the possibilities of scholarship and collaboration. All authors in this book are proof that creative writing matters and can be rewarding over the long haul, and that there exist many ways to do what we do as writers and as teachers. I tell my students that their critical writing should be in conversation with the existing scholarship on the topic, and the contributors to this book have put that into practice in a literal manner. *What We Talk about When We Talk about Creative Writing* captures a wide swathe of ideas on pedagogy, on programs, on the profession and on careers.

The Academy as Creative Space

Creative writing remains a newcomer to the academy as a separate discipline, with first distinct coursework offered in the late 19th century and distinct programs burgeoning only in the last few decades. The arts challenge day-to-day assumptions and traditions about what is academic. Too often we talk as if we, and our wild ways, still don't belong. Colleges and universities are, however, ideal environments for fostering creativity and, therefore, for practicing creative writing. Pedagogy and practice go hand in hand, reinforcing each other. To recognize and embrace academia as a creative space empowers us.

Steven Johnson, author of *Where Good Ideas Come From* (2010), argues that the coffee house of the late 17th century served a crucial role in the Enlightenment. The space itself allowed people with various interests to gather together, share their thinking and test out possibilities. Johnson calls this sort of space 'The Liquid Network', in part because the environment that nurtures creativity is one where ideas flow somewhat unpredictably and where ideas are valued. Contemporary science laboratories function this way, with smart people gathered in a physical space tossing around ideas, questions and frustrations in a seemingly willy-nilly manner. If we apply Johnson's well-researched notions to this book, the contributors to *What We Talk about When We Talk about Creative Writing* can be seen as a critical mass of creative people coming together to accomplish more together than we might individually. Working through topics collectively, we've spurred each other on, supporting and challenging each other into discovery.

Interestingly, Johnson's notions of creative culture sync up well with Richard Florida's arguments in *The Rise of the Creative Class* (2002) and *Who's Your City?* (2008). Some creative endeavors, such as writing, demand periods of isolation, and a given individual may be extraordinarily creative in isolation. But Florida and others argue that the myth of the writer scribbling alone in her garret is long gone. He points to communities built on weak connections, something akin to but more dispersed than Johnson's liquid network, as important for nourishing creativity in society.

Florida's ideas have influenced policies, though more recent scholarship on the creative industries has criticized Florida's loose application of the term *creative* 'as a single, unified entity' (Campbell, 2011: 18) and distinguished his *creative class* from the *creative industries*. Roberta Comunian and her coauthors have examined the relationship between place and creative industries, with particular attention to infrastructure and area governance policies. Our project acknowledges this scholarship in creative industries and puts into practice connectedness and individual and group interaction that Comunian *et al.* might consider 'soft infrastructure' (2010: 6).

UK scholar Daniel Ashton examines universities as playing the primary role in supplying the creative industries with talent and skills. Importantly, he points out that, although degrees related to the creative industries are not a guarantee of a job, 'for those trained in the arts and cultural humanities fields, having an interesting creative job is part of their social identities' (2015: 401). I would argue that this social identity as a creative person who wants to engage in creative work with other creative people is central to creative writing as an academic discipline. Florida remains relevant to this book's discussion because he focuses on people: 'When people – especially talented and creative ones – come together, ideas flow more freely, and as a result individual and aggregate talents increase exponentially: the end result amounts to much more than the sum of the parts' (2008: 66). That aligns with Johnson's claim that a critical mass of creative people fuels the creativity of creative people. Ideas 'rise in liquid networks where connection is valued more than protection' (2010: 245). In an interview on *The Daily Show*, novelist John Irving captured the importance of a creative writing program to his career well when he said that it saved him time. Creative environments, like MFA programs, are both buzzing and patient. As we developed this book, we employed these principles of collaboration that make our work more than the sum of its parts and this moved us further as a group more quickly than we could manage individually.

In *Patronizing the Arts*, Marjorie Garber argues that the university is an ideal place for artists and other makers to flourish because 'universities are full of experts' (2008: 189), 'are already accustomed to managing grants'

(2008: 188) and offer 'space, materials, training, and assessment, as well as a tolerance of imagination, "genius," stubborn dedication, or eccentricity' (2008: 188). In other words, the university has the basic things writers need, just as it has the basic things scientists need. Creative writing is as integral to academia as is science, and our methodologies and creative work are as valuable as cultural contributions and growing bodies of knowledge. While this book challenges some traditional notions of what constitutes scholarship, it supports Garber's assertion that the arts can shape and be shaped by academia. In this book, contributors take advantage of this wealth of expertise as we accommodate some expectations of scholarship, while reshaping what scholarship looks like.

In Robert Frost's poem 'Mending Wall,' the speaker tells his neighbor, who is desperate to repair the stone fence, that he shouldn't worry that the apple trees are going to invade and gobble up the pine cones. The speaker prods further, saying, 'Before I built a wall I'd ask to know/What I was walling in or walling out,/And to whom I was likely to give offense' (1972: 17, lines 32–34). That's exactly the concern of creative individuals. We don't like to wall out ideas, and we needn't let our ideas be walled in. We welcome the collisions inherent in community as much as we seek the isolation necessary to write, and other disciplines can benefit from seeing what we're up to. In other words, *What We Talk about When We Talk about Creative Writing* offers a new model for scholarship, for creative writing as a widening discipline and also for other disciplines that value the single-author model to the exclusion of other useful possibilities that take advantage of the liquid network that is academia.

Frost opposed all sorts of experimentation and the questioning of formal conventions, but Frost's words often seem to encourage innovation and figuring out as we go: 'And then to play. The play's the thing. Play's the thing. All virtue in "as if"' (353). The creative process rests upon *as if*, and the highest ideals of the academy – akin to what Fareed Zakaria calls 'the intellectual adventure' (2015: 61) in which 'writing makes you think' (2015: 72) – encourage us all to contemplate *as if* instead of settling for *as is*.

As if – and the creative process it represents – makes us human. Albert Schweitzer, though he was not talking about creativity, asserted, 'As soon as man does not take his existence for granted, but beholds it as something unfathomably mysterious, thought begins' (2008: 157). *As if* pushes us into thought, forces us not take ourselves or the world around us for granted. By putting ourselves into conversation, every contributor was faced with the *as if* presented by other voices, other perspectives, other contexts than his or her own. A single author in control of an argument can work toward a pat answer; we could not. This book is premised on notions that creative writing is stronger for its position in the academy and that creative writing teachers and scholars must be aware of the *as is* – the status quo – of the academy in order to create the *as if* that opens us up to innovation, alternatives and complementary perspectives.

Adaptations of Ethnography

What We Talk about When We Talk about Creative Writing is purposefully constructed as conversation, in large part because, as outlined in the previous section, innovation emerges from collision – from talk – and the university is full of smart people testing out interesting ideas. Creative writing, a discipline of practice, need not use exclusively the modes of more traditional academic disciplines to do its scholarly work. The conversation mode here is, in part, a challenge to and an addition to traditional academic discourse and positivistic research.

Wendy Bishop contributed to *Power and Identity in the Creative Writing Classroom* shortly before she died, so it seems significant to allow her ideas to shape – and even be misshapen in – this new collection. She advocated what she called 'I-witnessing' in a 1992 article. In that piece, she points out that it's especially difficult for a novice ethnographer to be taken seriously because of the ethical and emotional appeals inherent in such work but that someone who has developed standing in a field – and, I would argue in the case of creative writing, a field that has earned standing – can embark on such work. The 10th anniversary of *Power and Identity in the Creative Writing Classroom* is, then, a good time to adapt a method that draws from and resembles ethnography, to take the scholarly risk that the novice cannot.

Bishop outlines numerous challenges that ethnography faces. The conversation essay negotiates these challenges. Bishop was concerned, for instance, that, in order to pass muster in a context that values positivistic research, the data should be 'representative, reliable, whole' (1992: 148). But she discovered that, even early in the process of deciding what to record and how to document, she was already falling short of that standard. By the time she tackled the report toward the end of the project, she was grappling with the realization that 'all research methods and research reports are rhetorical, that is, all use the reliable triad of classical persuasion: *logos,* the appeal to reason, *pathos,* the appeal to emotion, and *ethos,* the appeal of personality or character' (1992: 149). Yet creative writing is a discipline more comfortable steeped in the rich combination of logos, ethos and pathos as well as at ease with the worth of voice and point of view, or what Bishop calls 'human subjectivity [...] and author-saturated reconstructions' (1992: 153). Despite risking postmodernist criticism, why not make meaning the way we are trained to make meaning as creative writers, as story-tellers, as teachers?

Ian Barnard is another rhetoric-composition scholar who grapples with ethnography. One of his greatest concerns with ethnographic research is that 'power relations between ethnographer and subject(s) reinforce existing inequities' (2006: 96). Although there may be no getting around this problem, the conversation essays here offset power inequity because all participants speak for themselves and interact with each other directly.

This book adapts notions of ethnography, rather than being ethnographic research itself. As the editor, I am the ethnographer and, thereby, responsible for the final version. Certainly, for some essays, I asked an initial set of questions to which all contributors to that essay responded; then, I recast those responses as conversation and added my own responses to the same questions. That positions co-authors of these essays ethnographic subjects of sorts. Yet I am also positioned as an ethnographic subject, for I participated as a contributor as well. In other essays, the conversation emerged piece by piece as the document was passed back and forth. Authors in these essays share almost equal power. No matter the starting point, all authors are experts and had opportunities to clarify and edit, a power that subjects in ethnographic research rarely have because interpretation is left entirely to the researcher. In fact, contributors often edited each other as the chapters moved along.

Perhaps, then, the reader is the real ethnographer, the one who interprets the conversation data for ultimate meaning and application in new contexts. Just as the authors here are consciously situated in particular circumstances, so are readers; the perspectives of readers will be at least as varied as the perspectives of contributors. Readers, in the end, will determine what is and is not meaningful, relevant and applicable to their own circumstances as creative writers in the academy. Though *What We Talk about When We Talk about Creative Writing* is not ethnographic research in its commonly understood sense, this book – the conversation mode – is influenced and inflected by the underpinnings of this type of research.

'To say that subjectivity is inevitable is one thing,' writes Barnard, 'but to imagine deploying one's subjectivity to draw attention to the limitations of the ethnographic project fundamentally redefines the purpose and status of ethnography' (2006: 103). That's what we've attempted in this book; we've deployed subjectivity, remained aware of limitations, and redefined the possibilities of scholarship. Allaying additional concerns Barnard poses about ethnography, here we each exhibit individual identity, the ethnographer's gaze, meaning-making and self-reflection, yet ultimately leave observation, interpretation and application of our comments to the reader. Barnard notes his own rethinking of a student project in which he initially thought elliptical elements and lack focus to be a weakness but realized that, when readers were taken into account, these elements became a strength (2006: 104). Though risky, the lack of neat consensus and tidy conclusion in this collection is a strength and an invitation to readers. Readers, we hope, will continue to explore the topics covered in this book, will take the ideas to their colleagues for discussions about their own programs, and will write journal articles and books that extend the conversations here.

A conversation is not comprehensive; it doesn't pretend to be. In addition, this mode highlights rhetorical qualities inherent in all research, making visible the usually hidden appeals to reason, emotion and personality. These qualities shape our writing and our teaching and, in this collection, are visible in our scholarly work. This approach may be seen as a direct challenge to positivistic research than hides the *I* and depends on what Bishop calls '*previously proven* scientific truths' (1992: 150). But creative writing is a discipline of *I* – of author – and our pedagogy is built on practice more than on what's previously proven. By not hiding our biases, our individual stakes in the issues, and our emotions and individualized meanings, the so-called data become useful in varied as well as common situations, as readers situate themselves among viewpoints. Bishop points out, rightly, that the line between my classroom and 'someone else's classroom but a classroom like those we have known' is 'a fine one' (1992: 151). The authors of this collection are I-witnessing together. Readers, too, should become I-witnesses, interpreting in ways that apply to their own situations.

Borrowing from Arts-based Research

While the conversation essay should not be the only way to do our scholarship and is not the best approach for every question or context, it's a useful contribution to our body of pedagogy knowledge. In her book *Method Meets Art*, Patricia Leavy writes, '*Arts-based research practices* are a set of methodological tools used by researchers across disciplines during all phases of social research, including data generation, analysis, interpretation, and representation. These emerging tools adapt the tenets of the creative arts in order to address social research questions in holistic and engaged ways in which theory and practice are intertwined' (2015: 4). Just as *What We Talk about When We Talk about Creative Writing* is not ethnographic research so much as influenced or inflected by the principles of ethnographic research, this book is not exactly arts-based research so much as it is influenced and inflected by these principles of addressing our pedagogical and programmatic questions in holistic and engaged ways that acknowledge and promote the intertwining of theory and practice.

It seems important to note, as Leavy does, that arts-based research draws from feminist scholarship that argues the value of partial truths and truths steeped in context (2015: 10). Perhaps, it's no coincidence that only two men contributed to *Power and Identity in the Creative Writing Classroom.* One male colleague, when I invited him to contribute, replied bluntly, 'I have no authority in the classroom'. Though misguided and naïve, that response concerned me, for I realized that pedagogy was a feminized area of investigation. It also convinced me that this work is necessary and also necessarily disruptive as much as it is self-conscious. With this in mind, the conversation mode became an appropriately disruptive way for the contributors of this book to demonstrate partial, contingent and context-dependent truths.

Like ethnography, then, arts-based research challenges positivistic stances, objectivity, and hierarchy. The conversation essay shares these goals as well and asks academia to expand its notions of what constitutes scholarship. As the authors of these conversations grapple with questions and ideas specific to creative writing, the project also engages with the larger conversation about academic practices generally.

Importantly, both Leavy and Mark Turner point to story as the basic principle underlying thought. Turner writes, 'Narrative imagining – story – is the fundamental instrument of thought. Rational capacities depend on it. It is our chief means of looking into the future, of predicting, of planning, and of explaining' (1996: 4–5). Bishop also pointed out, 'Narrative can be effectively self-conscious' (1992: 153). If this is the case, shouldn't narrative play a role in our scholarship, especially if we use it to plan and not merely to summarize?

Leavy points to Turner and several others to argue that, as the field of neuroscience adds to our understanding of how we think and understand the world, 'narrative, stories, and the arts can play a major role in teaching diverse subject matters' (2015: 15). Narrative tricks us, as Turner points out, into feeling 'as if we are doing no work at all' (1996: 6), so its foundational role makes it seem not rigorous when, in fact, it is merely deeply embedded. Narrative may seem, at first glance, out of place in the academy, but it's part and parcel of creative writing. In this book, then, we tell each other stories in order to explain and plan as we consider pedagogy, programs, the profession and our careers.

What appeals most to me in Leavy's articulation of arts-based research is how such work is best judged. In conceiving of how to mark the 10th anniversary of this series and to move the field of creative writing forward, I considered writing a single-author tome. But one of the great strengths of *Power and Identity in the Creative Writing Classroom* is that it became more than the sum of its parts. I decided that *What We Talk about When We Talk about*

Creative Writing could make what Leavy calls a 'substantive or practical contribution' (2015: 272) – could advance knowledge and improve classrooms, programs and lives – more effectively as a set of orchestrated conversation essays. Barnard, a colleague of mine, expresses serious concern about teaching generally: 'Prescriptive standards, standardized testing, common syllabi, and outcomes become more important than ideas' and 'our teaching lags behind our theoretical ideas' (2006: 95). I want creative writing to keep up with itself; this book is one means of doing that.

Ultimately, Leavy asserts that *usefulness* is the most appropriate criteria for judging an arts-based research project. 'Research should not circulate in the hands of an elite few with highly specialized education,' she writes. 'Moreover, times have changed, and there have been widespread calls for researchers to serve the communities in which they are enmeshed' (2015: 27). Even though she admits that arts-based research 'puts us in a messy terrain' (2015: 285), Leavy advocates that, despite the academic mess, we should switch from asking whether research is good to asking what it is good for (2015: 273). This collection, by operating as engaged voices and perspectives, is designed to be useful, to matter to the larger field of creative writing and to individual writer-teachers and, by extension, to their students.

Creative Writing as a Mangle-ish Discipline

Another approach underpins my thinking and decision making in this book: the mangle of practice. While this understanding of creative writing deserves its own article or even a book, this approach opens up here a different way of thinking about what we're up to – what we're talking about when we say, *creative writing*. Andrew Pickering, in his book *The Mangle of Practice*, outlined a new way to understand science as a practice. Since creative writing is inherently a practice-based discipline far more overtly than science, it has long struck me that his notions can help us understand ourselves, our pedagogy and our programs. Pickering makes an even more assertive claim for rethinking how we are performing scholarship when, in the introduction to the edited collection *The Mangle in Practice*, he advocates 'a shift in interpretative sensibilities, an argument that scholars should take interest in decentered and emergent processes rather than recycling implausible devices to obscure their existence' (2008: viii–ix). The project of conversation essay attempts a shift in this vein.

One important aspect of Pickering's approach is that he is after 'a *real-time* understanding' (1995: 3). The orchestrated conversation essay has the feel of real-time discussion, but it's helpful to keep in mind that this is an illusion we created. Still, this book is indeed a snapshot – or, rather, a photo album – of our discipline at this particular time, as close to real-time as we could manage. In addition, these conversations capture the *'temporally emergent'* (1995: 14) nature of what we do. In other words, instead of offering pat conclusions that might be mistaken to be true across time and contexts, these conversations make visible the not knowing in advance, the need to explore as we work, and the need for what Pickering calls 'tuning' (1995: 14), in the sense that we tune a radio to catch and clarify a signal. Sometimes, we don't know what we want or need to hear until we happen upon it, and then we're suddenly singing along.

Mostly, Pickering's mangle is concerned with agency and tuning, or with the dance of agency through resistance and accommodation. This dance of agency is a form of modeling, which he defines as 'an open-ended process with no determinate destination' (1995: 19) and which sounds to me like what we do as writers and also as teachers of creative writing, especially in relation to the workshop. Modeling begins with the known as a way into the unknown – and isn't that at the heart of creative writing? Out of this modeling process can emerge 'an indefinite number of future variants' (1995: 19). In other words, creative writing as a field represents a sort of many worlds theory in which each choice leads to multiple outcomes because we each make pedagogical (or writerly) decisions in a particular context.

In much of his work, Pickering focuses on the dance of agency between the human and the machine, but he also acknowledges disciplinary agency as 'the sedimented, socially sustained routines of human agency that accompany conceptual structures' (1995: 29). The dance between human agency and disciplinary agency – concepts of the workshop, AWP Hallmarks, institutional policies and expectations, etc. – is really that with which we're grappling in this book. *Conversation,* after all, is from the Latin meaning *turning together;* conversation is, then, a dance that, in this case, represents the dance we do with the discipline. Our dance is with established conceptual systems, in which we have what Pickering calls *'free moves'* when we assert our agency and *'forced moves'* when we 'become passive in the face of [our] training and established procedures' (1995: 116). In thinking about these terms, don't confuse *free* with being better than *forced* but, rather, think as if you were composing a sonnet by negotiating the resistance and accommodation of a set of particular constraints. A free move, Pickering asserts, is designed 'to invoke the forced moves that follow from it' (1995: 117). Free and forced moves create the dance that leads to a new iteration.

The creative arts work in a similar way to agile software development; *agile* describes creative writing and also creative writing pedagogy, and the conversation essay captures that agility. Brian Marick, in his contribution to

The Mangle in Practice, asserts that agile software development is 'a mangle-ish style of work that suits certain people, and Agile projects allow those people to be happy at work instead of bitter, cynical, and discouraged' (2008: 183). Not everyone builds software the same way; both traditional and agile approaches work. Agile designers create software that supports a set of fea-tures without planning for specific, predicted changes in the future, and then they build on that software to support another set of features and so on. The agile designer works on the next stage without fretting about the final out-comes; Marick writes, 'They have arrived at that capacity by tuning them-selves to a constant stream of deliberately unexpected change requests, explicitly assuming that the dance of resistance and accommodation will never end' (2008: 194). I am a teacher in flux, just as I am a writer in flux, so agility leaves me rarely flummoxed and often enthused as I figure out how to write and to teach over and over again. Moreover, Marick asserts about programmers what I surmise about agile creative writing professors: 'Agile programmers become the kind of programmer who makes the right decisions without being nudged by a chart' (2008: 198). This agile process depends on constant communication. That increased communication – talking with each other, sharing ideas – makes creative writing pedagogy agile, in the sense of being responsive and innovative.

The orchestrated conversation strikes me as a good way for the mangle-ish tendencies at the heart of creative writing to guide us from the known to the unknown. 'The constitutive part played by disciplinary agency in this dance,' Pickering writes, 'guarantees that the free moves of human agents – bridging and filling – carry those agents along trajectories that cannot be foreseen in advance, that have to be found out in practice' (1995: 139). Whether composing a sonnet or walking into a classroom, we make some-thing in real time through practice.

Much scholarship does not appear this way, however. Pickering suggests that traditional scholarship, while it produces knowledge, often misrepre-sents what's really happening in science practice; scholarship is often retro-spective, walking the reader through a linear progression, reconstructed after the fact, toward a conclusion the researcher has already made. Pickering sug-gests instead, 'an *ontology of becoming*' that occurs 'in the thick of things, in the intersection of the human and the nonhuman, in a trial-and-error search process that is open ended and forward looking' (2008: 3) Here, in this book, while we certainly edit for clarity and against simple repetition, we retain this making of scholarship in orchestrated time and figure it out as we go; we are in the midst of becoming. *What We Talk about When We Talk about Creative Writing* is about being in the world, in the thick of things, as teachers and as writers.

Writer-Teachers in Conversation

Importantly, no conversation essay in this collection is a transcript of an actual conversation. Although the open-endedness of conversation – the not knowing ahead of time exactly where we're going so that conclusions or possibilities can emerge – is an advantage in ethnographic, arts-based, and mangle-ish research, organization and editing make essays useful as pedagogy scholarship. These chapters, then, are orchestrated and constructed essays in the form of conversations so that we could each have our say in our own words and allow our ideas to interact while also providing a structure suitable for readers and for adaptation of concepts and plans to new environments. Appropriate here is Barnard's discussion of voice in *Upsetting Composition Commonplaces:* 'So, an understanding of voice as actively constructed nevertheless needs to simultaneously attend to (and sometimes even value) the unexpected play of language and the meanings that writers can't control – not as obstacles to be revised away, but as inevitable complications of our constructions of voice, as additional dimensions of pleasure and danger in our texts' (2014: 88). The conversation essay allows great flexibility for interruption, response, and re-envisioning as we each took into account what others wrote and took advantage of the collisions we saw happening as we drafted and edited.

This book's title draws from the title of Raymond Carver's story 'What We Talk About When We Talk About Love.' In this story, four characters sit around drinking gin and talking about the ways love works in their lives. It's a sad story in many ways, and it ends with the group discussing the possibility of going out for dinner without anyone mustering the gumption to move. So, that's the opposite of what we're doing in the book. Sure, we're sitting around talking, at least metaphorically, in emails and Word drafts. But readers will see a great deal of gumption and movement in *What We Talk about When We Talk about Creative Writing*. In an earlier version of Carver's story, published later in *The New Yorker,* the narrator says, 'There was suddenly a feeling of ease and generosity around the table, of friendship and comfort. We could have been anywhere.' That's what we've made with this book: generosity and companionship, together as writers and teachers. The conversation essays invite readers to take up the discussions, to consider what they are doing as writers and as teachers and why – to take the ideas from this book and adapt them anywhere they belong.

When Multilingual Matters expressed interest in a 10th anniversary celebration, it seemed fitting and ethical to include all the authors who contributed to that earlier collection (though Wendy Bishop had passed away and two authors had retired) and also invite new voices into the mix. Some of us had already published conversation essays together; some are writer-teachers with whom I've never worked before and whom I've not yet met in person. Development of chapter topics and grouping contributors went hand in hand.

The first section of this book focuses on pedagogy and connects most directly with the earlier *Power and Identity in the Creative Writing Classroom.* In 'Where Are We Going in Creative Writing Pedagogy?' Cathy Day, Stephanie Vanderslice and I discuss changes in creative writing pedagogy over the last decade, remaining resistance to this work, and some emerging developments, including the rise of the digital. Larissa Szporluk and I, in 'Good Counsel,' grapple with how students learn over time and through practice, as we discuss philosophical underpinnings and practical approaches to our teaching. In 'Writerly Reading in the Creative Writing Course,' five of the original book's authors discuss the relationship of reading to creative writing, the different ways we and our students read, and practical matters like class discussion of reading.

The second section looks beyond our classrooms to our programs. In 'Text(ure), Modeling, Collage,' I explore with a visual artist and a graphic designer concepts of *studio* and *workshop* as well as the ways our undergraduate and graduate programs align and vary across creative disciplines. With much written recently to attack MFA programs, 'More Than the Sum of Our Parts' is a crucial addition, for we emphasize the variety, dynamic energy, and potential that exists in graduate programs, both MA and MFA, both residential and low residency. Most creative writing courses, however, are at the undergraduate level; Katharine Haake, Argie Manolis and I, all of whom have held administrative positions as well, discuss struggles in developing and strengthening undergraduate programs, how the AWP Hallmarks do and not work in different institutions, and innovative possibilities such as service-learning. In 'The Program Beyond the Program,' my own colleagues at Chapman University talk with me about projects beyond the curriculum; this contribution is probably the most overtly ethnographic, as it offers a snapshot in time of one institutional culture in which we each negotiate a similar dance of agency differently as we move through resistance and accommodation.

The third section, 'On the Profession,' goes broader still. The first chapter, in three pieces, draws from multiple perspectives, including some of the leading experts in creative writing pedagogy, to address some of the criticisms lobbed at this field and to set to rest some of the recurring questions creative writing faces. The other essay in this section, 'Terms & Trends,' brings new scholars into conversation to discuss how we talk about what we do as scholars and what the future might or should hold, including what we make of creative writing studies.

The fourth section is most personal, as we discuss our careers as creative writers in the academy. 'Peas in a Pod' leans most toward the ethnographic, as four of us who graduated at roughly the same time from the same college trace how differently our careers panned out based on the opportunities we had and the choices we made. 'The First Book' brings together poets Nicole Cooley, Kate Greenstreet, Nancy Kuhl and myself to examine that seemingly all-important leap to the next stage of one's career; publication of the first book is a more complex event than any of us had imagined until it happened, so we tease apart its various meanings and momentums. Finally, Karen Craigo and I talk frankly about career stages and trajectories, including how gender and age play a role; readers, we hope, will think seriously about their own agency and the dance created by resistance and accommodation that shapes their careers.

The overlaps one notices among essays are part of the interwoven fabric of the field of creative writing and are, to my mind, a strength. This book is designed to cover broadly what we mean when we say *creative writing,* and the sections – on pedagogy, on programs, on the profession, on careers – indicate that wide scope and a useful way to organize the concepts that the term *creative writing* suggests. Importantly, this book's conclusion points to areas in which our discipline and this book fall short and to how we might address issues of identity and inclusiveness as well as the relationship of creative writing to academia and to the larger society and culture. Just as *Power and Identity in the Creative Writing Classroom* was 10 years ago, *What We Talk About When We Talk About Creative Writing* is a stay against confusion. As writers challenging traditional academic approaches, we take risks by admitting confusion exists, and we are better for it. The perspectives readers will find here are as contingent and shifting as they are thoughtful, tried and true.

References

Ashton, D. (2015) Creative work careers: Pathways and portfolios for the creative economy. *Journal of Education and Work* 28 (4), 388–406.

Barnard, I. (2006) Anti-ethnography? *Composition Studies* 34 (1), 95–107.

Barnard, I. (2014) *Upsetting Composition Commonplaces.* Utah State University Press: Logan, UT.

Bishop, W. (1992) I-witnessing in composition. *Rhetoric Review* 11 (1), 147–157.

Campbell, P. (2011) You say 'Creative,' and I say 'Creative'. *Journal of Policy Research in Tourism, Leisure and Events* 3 (1), 18–30.

Carver, R. (1981) What we talk about when we talk about love. *What We Talk About When We Talk About Love: Stories* (pp. 137–154). New York: Knopf.

Comunian, R., Chapain, C. and Clifton, N. (2010) Location, location, location: Exploring the complex relationship between creative industries and place. *Creative Industries Journal* 3 (1), 5–10.

Florida, R. (2002) *The Rise of the Creative Class*. New York: Basic Books.

Florida, R. (2008) *Who's Your City?: How the Creative Economy Is Making Where To Live the Most Important Decision of Your Life*. New York: Basic Books.

Frost, R. (1972) *Poetry & Prose*. New York: Holt, Rinehart and Winston.

Garber, M. (2008) *Patronizing the Arts*. Princeton, NJ: Princeton University Press.

Irving, J. (2005) Interview, The Daily Show with Jon Stewart. Comedy Central, 17 August. See http://thedailyshow.cc.com/videos/36k9p4/john-irving (accessed 13 May 2016).

Johnson, S. (2010) *Where Good Ideas Come From: The Natural History of Innovation*. New York: Riverhead Books.

Leahy, A. (ed.) (2005) *Power and Identity in the Creative Writing Classroom: The Authority Project*. Clevedon: Multilingual Matters.

Leavy, P. (2015) *Method Meets Art: Arts-Based Research Practice*. New York: The Guilford Press.

Marick, B. (2008) A manglish way of working. In A. Pickering and K. Guzik (eds) *The Mangle in Practice: Science, Society, and Becoming* (pp. 185–201). Durham, NC: Duke University Press.

Pickering, A. (1995) *The Mangle of Practice: Time, Agency, & Science*. Chicago: University of Chicago Press.

Pickering, A. (2008) New ontologies. In A. Pickering and K. Guzik (eds) *The Mangle in Practice: Science, Society, and Becoming* (pp. 1–14). Durham, NC: Duke University Press.

Schweitzer, A. (1998) *Out of My Life and Thought: An Autobiography*. Trans. Antje Bultmann Lemke. Baltimore, MD: Johns Hopkins University Press.

Turner, M. (1996) *The Literary Mind*. New York: Oxford University Press.

Vanderslice, S. (2005) Afterword. In A. Leahy (ed.) *Power and Identity in the Creative Writing Classroom: The Authority Project* (pp. 205–214). Clevedon: Multilingual Matters.

Zakaria, F. (2015) *In Defense of a Liberal Education*. New York: W.W. Norton.

Part 2
Pedagogy

2 Where Are We Going in Creative Writing Pedagogy?

Cathy Day, Anna Leahy and Stephanie Vanderslice

Can creative writing be taught? Yes, we're not charlatans, though teaching looks different in creative writing than in other disciplines. Should college-level teachers of creative writing be practicing writers? Yes. Though being a great writer doesn't make you a great teacher, creative writing teachers are strengthened by engaging in the practice themselves. Is the workshop monolithic? No, the workshop is an adaptable model. Why do thousands of creative writing instructors who teach courses professionally proceed as if this growing body of pedagogy doesn't exist? It's been 10 years since the authors of this chapter contributed to *Power and Identity in the Creative Writing Classroom*. This chapter examines the current state of creative writing pedagogy, including the tension that creative writing has with theory, and proposes several areas for further investigation and expansion, including digital modes.

Anna Leahy: Our body of work in creative writing includes novels, stories, poems, essays, plays, and all variety of creative pieces we make. Some of the body of knowledge in creative writing as a field, however, is pedagogical; some verges on how-to, and some includes textual analysis and criticism. Our body of knowledge is the equivalent of what other fields call *theory*. It's tricky to call it *theory,* though, because we are a practice discipline.

I recently read James Woods's *How Fiction Works* (2009) and Sven Birkerts's *The Art of Time in Memoir* (2007). Woods analyzes third-person close point of view, for example, as 'free indirect style,' grasping that author and narrator share certain sentences. He's not just offering a tried-and-true textbook definition, but adding to the understanding of fiction. Birkerts discusses, among other things, the difference between autobiography – a kind of historical writing – and memoir as creative nonfiction. These examples are theoretical and similar to literary scholarship.

Cathy Day: This kind of 'writing about writing' is what Tim Mayers called 'craft criticism' in his book *(Re)Writing Craft.* He defines this body of work as 'critical prose written by self- or institutionally identified 'creative writers'' in which 'a concern with textual production takes precedence over any concern with textual interpretation' (2005: 33). He includes pedagogy and how-to in this category as well.

Stephanie Vanderslice: Susan Bell also uses this approach in *The Artful Edit* (2007), which discusses the editing of great literary works in terms of what writers can learn about craft. For example, she introduces the concepts of micro-editing and macro-editing via a close examination of the actual editing of *The Great Gatsby.* Interspersed between *The Artful Edit's* chapters, moreover, are testimonials from various writers on the ways in which the editing process works for them. Reading this book, I saw great possibilities for structuring a whole course around it and books like it that help student writers develop an editorial consciousness beyond the nuts and bolts. Certainly, I wish I could have had that kind of course in my creative writing education. This growing body of knowledge can shape the future of our academic field.

Anna Leahy: We agree that this body of knowledge is growing, and additional publishers have recently taken note and jumped on board. But we also agree that there remains resistance to pedagogy scholarship in our publications and professional venues.

Cathy Day: Honestly, I think one reason why more creative writers aren't engaging in this pedagogy conversation is because of that word: *theory.* These days, there's a distinct polarization between the critical and the creative, and this discipline – creative writing pedagogy – sits in that divide. One side thinks we aren't theoretical enough, and the other side thinks we're too theoretical. We need to bring more writers from both sides into this space.

I heard James Kincaid speak about this subject. He's the Aerol Arnold Chair in English and Professor of English at USC, a serious literary scholar who also writes and publishes fiction. He said that bridging the critical/creative divide doesn't necessarily mean that writers in academia must learn to 'talk theory,' but rather (or also) that English departments should incorporate creative writing into the foundational experience of English studies.

Stephanie Vanderslice: When thinking about the place of creative writing in English studies, it's important to remember that the role of creative writing varies from institution to institution, from a course that fills a general education requirement for thousands of students at some schools, to a small, single course limited to majors or requiring instructor permission to enroll. This same variability is present in the range of courses available; smaller departments may have one multi-genre creative writing course, whereas larger departments with a creative writing major may have genre-specific workshops, forms courses, new media courses, and so forth. We shouldn't talk of the field as if it's uniform throughout.

Whether creative writing should be foundational in English studies deserves further examination. It would be worth looking at the benefits of this approach through the perspective of professors who teach such foundational courses and the students who take them. In the United Kingdom, creative writing is definitely considered one of many lenses through which English majors study literature, but the benefits seem to be rather assumed and not yet well studied there.

As a member of a writing department that is, in my university, separate from the English department, I would advocate for an optional creative writing course in the general education curriculum. Books like Daniel Pink's *A Whole New Mind* (2006) convince me that, in the post-information age, the ability to convey information via a compelling sense of narrative and story will be a critical skill for all college students. Examples of this phenomenon are everywhere; from digital storytelling to blogging, narrative is at the core of information in the 21st century.

Anna Leahy: The rich variety across institutions and the continuing growth of programs extend what has already been deemed a boom time for creative writing. Mark McGurl's book *The Program Era* opens with the assertion 'that the rise of the creative writing program stands as the most important event in postwar American literary history' (2009: ix). Some see the ubiquitous creative writing course as the downfall of literature.

Cathy Day: While some see the exponential growth of creative writing programs and online writing communities as a harbinger of doom, it's a cause for celebration that so many people feel authorized to write and are interested in learning to do so. As Richard Hugo wrote in *The Triggering Town,* 'A creative-writing class may be one of the last places you can go where your life still matters' (1979: 65).

Anna Leahy: That idea of mattering echoes a more recent article in AWP's *The Writer's Chronicle,* in which Steve Healey scrutinizes the position of creative writing in the academy. Sadly, he ignores much of existing pedagogy work: 'the field has tended to avoid thinking about how it teaches' (2009: 30). But I'm glad he asks us to think about dreaded capitalism, whether our teaching goals match students' life goals, and how other fields can benefit from our practices. We still need more documentation of what's really happening in our programs and classrooms.

Cathy Day: One thing I enjoy about being on Facebook and being digital friends with lots of other creative writing teachers is sharing information about what we do in the classroom, but occasionally swapping syllabi or lesson plans isn't enough. A few months ago I wrote a 5,000-word essay about moving from writing stories to writing books. It was part craft, part form/genre theory, part pedagogy. I faced two problems. One, there was no clear body of knowledge within which to frame my discussion, and two, I had little idea where to send this essay. We need more journals, more opportunities to talk to each other *professionally* about teaching.

Stephanie Vanderslice: Two other venues for this sort of work are *New Writing* published out of the UK and the Australian online journal *Text*. There are some great conversations happening about creative writing pedagogy in these journals. The articles in these journals are what we're talking about: not so much about craft, but about *teaching* craft. We need to develop an awareness of those venues here in the United States.

Anna Leahy: I'm glad we're talking across oceans. But because the British and Australian educational systems are different from ours, it's also important to develop visible venues here too. *Pedagogy* is a journal about English studies generally that is open to pieces about creative writing, but their backlog is long, and that's not enough. AWP launched a spot for some of this work a few years ago, a batch of essays in the members' e-link section of the website.

Cathy Day: This is why I chose not to publish my 5,000-word article there. They didn't want to put it in *The Writer's Chronicle*, which reaches many creative writing faculty and students; they wanted to put it in the e-link section, a less visible space for logged-in members. Certainly, this is their prerogative, but why write about teaching better if teachers don't read it? I elected to publish the article with an online magazine called *The Millions*, and it was widely read and discussed. It did some pedagogical good, but it wasn't legitimate, in the traditional academic sense, because it wasn't published as pedagogy scholarship.

Stephanie Vanderslice: *College English* and *College Composition and Communication* have also provided some space for these discussions. But creative writers shouldn't have to rely on those composition-oriented venues exclusively. The new *Journal of Creative Writing Studies* recently lanunched.

Cathy Day: This issue isn't solely related to the lack of journals out there, of course, or to the resistance to the term *theory*. There exists another reason why writers who teach creative writing are not more fully engaged in these issues: they can't afford to be because, at some institutions, working in this area doesn't count towards tenure and promotion in the same way as publishing creative work.

Stephanie Vanderslice: Joseph Moxley has a wonderful essay in *Does the Creative Writing Workshop Still Work?* (2010), in which he talks about why he hasn't engaged much in creative writing pedagogy since he published *Creative Writing in America* more than 20 years ago. Apparently, his institution told him he would get zero credit for editing that important book and that he should spend his time on more established critical disciplines for promotion and tenure.

I am fortunate to be at an institution where I am encouraged to do both creative and critical work. We need to remember, as we discuss professional and pedagogical issues, that different institutions have different missions and environments. We must continue to legitimize the field of creative writing pedagogy so that it complements the rest of our pursuits as writers.

Even so, teacher-writers are responsible for knowing what's going on. At my institution, for example, the teaching narratives in our promotion and tenure packages must be grounded in the pedagogy of the field. Many institutions require these sorts of teaching descriptions from individuals. These kinds of documents, then, could also demonstrate a teacher–writer's engagement with his or her teaching discipline.

Anna Leahy: I wouldn't encourage any creative writing professor to devote all her professional development time to pedagogy scholarship, at the complete expense of, say, poems or a novel. Anyone hired as a creative writer should remain engaged in the field as a writer, just as colleagues in other fields – biology, political science, art history – are expected to contribute scholarship to the growing knowledge in their fields and to the larger culture. But even in institutions that value publication over teaching, most of us are teaching regularly. As long as we're teaching, we remain responsible for articulating not just what we do, but also how and why we teach the way we do. I wonder how many of us actually do that in our annual reviews.

Stephanie Vanderslice: In articulating what we do and how we do it, one of the most interesting and, perhaps, important issues to discuss as we go forward are the ways in which we respond to students' creative writing. There exists much more to examine about how we respond – in writing and orally – and especially why. What leads to the most improvement? This issue is an old staple, in some ways, but it is newly complicated by the rise of program assessment as part of institutional accreditation over the last decade or two.

As a faculty member in an independent writing program, we have been occupied with assessment from the beginning. Our program was founded in 1996 under some controversy, so the issue of whether we were producing results was a factor early on. We've looked at the issue in a number of different ways and have finally settled on an exit portfolio system from our general education writing courses, our writing major, and now our creative writing major. I give our assessment committee a lot of credit; this is not an easy issue with which to grapple, and many faculty can be very suspicious of the A-word. While we've finally come up with assessment plans, these are constantly evolving as we continually ask ourselves what we are able to assess and what we want to see in our students' work. Once formed, the models require ongoing reflection and fine-tuning.

Cathy Day: I hope we aren't losing readers at this point, just because we mentioned assessment. Stick with us, reader, because we're covering a lot of ground.

Assessment has been good for creative writing programs because it's forced what I'll call first-generation writers in academia to talk openly about what they're doing in the classroom and why. The three of us represent that second generation, whose journey into academic teaching was informed by our shared experience teaching composition as teaching assistants. And it's fallen on our generation to handle the assessment tasks.

I've observed this process at two different schools; both times, the experience was ultimately enriching. Once you get past the jargon – learning goals, outcomes, rubrics, and matrices – you discover commonalities among colleagues and develop a shared sense of purpose. About 10 years ago, I was teaching at a college that ramped up assessment at the same time that I was developing a creative writing minor. I had to articulate a rationale for course levels, and that document, created out of bureaucratic necessity, became a list of craft proficiencies – basic, intermediate, and advanced – that I've used every semester since then to explain my expectations and grading policies. My students appreciate this transparency, and it's allowed for a better learning environment in which they can thrive. At both schools, we ended up – after some fussing and resistance – with a far more cogent curriculum than the one with which we started.

Anna Leahy: When creative writing programs were being formed a few decades ago, discussion about how it all adds up must have occurred, but that fell off or wasn't done across institutions, and a great deal became taken for granted. The catalog and syllabus are legally binding documents, so, in practical terms, it's a good idea for us to back them up with what happens in our courses. Assessment reinvigorates that discussion about pedagogy and the profession.

That said, I have grave concerns about how assessment is practiced (and wrote about it at *Inside Higher Ed*), namely that current practices loosely apply social science methodology to the arts and humanities. I hesitate to turn to composition studies for guidance because that field is heavily influenced by social science methodology and because that's a field often without an undergraduate major. We shouldn't start with the tools of another trade. Instead, let's begin with issues in our body of knowledge, then develop methods and tools to answer our field's questions.

Cathy Day: My general impression is that the best way to get so-called cred in academia – and now that, in part, means assessment – is to model ourselves after composition studies, but by doing so, we lose touch with our identity as working artists.

We should look outside the English department and turn to studio art departments for further guidance. As Madison Smartt Bell says in the introduction to his textbook *Narrative Design*, 'The teaching of music and visual art as crafts in some systematic fashion is centuries old; it goes back as far as Renaissance ateliers, even to the medieval guilds. There is no long-standing tradition of guilds or ateliers for fiction writers' (1997: 3).

Stephanie Vanderslice: As Wendy Bishop would have said, *There's an essay in that.* We've referenced other arts for years. It's time to really take a look at how other arts, like music and visual art, are taught and how some of those methods might be applied to creative writing.

Anna Leahy: This conversation led me to talk with two artists at my institution (see this book's chapter with Halloran and Jaenichen). Every discipline has its own priorities, and ours tend to be habits of mind. That's good reason to talk across the creative arts (or even medicine as a practice discipline, in which advanced students learn by doing). It's easier to measure, say, acquisition of terminology in biology than to measure thinking for oneself, which *Classroom Assessment Techniques* (Angelo & Cross, 1993) lists as one of the three top teaching goals English faculty report having. Faculty lead busy lives, so it's tempting to assess what's easiest to measure instead of what's most important.

AWP has begun to tackle assessment, with some conference panels. Such an organization could provide us with guidance that can be adapted across institutions. Without scholarship, we'll likely each keep cobbling together something do-able that satisfies given administrators, without taking advantage of doing something really useful for the discipline as a whole.

Cathy Day: Let me step away for a moment to approach the fourth wall – to step outside our conversation with each other. You – YOU, reader of this dialogue – I fear that right about *here* in this pretty important conversation we're having about what we do, about what *you* do for a living, your eyes are glazing over as you encounter words like *assessment* and *rubric*. Am I right? Well, how would you feel if your physician skipped the boring stuff at her professional medical conference? How would you feel if the *Journal of the American Medical Association* stopped publishing because the jargon got too dry to keep doctors' interest and because they figured each doctor could figure it out on his or her own?

That's the sort of thing we're talking about here. We're talking about issues that matter. We're talking about our professional obligations. In common parlance, don't be part of the problem. Be part of the solution. Okay, let me slip back into the conversation.

Stephanie Vanderslice: *Rubric* has become a distasteful word, hasn't it? Rubrics might work in program assessment, but narrative response is much more effective for individual evaluation. We shouldn't lean too much on rubrics in creative writing (music to many readers' ears!), in part because they can be overly fault-finding, which doesn't help writers at any level. The writers who are doing well don't really find out why and even what they, individually, could be doing better, and the writers who are having problems don't get those individual problems addressed.

I'm becoming very interested in different types of response and how they help writers advance. This is especially important when teaching undergraduates, and response needs to be very formative at this stage. As opposed to summative response, which is the grade the student gets at the end of a unit or semester that gauges the student's mastery of a skill or discipline, formative response is the actual feedback that helps the student to improve over time. In teaching creative writing, my thoughtful oral and written response to student work is much more important to their growth than the grade I record or the boxes I check on a rubric.

But I'm noticing anecdotal differences in how students receive the response styles of the different teachers in our creative writing program, and that's really something worth investigating: how students receive response and whether and how they implement it to improve their work. The sooner students learn how to use feedback well, the better for their work and their development as writers.

Anna Leahy: It's crucial to distinguish *assessment,* a term used here in the United States to refer to program appraisal, and *evaluation,* which describes grading student work. And formative response is yet another distinct activity. The British seem to use *assessment* to describe all of it, but we shouldn't conflate a curricular program with individual student writing.

When we respond to student writing, we must strive to be neither a Bobby Knight (Mary Swander dismantles that approach in her essay in *Power and Identity in the Creative Writing Classroom*) nor a Pollyanna. Both extremes involve, to too great an extent or too directly, self-esteem. As I've written elsewhere, echoing John Gardner and Wallace Stegner, the self is always already part of the writing process, but can and, I think, should be mostly beside the point in workshop exchanges. That's not easy, though.

Colleagues who've observed my classes have been surprised that students energetically discuss weaknesses with great specificity. Narrative feedback – written or oral can open conversation and potential. Because the real challenge in my courses is the revision I require, talking about weaknesses or obstacles becomes a mutual leg-up – motivation – that students give each other to face that challenge. Students learn not to be afraid of making mistakes; they become more comfortable being shown shortcomings so they can work on them. Playing to our strengths isn't bad, but cognitive scientists assert that we learn from mistakes. That's a good habit of mind for students to carry beyond earning their degrees.

Cathy Day: We do need to consider what our students will do after graduation and what experiences will help them succeed later. One area to which we might look is digital media writing, but creative writing programs seem slower to do so than our colleagues teaching composition. Why is that? Over the last few years, my students' work has become increasingly multimodal. They tell stories with pictures and graphic novel frames and drawings and links to YouTube videos. They tell audio stories and video stories that ask us to read in a different way.

Rather than prohibit this hybridity, I've challenged myself to catch up, to understand and utilize new modes of expression – in the classroom and in my own writing. Many schools offer composition courses in digital writing (narrative via blog, podcast, video, and website). I've been closely following what's happening at Stanford University's undergraduate creative writing program, where creative writers Adam Johnson and Tom Kealey teach a new media writing course titled 'Storytelling Through Any Means Necessary.' A considerable generational divide exists between those comfortable and conversant in old media vs. new media, and I'm interested in trying to bridge that gap somehow by creating a textbook (Burroway 2.0? Or even 3.0 now?) or a conference (Breadloaf 2.0?). This is a big reason why I accepted a new position at a school dedicated to emerging media initiatives.

Anna Leahy: Recent discussions in popular venues and books like Nicholas Carr's *The Shallows* raise concerns about embracing digital projects part and parcel. Some initial studies in brain science indicate that digital modes may be at odds with some habits of mind – curiosity, concentration – I'm working to cultivate in students. I'm not against digital modes, but until I understand them better, I don't want to inadvertently introduce contradictions into my pedagogy.

Since we first had this conversation, I've dabbled in digital media. I wanted to see whether the nonlinear Prezi could be useful for mini-lectures, to generate discussion, or to allow students to document their writing process in a digital portfolio. Since I started blogging and found that weekly habit useful for myself, I developed a month-long draft-a-day assignment using blog software. These efforts worked so well that I contributed a chapter (with co-author Douglas Dechow) to *Creative Writing in the Digital Age.* And others at my university have developed several digital humanities courses open to all arts, humanities, and social science students but designed especially for undergraduates and graduate students in creative writing.

Stephanie Vanderslice: Digital media is something I, too, have begun to incorporate in my creative writing courses. The National Writing Project has really embraced digital media and web 2.0 in teaching writing; in fact, they have a term for this aspect of their organization, 'Digital Is' – as in, digital just *is* in the 21st century and we need to get used to it.

It was reading the book *Teaching the New Writing* (Herrington et al., 2009), co-published by Teacher's College Press and the NWP, that I came to understand that it's absolutely essential that we catch up and understand that multimodal composition needs to be incorporated into courses at every level – not only because students must know these skills in order to communicate in the 21st century, but because they are already using them outside the classroom. Since reading this groundbreaking book, I've made changes to all my courses to include some kind of digital component. For example, I have always required my introductory creative writing students to read a book on the writing life (from a list I provide) and present it to the class. Now, these presentations must be digital. In my creative writing pedagogy course, students must write a literacy autobiography; now I require that these be digital stories or digital literacy autobiographies. Not surprisingly, most students are remarkably enthusiastic about these components and often have a greater facility with the technology than I do. I might give them suggestions, like Prezi, Glogster, or Microsoft's Digital Storyteller, to get them started, but they usually find on their own the technology suited to the story they want to tell.

This issue seems to present itself urgently as the next frontier in creative writing pedagogy. How and why do we assign it? How do we assess it in terms of creative writing? A lot of programs are quite far along in this endeavor; in fact, Virginia Tech requires a digital story in a student's exit portfolio. We need to start experimenting with the workshop model to accommodate digital modes.

Anna Leahy: Based on my own experience and on anecdotes from librarians, students have a surface-level, casual understanding of the technology they use. That's a reason to bring technology into the classroom: to help students think critically and creatively about technology they're already using.

Digital modes are not a replacement for what we're already teaching, though. Instead, they offer new, additional – often nonlinear – ways to tell stories, use imagery, and think creatively. There exist some spectacular digital humanities projects in the journal *Vectors* – you have to see it to understand its scope. The potential is huge, but these projects raise concerns. Higher education struggles to support and fully count collaborative work. We cling to traditional relationships between form and content and haven't learned how to read or value content in innovative forms without worrying that we're merely being dazzled. We resist valuing archival work, even when a digital archive offers new ways to ask critical questions. Importantly, going digital requires time and money.

Stephanie Vanderslice: Time – time to learn technologies that are arriving at an exponential rate. This was probably the main factor in my reluctance to include much technology in my courses; I didn't have the time to keep up with everything that was out there and that kept on coming. *Teaching the New Writing* convinced me that I didn't *have* to learn a new technology in order to evaluate my students' use of it and gave me some tools for evaluating and responding to digital media in general.

Cathy Day: Lately, I've been asking myself a lot of hard questions about teaching fiction, the efficacy of the workshop model for different traditional modes, and how digital tools might foster the writing process. Why do we call a class 'Fiction Workshop,' if it's really 'Short Story Workshop'? Does the workshop model privilege the short story over the novel because it's a more manageable form, akin to the critical essay? Can we tinker with the workshop model to accommodate big things as well as short stories?

Perhaps I'm asking these questions because I've just finished a five-year stint teaching in an MFA program. Most of my students arrived in my classes already craft proficient, ready to embark on larger projects. A thesis, a book, a big thing. The budding novelists told me they considered workshop courses a hindrance. They try to workshop novels-in-progress and submit early chapters, and then are required to revise and resubmit, which they do, over and over again, sometimes never moving forward. Others said they go through the motions by writing short stories about which they don't particularly care, in order to fulfill their workshop requirement, while working privately on their novels, only sharing their real project with their thesis advisor and perhaps a few trusted readers. What is the point of pursuing creative writing instruction if that instruction gets in the way of writing the book you've always wanted to write?

Anna Leahy: We must consider how labels and goals shape course structure, in-class activities, and students' learning. Also, the semester timeframe and class meeting schedule are arbitrary constraints imposed upon us. It's challenging to figure out how the workshop model can be adapted for different course topics and levels, as well as for these timeframe configurations. How, for instance, might a novel workshop function more like the writing group that many published novelists have? At least one of my fiction colleagues requires little, if any, revision; his course is about production.

Cathy Day: I'm trying some new methods in graduate and advanced undergraduate workshops, organizing them more like group independent studies. I ask my students to write up an independent study proposal and share it with the entire class on what I call a *process blog*, which they maintain throughout the semester. I've also stopped asking for stand-alone stories. Now, I ask for pages. When we ask for stories, not pages, our students respond as if they are writing a paper, trying to meet page requirements and page limits – swelling very small stories, shrinking very big stories – rather than working to find the right and appropriate form for the particular story they're trying to tell. Sometimes, I'll require a 50-page manuscript as the final project, which can be the beginning of a novel, a novella, a few connected stories, a few unconnected stories, 50 one-page stories, etc. They only have to workshop 20+ of those pages, but they must present it to us like a book manuscript: cover page with title and contact information, table of contents, epigraph, even maps and photographs, if they wish.

And I've tried something new: whole class participation in National Novel Writing Month. Students write 50,000 words during the month of November, then revise 25 of those pages for their final grade. You could say that my current pedagogical stance is about figuring out how to teach my students that writing isn't just something they do for school, but is a way of life. For a long time, I just taught craft, which is what most of us do, I think. Now, I'm also interested in showing them how to create a literary life for themselves, if that's what they want.

Stephanie Vanderslice: More and more programs seem to be involved in NaNoWriMo, and, having participated in it myself and having seen even undergraduate students getting involved on their own, I see the value of what NaNoWriMo communicates: getting pages drafted is an important part of the daily writing life. That project also communicates the value of process, of exploring and writing those pages, even though some of them might not ever see the light of day. But they're all part of becoming the writer you want to be, rather than fussing over an individual story or poem to make it perfect before going on. Both approaches are needed in the creative writing classroom, but we often don't have enough of the former: the process, the messy part.

Cathy Day: Because process is hard to grade.

Anna Leahy: Poetry workshops are often structured as one-poem-at-a-time because a collection of disparate poems can get published. There exists a trend toward the cohesive collection, though, and I'm interested in sequences – connected poems – in my own writing. When I was an MFA student, Stanley Plumly launched a workshop with John Keats's odes defined as a series. John Tribble, editor of *Crab Orchard Review,* hosted an AWP panel focusing on coherent collections. Beth Ann Fennelly has written about 'the winnowing of wildness' – or lack of disparateness – in first books.

In this wake, I developed a graduate course with a chapbook as the final project. *Ordering the Storm* (Grimm, 2006) is a great resource; we also read several chapbooks. One aspect students appreciate – and which I expected them not to appreciate – is the requirement to submit a formal proposal. They can revise proposals, so no one is stuck with a project that changed as they drafted and revised. Students are motivated by having articulated a big thing up front. The course has a different kind of energy.

On the other hand, maybe such a course overemphasizes professionalization and the goal of publication, when I want students to take risks and attend to language and form in each poem.

Cathy Day: You're absolutely right. My graduate students were extremely professionally motivated, and I'm sure I was responding somewhat to their anxieties – helping them get their books ready for agents and editors.

Stephanie Vanderslice: Programs like the one at UNC-Wilmington recognize that, for better or for worse, the market is heavily focused on longer works and thus several courses there help students to create longer pieces in innovative ways. In addition to several courses that address varying approaches to writing the novel, they also offer a course in documentary poetry that focuses on collections and a course focused on award-winning first collections, which serves the additional purpose of helping students become aware of the first book awards out there. Finally, they have an introductory and advanced courses in book design that, while more focused on the publishing industry, give budding authors a sense of the process of book publishing. Curricula like these demonstrate there's room for both kinds of courses, those that focus on longer works and those that focus on stories, essays, or poems, as well as those that focus on exploration and invention and those that focus on the business.

Anna Leahy: When we discuss these issues, we need to keep teasing out the differences between MFA and BFA or BA curricula. Because of the risk of professionalization or narrowing, I wouldn't structure an undergraduate course around a chapbook project, though a series or sectioned poem might fit an advanced undergraduate course. We can't accomplish everything in every workshop, and I want undergraduates especially to experiment and try things just to see what happens, not merely find a single voice or style that works.

The mistaken (or outdated) concept of a monolithic workshop and, as Donald Hall called it, McPoem may exist because we haven't yet articulated enough of what we actually do in different courses. In May 2010, *Inside Higher Ed* ran a piece about an approach to teaching by a Duke University English professor that 'attracted attention nationwide.' The course was structured around contracts, standards, peer response, and revision – all pedagogical elements long used in creative writing. Cathy Davidson said that the experience exceeded her expectations and that 'students took more risks,' participated, and pushed each other to improve. She admits that she 'worked like a dog,' commenting right along with her students on every blog post that was a short essay on the week's topic (quoted in Jaschik, 2010). Good for her, but I'm flummoxed as to why creative writing teachers haven't been lauded daily for decades, since this stuff is old hat to us.

Oddly, one measure of the approach's success was that Davidson expected every student to earn an A (15 of 16 already had when the article was posted), because students revised work that didn't meet the standards. That's what my students do in their portfolios or final projects, and I'd written about the so-called easy A in *Can It Really Be Taught?* (Leahy, 2007) back in 2007. For Davidson, there were no cries of grade inflation or lack of rigor as we've faced in creative writing, but rather an acceptance that students rose to the course's rigorous challenges.

Stephanie Vanderslice: That story does sound familiar. An overwhelming theme of *Does the Writing Workshop Work?* is that undergraduate workshops really benefit from a combined approach that introduces students to peer review but also introduces them to the various forms of invention. My students and I do a significant amount of in-class writing, especially exercises around a concept I'm trying to teach, like rhythm or structure. For example, we might work individually on pieces (and they can be in any genre) that must all incorporate the same line a certain number of times. It's worth remembering, too, that, as they come to us with different backgrounds in writing, sometimes even advanced students could do with a little instruction in invention and recursive revision before they develop the assumptions that lead to writer's block – e.g. good writers don't need self-assignments, their work is always the result of divine inspiration or the dictation of the muses.

Anna Leahy: More than a little instruction, I'd say. Larissa Szporluk and I have a conversation essay in this book about imitation, invention, and deep imagination. Revision is a very important aspect of my approach as a teacher, which scares students at first, but almost always ends up making them proud of their work – and interested in others' writing.

Stephanie Vanderslice: Actually, that essay is a great example for new writers of the all the ways in which a piece of work is born, via a combination of practices and habits of mind. Most illuminating for students are the many ways in which juxtaposition – of inspiration, forms, ideas, subjects, and on and on – almost always leads to interesting new work.

Cathy Day: Something else changing in creative writing curricula and/or co-curricular projects is what Dinty W. Moore, Lori A. May, and others call *literary citizenship.* Many programs require creative writing majors to take a course that's akin to service-learning: tutoring young writers, administering a visiting writers' series, partnering with community organizations, etc. According to AWP, there are more than 800 degree-granting creative writing programs in this country – an amazing number! – so it's important to think about how we, as writers and teachers of creative writing in those hundreds of programs, can channel all that interest constructively. Creative writing programs, in their current manifestation, are laboratories in which writers are cultivated, but we're also cultivating future readers and teachers and editors and bloggers and book reviewers and book buyers – citizens in the vast literary culture. I'm more conscious of this role we have as creative writing teachers, but I'm sort of making it up as I go along.

Anna Leahy: I've been using the term *nerd* to refer to the habits of mind that I want to cultivate in my students, because I want them to be curious, to think divergently, and to try new things. I want them to be creative thinkers generally.

Literary citizen may be a more discipline-specific term, but broader, too, in the sense of connecting with the larger community and culture. Isolation, because it's required to do the writing itself, can all too easily be viewed as the most important part of the endeavor. With tens of thousands of students, creative writing programs can nourish a culture that appreciates the arts and humanities as human endeavors.

Stephanie Vanderslice: I could have used that term as I was finishing my recent book, *Rethinking Creative Writing in Higher Education*, but it hadn't yet caught on. The whole last chapter is about that issue, about how creative writing programs need to connect with the community and form a sense of civic responsibility among the next generation of writers. A brilliant example of this, which exists completely independent of creative writing programs, is Dave Eggers's brainchild 826 National. This project oversees community writing centers run by writers in cities all over the United States.

These kinds of connections are mutually beneficial, for the community and for the writer. And they help to create the next generation of readers! *Literary citizenship:* this term is now becoming part of the creative writing lexicon. The next generation of writers and pedagogy scholars can take this up and see where it leads us. It may well be the primary way to keep re-envisioning our discipline.

References

826 National. See http://www.826national.org/ (accessed 13 May 2016).
Angelo, T. and Cross, P. (1993) *Classroom Assessment Techniques,* Hoboken, NJ: Jossey-Bass.
Bell, M.S. (1997) *Narrative Design: Working with Imagination, Craft, and Form* (p. 3). New York: W.W. Norton.
Bell, S. (2007) *The Artful Edit: On the Practice of Editing Yourself.* New York: W.W. Norton.
Birkerts, S. (2007) *The Art of Time in Memoir,* Minneapolis, MN: Graywolf.
Carr, N. (2010) *The Shallows.* New York: W.W. Norton.

Grimm, S. (ed.) (2006) *Ordering the Storm*. Cleveland, OH: CSU Poetry Center.
Healey, S. (2009) The rise of creative writing & the new value of creativity. *The Writer's Chronicle* 30.
Herrington, A., Hodgson, K. and Moran, C. (2009) *Teaching the New Writing: Technology, Change, and Assessment in the 21st Century Classroom*. New York: Teacher's College Press.
Hugo, R. (1979) *The Triggering Town*, New York: W.W. Norton.
Jaschik, S. (2010) No grading, more learning. *Inside Higher Ed:* 3, May. See http://www.insidehighered.com/news/2010/05/03/grading.
Leahy, A. (2007) Creativity, caring, and the easy A: Rethinking the role of self-esteem in creative writing pedagogy. In K. Ritter and S. Vanderslice (eds) *Can It Really Be Taught?* (pp. 55–65). Portsmouth, NH: Boynton/Cook.
Leahy, A. (2009) Cookie-cutter monsters, one-size methodologies and the humanities. *Inside Higher Ed* 29 January.
Leahy, A. (2010) Who wants to be a nerd? Or how cognitive science changed my teaching. *New Writing: International Journal for the Practice and Theory of Creative Writing* 7 (1), 45–52.
Leahy, A. and Dechow, D. (2014) Concentration, form, and ways of seeing. *Creative Writing in the Digital Age*. New York: Bloomsbury.
Leahy, A. and Szporluk, L. (2010) Good counsel: A conversation about poetry writing, the imagination, and teaching. *Mid-American Review* 30 (1&2), 57–69.
Mayers, T. (2005) *(Re)Writing Craft: Composition, Creative Writing, and the Future of English Studies* (p. 33). Pittsburgh, PA: University of Pittsburgh Press.
McGurl, M. (2009) *The Program Era*. Cambridge, MA: Harvard University Press.
Moore, D. (2008) *Brevity*. See http://brevity.wordpress.com/2008/08/14/be-an-open-node-blake-butler-on-literary-citizenship/.
Moxley, J. (2010) Afterword: Disciplinarity and the future of creative writing studies. In D. Donnelly (ed.) *Does the Writing Workshop Still Work?* (pp. 230–238). Bristol: Multilingual Matters.
National Writing Project. See http://www.nwp.org/.
Pink, D. (2006) *A Whole New Mind: Why Right Brainers Will Rule the Future*. New York: Riverhead.
Swander, M. (2005) Duck, duck, turkey: Using encouragement to structure workshop assignments. In A. Leahy (ed.) *Power and Identity in the Creative Writing Classroom* (pp. 167–179). Clevedon: Multilingual Matters.
Vanderslice, S. (2012) *Rethinking Creative Writing in Higher Education*. Cambridge: Creative Writing Sudies.
Woods, J. (2009) *How Fiction Works*. New York: Picador.

3 Good Counsel: Creative Writing, the Imagination, and Teaching

Anna Leahy and Larissa Szporluk

'Good Counsel' acknowledges the role talent may play in an emerging writer's growth, but argues that guidance, mentorship and reading play important roles as well. As teachers and as practitioners of the art, we can and should guide students in their growth over time and show our students ways they can continue to grow as writers even beyond our influence. Drawing from a variety of theoretical and philosophical stances, from Aristotle to recent developments in cognitive science, Anna Leahy and Larissa Szporluk define three stages of artistic learning fostered in our classrooms: imitation, invention and deep imagination. They also discuss specific approaches and assignments that foster each type of learning.

Anna Leahy: As a student *being taught* in workshop classes, *Can creative writing be taught?* seemed an odd query. I now understand that creative writing as a discipline was a relative newcomer to the academy, and, since 1975, the number of programs quadrupled across the United States. So, that early question was important for the field and its practitioners to address.

I was baffled, however, in 2007 by the opening line in Francine Prose's *Reading Like a Writer*: 'Can creative writing be taught?' A year later, an essay of mine appeared in a book titled with the same question: *Can It Really Be Taught?* (Ritter & Vanderslice, 2007). Why can't we move beyond that question? That question asserts that talent is the central component in the artistic – or creative – process, for only if talent is the end-all-be-all can teaching be beside the point. We remain invested in the Romantic model of the inspired poet, with a popular emphasis on William Wordsworth's notion of overflowing emotion, rather than on its balance with recollection in tranquility.

Larissa Szporluk: Talent is essential but can't operate alone to produce great poetry. Character, luck, stamina, etc. – in short, life – all factor in. Life is the central component in the creative process. But I do think that an absence of so-called talent makes the artist's task more strenuous.

Anna Leahy: If we look to discoveries about cognition, talent or genius may not be meaningless but is not as important as we've believed. In an article entitled 'Unleashing creativity,' Ulrich Kraft topples the Romantic myth: 'Scientific understanding of creativity is far from complete, but one lesson already seems plain: originality is not a gift doled out sparingly by the gods' (2005: 18).

More recently, Malcolm Gladwell, in a *New Yorker* article (2008), asserts that genius – and its presumed companion, precocity – is not the sole path to creative productivity. Instead, Gladwell suggests the 'experimental innovator,' a curious, driven individual who works hard over decades. Gladwell concludes 'sometimes genius is anything but rarefied; sometimes it's just the thing that emerges after twenty years of working at your kitchen table.'

Larissa Szporluk: One resource that I find helpful when exploring these questions is Longinus's treatise, *On Great Writing (On the Sublime)*. Though he lived 20 centuries ago, his statements are applicable today. After contesting Caecilius's statement 'Great writers are born, not made, and there is only one kind of art: to be born with talent,' Longinus argues that talent is

> not usually random or altogether devoid of method [...]. Great qualities are too precarious when left to themselves, unsteadied and unballasted by knowledge, abandoned to mere impulse and untutored daring; they need the bridle as well as the spur. Demosthenes shows that this is true in everyday life when he says that while the greatest blessing is good fortune, the second, no less important, is good counsel, and that the absence of the second utterly destroys the first. We might apply this to literature, with talent in the place of fortune and art in that of counsel. The clinching proof is that only by means of art can we perceive the fact that certain literary effects are due to sheer inborn talent. If, as I said, those who object to literary criticism would ponder these things, they would, I think, no longer consider the investigation of our subject extravagant or useless. (2012: 62–63)

Teachers and poets should be obsessed with the mysteries of great writing and ponder the question of talent. We want our students to have confidence in the whole teaching-of-creative-writing endeavor because we ourselves have benefited from it. Right? Longinus is convincing. It is too simplistic to state that talent is the only consideration. We can insist that the 'good counsel' in our current creative writing climate is a good teacher, one who has an excellent understanding of the writer's art.

Anna Leahy: When you – and Longinus – refer to 'good counsel,' that points to mentorship as an experiential form of teaching, as the role of the engaged creative writing teacher in workshop-based pedagogy as well as in our individualized conversations with our students.

But reading also is good counsel. In the collection *Women Poets on Mentorship,* Beth Ann Fennelly writes about Denise Duhamel's poem 'Bullimia': it 'changed my writing because it gave me the courage to be unsavory, if that's what a poem called for. I decided to stop being so self-conscious in my poetry' (2008: 15). Fennelly didn't have to meet Duhamel to be mentored by her poems. Likewise, Joy Katz read Sharon Olds's *Satan Says* before she met Olds. Like Katz, my undergraduate self found Olds 'accessible,' 'grotesque,' and 'like me' (even though I wasn't really like her). And as did Katz, I faced 'my poetry teacher's skepticism' (2008: 75); a dissertation director struck Olds from my reading list, presumably because she wasn't important or serious enough (I changed directors). I was riveted not merely by the subject matter and the 'room for me to write without self-consciousness' (2008: 77), but also by her enjambment, organizing syntax, and pacing to shade meaning and create emphasis.

Larissa Szporluk: Hidden mentors – those writers and works that we admire from afar. Virginia Woolf was Sylvia Plath's most influential hidden mentor. A poet like Emily Dickinson seems to have depended almost entirely on hidden mentors, like the Bible and Shakespeare.

Anna Leahy: That's not to say active mentorship isn't important, too. My MFA thesis director asked me bluntly, perhaps because I'd become enraptured with short, Olds-like, enjambed lines, 'Will you ever write a 10-syllable line?' He also told me, perhaps because self-consciousness had crept into my work, 'You never write a bad poem' – a back-handed compliment about my lack of risk taking. Now, I say something like that when I hope a student is ready to be nudged.

Another way to think of mentorship is to understand (echoing the 'signature pedagogies' discussed by Carnegie Foundation's Lee Shulman) creative writing as an ethical, professional community sustained by mentors of all sorts who guide student writers. Mentorship demands much of teachers and of literature, but it also demands that emerging writers be active, take risks, internalize expectations, and individuate themselves.

Larissa Szporluk: Longinus would wholeheartedly agree with you; in fact, he himself substitutes 'counsel' with 'art.' Mentorship can be defined as need be – that which drives you to be brave, for example. But all of this brings us to the more pressing question: if mentorship can act as a kind of stand-in for talent, what kinds of mentorship activities are especially effective in fostering truly innovative and skillful writers? Are there general applications for success or is this strictly an individually determined relationship?

There are some general modes for successful mentorship – not infallible, of course, but certainly time-tested. Imitation, for example, was an ancient teaching tool, dating back to Aristotle. Imitation is the most effective teaching tool for languages and music. Encouraging imitation is good counsel for students of poetry. It is much more effective than lecturing on the qualities of a great poem. Simply ask your students to imitate a great poem, and they will be forced to ask themselves the essential questions about language and composition as they go about it, appealing to the puzzle-solver within, which ameliorates the process.

Anna Leahy: I wonder whether imitation took on particularly negative connotations in the 20th century, especially in the United States, as the individual gained primacy and as technology introduced a new notion of *copy*. Not only do we think of a copy in terms of the photocopier – or a person presses a *Save As* button and a replica appears – but copying is also linked with cheating. When poets discuss imitation, however, we are not referring to copying but, rather, to a complicated investigation, an in-depth questioning of language and style.

Larissa Szporluk: As a young poet, I smirked at the idea of imitation, believing that it would somehow soil my determination to be original. I was guilty of that Romanticism you mentioned. Call it anxiety of influence, as Harold Bloom did – a shallow form of it.

As a teacher now, I find imitation exercises to be fantastic shortcuts to the creative process. I'll ask students to imitate a Hopkins poem for example and suddenly they're using alliteration and consonance and internal rhyme and performing technical feats and learning much more than they would by just listening to me discuss Gerard Manley Hopkins. Poetry is active and should be taught actively.

Anna Leahy: In an issue of *College English* about the status of creative writing (with which I disagree on several other points), Mary Ann Cain suggests an exercise she calls 'intertexting'; students copy a passage from Ernest Hemingway in one column and then, in the other, fill in what might be missing, from adjectives to character backstory. That's a version of imitation.

Sandy Feinstein, in *Power and Identity in the Creative Writing Classroom,* states, 'For the most part, students are unaware of what they don't know about their language and how what they don't know matters in writing' (2005: 192). That's why creative writing can be taught; teaching is often about making students aware, pointing them in a direction, and showing them ways to figure out new things. Feinstein uses less well-known poetry – epigrams of Anyte, Sappho's fragments, and poems by Lady Mary Wroth – to tease apart how different poets of different times explored *love* in different forms. Imitation helps us discover what we don't know about language and how one concept or form might be conceived in many ways.

Imitation tasks challenge students to actively examine a supposed master to figure out for themselves how the text is put together. One risk of imitation could be the reification of genius – or the fixing of such a quality through a few examples. In practice, as with Cain's exercise, Feinstein's, or yours, imitation instead provides access and experimentation, the sort of thing Robert Frost thought essential to writing: 'Play's the thing. All virtue in "as if"' (1966: 353).

Larissa Szporluk: Some might point out additional risks to imitation. The McPoem that Donald Hall scorned? Homogeneity? Never! The McPoem is created by bad group criticism, not by imitation. By bad group criticism, I mean the occasional group tendency to recommend blunting one's edges, excising one's strangeness, and, for heaven's sake, murdering one's so-called darlings. Clean a poem of its original elements and you have a McPoem because it's a consensual product, one created by cutting rather than building. It's safe, it's cheap, and, in the end, it's worth whatever a cheeseburger goes for these days.

Anna Leahy: Homogeneity often strikes me as a straw man held up to argue against the workshop, as if it's a monolith instead of the varied practices that exist across our courses and programs. Instead of ending up with McPoem, students in a dynamic workshop are likely to expand their concepts of what and how a poem can be. The collective wisdom of a classroom offers more than the sum of its parts, and students work against uniformity.

Nancy Andreasen, in *The Creating Brain,* says, 'It is more difficult for the creative brain to prosper in isolation' (2005: 128). The act of writing requires solitude, of course. Perhaps, we should pay more attention to that need for isolation, not in terms of the Romantic model, but because we have difficulty being alone in our world of streaming movies, cell phones, and Facebook. But creativity flourishes in the balance of solitude and community. Andreasen claims, 'Put simply, creative people are likely to be more productive and more original if surrounded by other creative people. This too produces an environment in which the creative brain is stimulated to form novel connections and novel ideas' (2005: 129). The workshop is thoughtful pedagogy; it acknowledges a balance between the individual, a peopled environment, and a literary tradition.

Larissa Szporluk: Imitation is part of that balance. Imitation opens something up in a poet – the discovery of the musculature of sound for example – it doesn't shut a poet down. Conscious imitation is safe. It's the subconscious kind of imitation that is potentially dangerous.

Subconscious imitation occurs when there is too much identification with another poet – too much emotional identification. I had an unpleasant experience with it myself and honestly did not fully realize that I was trying to change my natural way of thinking to fit this deeply intellectual poetic model I had latched onto. It was like a weird crush, now that I think about it. Weird and destructive, like my childhood admiration for a boy that drove me to develop an overbite – because he had one. Now that's pathetic. But the same thing happens to artists, to their psyches. A sick admiration like that can lead to a subconscious imitation, which is dangerous to one's originality and potential flowering of talent or genius.

And that is why invention, what I consider the second stage of creative development, is so important – not only as a means of breaking out of the potentially dangerous imitation mode, but as a way to begin to identify one's particular brand of inventiveness. For example, if a poet is excited about juxtapositions – two or more incongruent things co-existing in a poem – then that would be an area of invention to attend to. He or she might want to test the limits, almost like a science experiment: can I write a poem with 20 sheep in it and a cucumber and a mass murderer and an enormous sunflower that cries at night? Can I pull off a poem like that? Or, if the special interest is in forms and the poet is bored by the traditional ones, she may want to invent a form of her own, as Billy Collins did with the paradelle. As a teacher, I encourage that kind of exercise. Good prompts urge the inventor within to the forefront and that is why, although they can be annoying, prompts have a natural place in the creative writing classroom.

Anna Leahy: Yes, both imitation and invention get the poet out of her own head, looking away from her own navel. The novelist John Gardner wrote,

'None of these writers [ancient poets, Daniel Defoe, Henry Fielding, etc.] sat down to write 'to express himself.' They sat down to write this kind of story or that, or to mix this form with that form, producing some new effect' (1983: 21). Invention gets the poet out of herself. Flannery O'Connor wrote, 'No art is sunk in the self, but rather, in art the self becomes self-forgetful in order to meet the demands of the thing seen and the thing being made' (1970: 82). Prompts introduce the possibility of self-forgetfulness. They focus on the thing being made.

As a student, I once forced myself to write one-sentence poems; I made them as long as I could. Another time, a friend and I assigned each other titles; she assigned me 'Recidivism.' That title led me unexpectedly to an abusive priest when I realized that the inmates I'd taught at a correctional facility wore the same uniform as the boys at my elementary school. One of my students a few years ago gathered her writing group in an alcove on campus where names appeared on bricks; they wrote narrative poems about the imagined lives of these strangers.

Even prompts about the self can force us to take an unfamiliar perspective. Marilyn Annucci adapted a Facebook meme called '25 Random Facts about Yourself' as a first-day-of-class exercise, so I used her idea. Students wrote often funny, sometimes heart-breaking tidbits. They attended not to theme, emotion, or the self as much as to juxtaposition, detail, and tone.

Something imposed externally can show us the inventor within, who we are as poets.

Larissa Szporluk: What does invention *mean*? If you invent a machine that sterilizes and dries plastic bags so they can be used indefinitely, then you have (1) identified a need, (2) visualized a solution, and (3) realized the solution with material applications. Are poems the same?

For useful poetic inventions, must we identify a need? I'm beginning to think *yes*, because otherwise, invention, like imitation, risks banality. Invention can be done for its own sake only, and while the benefits are technical and can be pleasurable, the result is not an important poem. Wallace Stevens makes an interesting distinction when he criticizes quasi-surrealist poetry: 'To make a clam play an accordion is to invent not to discover.' (1991: 277). Discovery, then, is the integrity that is missing in mere invention for the sake of novelty. Important invention involves bringing to light something hitherto unknown or unimagined. Classroom prompts, or prompts in general, can often lapse into a more imitation-like state or into what we call going through motions, unless a sense of discovery or necessity accompanies it or develops somewhere along the way.

So, invention can be play, as you mentioned via Frost, but the poet must, at some point, move into discovery. That's the path to deep imagination.

Anna Leahy: Poet Glyn Maxwell writes, in his book *On Poetry*, 'Let's start again with nothing. Let's start with poetry's inventions that are absolutely required – their names are *something* and *nothing* – and see what comes of them' (2012: 10). Imitation, invention, and deep imagination are ways to negotiate the relationship between something and nothing.

Invention can intervene (or be imposed) at any time in the writing process, too. I've written elsewhere about a student whose aunt was diagnosed with breast cancer while she was in my class. She believed she owed it to herself and her aunt to document – to witness, as poets say – the situation. Of course, the first draft was abstract and filled with clichés designed to capture emotion, and the post-workshop revision was differently empty. It read like a sympathy card. I asked her to write a version in which Barbie had breast cancer. My student was unconvinced (and initially unaware of the potential irony of a Barbie with breast cancer), but she promised to give it a try. She expected Barbie to make her aunt's cancer too light a subject; instead, it allowed her to discover her complex feelings.

Larissa Szporluk: Invention, good invention, is the marriage of two previously disconnected things. Once married, they become their own entity, although the traces of their previous existence might remain (and are usually especially apparent to the poet). Often readers can see the poet's process: there is transparency involved in the invention.

Here's another example. Poets can be inventive when they're revising, especially when they're dealing with a surplus of bad poems. So I have a bad poem with long lines, weak emotion, mainly fluff, but I have a couple of good phrases in it, and I remember there was tremendous goodwill behind the writing of this poem. I felt, at the time of the writing, that I genuinely wanted this poem to be written. Then I also have a new poem with curiously short lines that, on the whole, leaves me cold. But the short lines are really compelling because they create, all by themselves, a feeling of trepidation. Ah-ha. I will bring the short lines to the fluffy, long-lined poem. The short line knocks the fluff around until a badly torn, bleeding, bizarre new angry syntax begins to suggest a possible new narrative. The poem is finally becoming interesting. Sparks are flying as I attack it. The short line has forced the language to be more responsible. Starkness has replaced the previously banal atmosphere. I have invented a way to energize two bad poems.

But is it great? No, of course not. It is interesting. It is inventive. It has energy. I could stop here. I could maybe even get it published somewhere because it is rather fetching and mysterious. And this is the impasse where we all linger: What will it take to make my inventive poem great? What is this deep imagination stuff that promises to transform the competent and interesting into the breathtaking? If I only knew from experience!

But I can try to guess – because I have seen it at work in great painting, have sensed its roots in great poems. It comes from a kind of falling through your work, almost literally, falling through to the other side of where it all began.

Anna Leahy: The poet Jane Hirshfield writes, 'Concentration can be also placed into things – it radiates undimmed from Vermeer's paintings' (2004: 3–4). She uses the word *concentration,* but she's talking about deep imagination, from a different perspective. Hirshfield also says, 'Before we can concentrate easily, we need to know where we stand' (2004: 11). Imitation and invention *invite* concentration – or inspiration or deep imagination or whatever we call it. The first two stages of creativity teach not only intellectual understanding but habits of mind. They invite what Hirshfield calls, 'a kind of fullness that over-spills into everything. One breath taken completely; one poem, fully written, fully read – in such a moment, anything can happen' (2004: 32).

We come back to a basic creative process. Some cognitive scientists, including Alice Flaherty, assert that divergent thinking (making new, often unexpected connections or leaps) and convergent thinking (conventional or planned connections) alternate in five stages: defining the problem, learning as much as possible, incubating at an impasse, discovering an idea that moves the process forward, and testing the ideas. Maybe imitation is both a means of defining the problem – how to write a poem based on existing poems – and also learning as much as possible through existing poems. Maybe invention is learning through practice, or the means to move forward. So, imitation (practicing craft based on existing poems) and invention (practicing through prompts) allow us to understand poetic conventions. Perhaps, we need to be conventional before – or as – we can be divergent or imaginative.

Larissa Szporluk: Yes, but we need to work with these conventions in unconventional, even imaginative ways from the very beginning, showing our originality in the first two stages. During the imitation stage, we are using the imitated poems as a form of contrast to what we have written thus far. That difference, usually one of perspective, must be retained. We don't want our original way of perceiving to get lost in the quest for technical prowess.

Similarly, in the invention stage, we don't want the art of invention to take precedence over the emotional responsibility of poetry. Of course, the hope is that after several years of these exercises, a poet will assume and move beyond inventiveness and not need to receive it from teachers and/or peers. In other words, we have to have a vision of what we're all about when we enter deep imagination, knowing where we stand, as Hirschfield says, because it's dark there, there are no rules, no guides.

Anna Leahy: There are no rules in deep imagination, but there may be deeply engrained mental habits that allow us to make our way in the dark. Athletes talk of being *in the zone*; that may be analogous to your idea of falling through. A baseball player must know what a great swing looks like and may even watch videotapes of himself to consciously change bad habits. In other words, a batter develops an intellectual understanding of batting. That's what imitation does for a poet, and that intellectual understanding of poetry weaves through the entire writing experience.

But as much as a batter *knows* what he needs to do in the batter's box, he also needs to practice that swing, over and over, with different pitches. Invention both makes us more consistent and also shows us how we can respond as *individual* poets to *individual* poems we are writing. Also, if a batter gets a hit just one out of every three at-bats, he's doing well. A poet doesn't write a great poem every time. It's not about perfection; there is no perfection, only the striving toward discovery.

What's interesting about this analogy is that great hitters often have streaks, stretches of being in the zone when time slows so they see the seams of the ball as it approaches. Hirshfield writes, 'By concentration, I mean a particular state of awareness: penetrating, unifying, and focused, yet also permeable and open. [… It] is felt as a grace state: time slows and extends, and a person's every movement and decision seem to partake of perfection' (2004: 3). Of course, hitters have slumps, too, something akin to writer's block. They go back to the coach, the videotapes, and the extra practice. As Flaherty, and numerous poets, assert, 'writing regularly, inspiration or no, is not a bad way to eventually get into an inspired mood.' The streak – what the Romantics called *inspiration*, what James Joyce called *epiphany*, what Mihaly Csikszentmihalyi calls *flow* – happens when the world falls away. The poet falls into intense concentration.

Imitation and invention, then, create conditions in which deep imagination – or inspiration – can occur. Andreasen, whom I mentioned regarding the individual and community, writes, 'The notion of the muse, or the need for inspiration, is much more than a metaphor.' In fact, she asserts, 'The capacity to focus intensely, to dissociate, and to realize an apparently remote and transcendent 'place' is one of the hallmarks of the creative process' (2005: 37).

Larissa Szporluk: I like your quote from Andreasen – the 'remote and transcendent place' – because I have always felt that the imagination is a place. When I was beginning to write poetry seriously, ages ago, and working on the poems that became *Dark Sky Question*, I could feel myself actually going to that place. For me, it was a small planet, completely barren. All my poems started there.

I like to think of each book I write as having a location in the imagination – the more defined, the better the book. My most problematic book, *The Wind, Master Cherry, the Wind* (2003), was, like the wind, all over the place – NOT a good location! Too frantic and whimsical. I couldn't *land* anywhere and that upset my concentration.

Occasionally, I ask students to describe their imaginations in spatial terms and the responses are always surprising and interesting. Visualizing the imagination is a way of solidifying your relationship with it. But that relationship is imbalanced, imagination having most of the power. The best we can do is to be open to it. Trying to control it is akin to caging the animal we love only to wonder why it looks so misshapen behind bars.

A few years ago, I had an epiphany of sorts about the imagination, albeit an embarrassingly simplistic one: deep imagination is the brief but total relaxation of all the senses. I say *brief* because this relaxed state cannot be sustained. When it occurs, total relaxation invites transportation. The senses become elastic. Transportation invites transformation: any time we go somewhere, we are susceptible to change.

The German film director Werner Herzog, a genius who seems to drip deep imagination, was apparently a strange child who spoke very little. His mother says of him: 'He is absolutely unable to explain anything. He knows, he sees, he understands, but he cannot explain. Everything goes into him. If it comes out, it comes out transformed' (2002: ix). I love that description. It captures the intensity of how the imagination functions: imagination WANTS to change the world. Not to control it, but to participate in its continuous creation.

In order to take in 'everything,' as Herzog does, it is essential that the self be unobstructed. Only through a relaxed state is this possible. I'm not talking about doing yoga and transcendental meditation around the clock. I'm talking about being about to engage universally with whatever piece of world you're in: Do you hear the laments from the dog kennel two miles away? Do those laments cross the forest? At the same time, does a walnut land in the road with a thump? Once inside of you, do the laments become the trapped cries of the soul of the walnut? Is the walnut yelling? Okay, this is getting silly, but you see where I'm going: transformation. The deep imagination is able to make instant combinations, instant hybrids of the elements of the sensed world. It does this almost without you.

Anna Leahy: The popular notion of so-called inspiration is that of impetus for a poem, but we are arguing that deep imagination results from imitation and invention. It's not a starting point.

Larissa Szoprluk: Imitation teaches you how to be original while using conventional techniques. Invention teaches you how to combine, how to associate, so that, when you encounter deep imagination, you trust what happens there. Deep imagination is where you surrender to creative energy; you follow along, and you use your skills instinctively, not consciously.

We could say that, in deep imagination, we use creative memory the way athletes in the zone use muscle memory. Being in the zone means being totally relaxed. When Michael Phelps won his gold medals, not a single muscle was tense (so they say). The body is no longer restricted by itself and becomes capable of incredible feats. Similarly, when a poet is in this state, the poem doesn't have boundaries, doesn't even have lines. The poem lives in a three-dimensional state and can wrap around trees or fall suddenly or go dark. It's alive. The only thing we can control, or work to control in this process, is the transfer from the deep imaginative space to the page.

Anna Leahy: So, we must learn to relax through effort, in order to become open to discovery. Stephen Dobyns, somewhat akin to Hirshfield, warns the poet 'not to censor or limit the work for reasons that stand outside the work' (2003: 9). To me, he also suggests that a poem balance between two worlds: a logical, literal reality and that world of deep imagination.

Glyn Maxwell asserts, 'You master form you master time. Well, you don't, but you give it a run for its non-exchangable money. Form has a direct effect on the silence beneath it, which is to say on the whiteness before and after it and where the lines end' (2012: 18). Form represents a logical, literal reality, whereas time – and timelessness – involve deep imagination.

Larissa Szporluk: I believe so many poems that are born and raised in deep imagination are killed on the page because the left brain gets activated when it sees words on that white sheet or blank screen, and that logical, conventional part of us rushes to organize them. As poets, we can try to ease the damage done by arranging, maybe even solidifying, a poem's lines in our heads first. In other words, we can line up the words like sheep, while they're all still alive. Then, only at the very end, in a final necessary move, we put them down in ink.

This makes for a terrific exercise for students. Write a poem entirely in your head. Bring it to class in your head. Share it with the class from your head. Only after you've spoken it to the class may you commit it to paper.

Compare the poem written in this manner with those that are grown on the screen or paper.
Perhaps I'm wrong. Perhaps there is no difference.

Anna Leahy: I don't know that I could do that exercise, but I see what you're after. I ponder poems longer than I used to before putting finger to keyboard (or, less often now, pen to paper). Seeing a poem onscreen creates boundaries, so lining up the sheep – and sheep do seem to want to be herded – may be increasingly important as we mature.

At some point, though, a poem incubating in my head starts to lose more than it gains there. Once typed, revision presents the poem as a new kind of problem and invites more play, which can push me back into imagination. That's the reason I emphasize revision as a teacher.

Perhaps, the deep imagination stage of the process is what cannot be taught in the more overt ways of earlier stages. We create conditions for imitation and invention, and students strengthen their thinking skills as we guide them. But deep imagination may require additional, ongoing practice to take advantage of these conditions. Of course, once a poet experiences deep imagination (or inspiration or poetic discovery), she'll probably want to experience it again.

Larissa Szporluk: I would argue that from that point on, she'll never be satisfied with less. I'll even go as far to say that in that first encounter with deep imagination, the real poet is born.

Anna Leahy: To be born is to be ushered into life, to become fully human. Add an *e*, and being a poet is something that is borne as well, something weighty we carry as part of ourselves.

References

Andreasen, N. (2005) *The Creating Brain: The Neuroscience of Genius.* New York: Dana P.
Cain, M.A. (2009) 'To be lived': Theorizing influence in creative writing. *College English* 71 (3), 229–241.
Dobyns, S. (2003) *Best Words, Best Order.* New York: Palgrave Macmillan.
Feinstein, S. (2005) Writing in the shadows: topics, models, and audiences that focus on language. In A. Leahy (ed.) *Power and Identity in the Creative Writing Classroom* (pp. 192–202). Clevedon: Multilingual Matters.
Fennelly, B.A. (2008) On Denise Duhamel. In A. Greenberg and R. Zucker (eds) *Women Poets on Mentorship: Efforts and Affections* (pp. 13–16). Iowa City: University of Iowa Press.
Flaherty, A. (2004) *The Midnight Disease: The Drive to Write, Writer's Block, and the Creative Brain.* New York: Houghton Mifflin.

Frost, R. (1966) *Poetry & Prose.* New York: Holt, Rinehart and Wilson.

Gardner, J. (1983) *The Art of Fiction: Notes on Craft for Young Writers.* New York: Vintage.

Gladwell, M. (2008) Late bloomers: Why do we equate genius with precocity? *The New Yorker* 20 October. See http://www.newyorker.com/magazine/2008/10/20/late-bloomers-2 (accessed 13 May 2016).

Hall, D. (2005) *Poetry and Ambition.* The Poetry Foundation. See https://www.poets.org/poetsorg/text/poetry-and-ambition (accessed 10 October 2015).

Herzog, W. (2002) *Herzog on Herzog.* New York: Faber and Faber.

Hirshfield, J. (2004) *Nine Gates: Entering the Mind of Poetry.* New York: Harper Perennial.

Katz, J. (2008) On Sharon Olds. In A. Greenberg and R. Zucker (eds) *Women Poets on Mentorship: Efforts and Affections* (pp. 75–78). Iowa City: University of Iowa Press.

Kraft, U. (2005) Unleashing creativity. *Scientific American Mind* 16 (1), 16–23.

Longinus (2012) On the sublime. In J. Tanke and C. McQuillan (eds) *The Bloomsbury Anthology of Aesthetics.* New York: Bloomsbury.

Maxwell, G. (2012) *On Poetry.* London: Oberon Books.

O'Connor, F. (1970) *Mysteries and Manners: Occasional Prose.* New York: Farrar, Strauss, and Giroux.

Prose, F. (2007) *Reading Like a Writer.* New York: Harper Perennial.

Ritter, K. and Vanderslice, S. (eds) (2007) *Can It Really Be Taught?* Portsmouth, NH: Boynton/Cook.

Shulman, L. (2005) Signature pedagogies in the professions. *Daedalus* 134 (3), 52–59.

Stevens, W. (1991) Materia Poetica. In J. V. Brogan (ed.) *Part of the Climate: American Cubist Poetry* (pp. 277–280). Los Angeles: University of California Press.

Szporluk, L. (2003) *The Wind, Master Cherry, the Wind.* Farmington, ME: Alice James.

4 Writerly Reading in the Creative Writing Course

Sandy Feinstein, Suzanne Greenberg, Susan Hubbard, Brent Royster and Anna Leahy

When New Criticism took its hits, so-called close reading fell out of favor, but writers continued to read closely to figure out how a text works and what decisions authors have made. Francine Prose and others have reclaimed careful attention to the text as reading like a writer. In *Power and Identity in the Creative Writing Classroom*, Sandy Feinstein suggested specific ways that reading provides breadth and depth in a creative writing class. This new conversation checks in 10 years later on what we call *writerly reading* and explores the role of reading as a crucial part of creative writing pedagogy and practice. The authors here grapple with issues of pleasure, cultural context, and practical application and discuss ways that reading works in different genres and to different ends.

Anna Leahy: In *Reading Like a Writer*, Francine Prose talks about reading as part of the way writers learn, perhaps the most important way we learn such things as 'the love of language' and 'a gift of story-telling' (2007: 1). Of course, a writer must write, but Prose says, 'For any writer, the ability to look at a sentence and see what's superfluous, what can be altered, revised, expanded, and, especially, cut, is essential.' (2007: 2). And that ability is cultivated by reading.

Sandy Feinstein: Reading like a writer can be, in the creative writing classroom, an act of reverse engineering: a taking apart of the parts – metaphor, images, meter, sound, noun, verb, adjective, etc. – to build it back together again in a way that works for each individual writer.

Anna Leahy: That's how I watched films when I took a film class in college, with heightened awareness of choices the director and actors had made, and, at times, I still notice a camera angle. Prose goes on to say, 'I read for pleasure, first, but also more analytically, conscious of style, of diction, of how sentences were formed and information was being conveyed, how the writer was structuring plot, creating characters, employing detail and dialogue. [...] I read closely, word by word, sentence by sentence, pondering each deceptively minor decision the writer had made' (2007: 3). The ways we learn to see and understand texts sticks with us.

That attentiveness to craft in the process of reading, even when reading is done for pleasure, is what I've long called *writerly reading*. Students learn and practice it in my classes but also, I hope, carry it with them beyond the end of the semester.

Susan Hubbard: Writerly reading describes productive, exuberant ways in which writers engage their minds with texts in order to find and make meanings and glean insights into craft and culture. It's a kind of close reading that explores larger cultural frameworks for textual interpretation and resists narrowness, formalism, and rigidity.

Sandy Feinstein: Writerly reading, then, is less content or plot driven than technique aware. The writerly reader, caught up in an idea or plot, will step back and reflect on how what happened happened. Or, to put it another way, the writerly reader considers plotting in a double sense – the strategies of building action and the reader's complicity in it. In this way, writerly reading looks at the micro as much as the macro. Even while impressed by big ideas and themes, the reader focuses on how these emerge through narration, character(s), juxtapositions of setting – that is, through construction done by the writer. Explaining his own development as a writer, the novelist E.L. Doctorow told an NPR interviewer (2004/2015), 'I was reading constantly everything I could get my hands on. And, you know, at that age [nine], something else happens if you're going to be a writer. You're reading for the excitement of it and to find out what happens next, just racing along. And then another little line of inquiry comes into your head. You say, well, how is this done?'

Brent Royster: If we look at a text as constructed, writerly reading is a deconstruction. When we read another writer, we tend to try to figure out what makes this artist tick. For example, as my students perform close readings of poems and essays, they tend to annotate exhaustively; I also encourage recitation and imitation. Sometimes, the questions students ask of a text are a device to get inside the skin of a reading passage so that – rather than taking it in, as we so often suggest happens – students are taken into the work itself. By performing within the parameters of another artist's work, we writers begin to recognize, understand, and adopt the styles and devices of another. At this crucial stage in the writing/reading process, we may adapt to our challenges and (mis)understandings and thereafter improvise within our ongoing craft.

Sandy Feinstein: This kind of reading likely comes more easily when reading poetry than fiction, partly because poems are generally shorter and partly because fiction is seemingly read more for pleasure – or even entertainment – than is poetry. Perhaps the most compelling reason that poetry appears to invite attentive reading is because it has been part of our training as a legacy of the New Critics. Cleanth Brooks's call to read closely offered a different way to read and teach literature in the 1940s and 1950s, and his adherents, such as Stephen Booth and E. Talbot Donaldson, listened and taught their students of the 1960s and 1970s to look deeply at structure and language in, even the grammar of, poetry. And their students, some of whom would become teachers themselves, were inspired by the magic of so-called well-wrought words and absorbed those lessons of reading as potential new directions for writing and instruction. Booth's teaching of 'close reading that tries to avoid resulting in 'readings' – in interpretations' (1994: 43) informs, for example, the experimental poetry of one of his former students, Stephen Ratcliffe, who, in *[where late the sweet] Birds Sang*, pulls words from Shakespeare's sonnets to shape a new sonnet sequence that prompts close reflection on what's missing as much as on what's there. As Ratcliffe, who teaches Shakespeare and poetry workshops at Mills College, concludes in *Reading the Unseen*: 'those "Words, words, words" (2.2.192) that "show" us things we do not see, construct a picture of the world, describe how things are ("there") and how they might also be (here) imagined' (1988: 14). In this way, poetry seems to invite the reader to be attentive to the micro – even the interstices or blanks spaces – as well as the macro.

Anna Leahy: Or as poet Glyn Maxwell writes, 'poets work with two materials, one's black and one's white. Call them sound and silence, life and death, hot and cold, love and loss [...] Call it this and that, whatever it is *this time,* just don't make the mistake of thinking the white sheet is nothing. It's nothing for your novelist, your journalist, your blogger. For those folks it's a *tabula rasa,* a giving surface. For a poet it's half of everything' (2012: 11). A poem invites attention to everything, even the spaces, gaps and absences.

Brent Royster: Of course, we all return to reading for pleasure. Pleasure is the hook that brings us in. But then, once we've landed it, as writers, we want to handle it, to find out how it feeds and what it's got in its belly. When the subject matter is meaty, we want to figure out how it was made. What are all these composite parts and how do they move forward to provide such delight? Reverse engineering indeed.

Let's say one wayward poem is simply a construct: rhythms and poly-rhythms and rhymes and elliptical language that crackle in its own making. That doesn't sound like pleasure, but it is pleasure that brings writers to the brink of wanting more, and, so, it is the artifice we deconstruct to remind ourselves of the artifice unmade – the wellspring of the mind that gives artifice its life.

Anna Leahy: As writers reading, practicing reverse engineering in our minds, we explore *how* and *why* – not the writer's intentions, but the writer's decisions – even more so than the *what* or meaning of a text. We ask our students to read with us in this way, too. Richard Goodman, in his book *The Soul of Creative Writing*, puts it this way: 'Reading, for a writer, is a practical matter. How do you know what can be done unless you've seen it done by others?' (2008: 107).

Susan Hubbard: This kind of close reading uses critical language that embraces concepts and terminology associated with other disciplines and art forms. In other words, writerly reading is not necessarily limited to breaking every text down into its parts, but goes further to consider its wider and deeper contexts as well.

Suzanne Greenberg: Writerly reading means being open to awe, allowing yourself to fall in love with a sentence or phrase or paragraph and even to wish you wrote it yourself. Writerly reading can be transformative. It's reading with an awareness of all your senses and letting the evaluative mind take a rest for a while.

Susan Hubbard: Aaron Copland's *What to Listen for in Music* draws important parallels between music and writing. Copland maintained that a thoughtful, disciplined apprehension of an art form enhances our understanding of it. While acknowledging that some audiences seek entertainment or escapism, he suggested that, as we become more aware of the ways in which artists handle their materials, we become 'intelligent listeners' who appreciate creative work at more profound levels (2011: 15). Such awareness is invaluable to writers.

Suzanne Greenberg: Many writers are intuitively aware readers. Writers imitate in the way visual artists have always imitated, standing in front of paintings in museums, their own easels propped up in front of them. Writers fall in love with books the way someone else might fall in love with Barcelona or kickboxing or religion or, yes, a type of music. I teach writerly reading as the way we fall in love with writing.

Anna Leahy: Though I've not before thought of reading as guiding my students to fall in love with writing – or that my role might be as matchmaker – that seems a strangely fruitful way to view teaching. I want my students to care about writing, about language, and about certain texts (though not necessarily the same texts) as much as I do.

In the collection *Creative Composition*, I wrote about perseverance, about how part of what I try to cultivate in students is grit or the ability to stick with the poem through drafts or through the writing life over the long haul. I quoted Malcolm Gladwell, Steven Johnson, and psychologist Angela Duckworth, who all talk about cultivation over time (2015: 175). Maybe I didn't dig deeply enough, didn't think beyond the intellectual to the emotional. For underlying those arguments is the idea that, to pursue something over time, you must love what you do.

Susan Hubbard: My classroom discussions and conversations with colleagues indicate that many creative writing students have learned much of what they know about stories from listening to music, navigating internet media, and watching television and films. Making connections among those familiar experiences and texts assigned in my courses is central to my pedagogy. It's useful to create courses that ask students to be conversant in several critical languages and to consider principles that are pertinent across differing arts and cultures.

Brent Royster: We read to constantly repopulate the storehouse of the mind that we have been populating since we became familiar with language and ideas. As writers, we are awestruck by beautiful language; maybe that's a kind of love. However, we are also dumbstruck by the power words hold to do something more: the power words and ideas and images hold to move an audience beyond simple sleight-of-hand. Heart. Whatever heart is. Mind. Whatever mind is. Over both, language itself can hold sway, and it is the recollection and reconstruction and composition and presentation of all these abstract words that writers tend to value, *über alles*.

In some cases, students may not even know of their own love of reading until they are presented with the special quiet relationship with reading, what Kurt Vonnegut so aptly termed 'Occidental-style meditation' (1990: 200).

Suzanne Greenberg: In addition, there are also less serene ways to consider writerly reading. As Sondra Perl and Mimi Schwartz write in *Writing True,* 'Writers read with a bit of the scavenger in their hearts [...] to study the craft that makes writing succeed (or not)' (2006: 166). I want to know what my students *got* from a piece of writing, what they could *take away,* which really translates into what they learned about aspects of the writer's craft.

Anna Leahy: Indeed, writerly reading is selfish: *getting* something, *taking* something. In a piece at *The Huffington Post* about reading, I point to Richard Bausch's adamant stand: 'You must try to know everything that has ever been written that is worth remembering and you must keep up with what your contemporaries are doing.' Talking about the relationship of reading and writing, 'He suggests that writers take the great work of others into themselves and, rather than analyzing like a literary scholar, get to know favorites by heart.' Though maybe I should, I don't expect that knowing by heart from my students or even myself, unless we define *by heart* loosely as having heartfelt favorites.

When writers read the work of others, we are perhaps greedy, but it's not merely out of self-interest (or at least not for very long) so much as it is part of the immersion in being a writer. Reading selfishly diminishes no one else's experience. Books are not cake – you and I can devour the same book, and there it remains for us and others to devour all over again.

Suzanne Greenberg: The scavenging Perl and Schwartz write about may be greedy – devouring is a wonderful concept – but it's also generous. The work we read in my classes isn't about ranking one through ten or a thumbs-up/ thumbs-down. Writerly reading in my classes is not about analyzing the themes or telling me the moral they thought the author was trying to get across. It's not about whether the book was easy or hard to read.

Anna Leahy: The way we orchestrate class discussions makes all the difference in cultivating such approaches to reading, in connecting analysis of published and peer texts with the writing process. Inadvertently or purposefully, this orchestration of discussion also prioritizes love of language over self-expression. Nancy Kuhl, in her essay about teaching in and outside of the academy, critiques the connection between creativity and psychotherapy as '[t]he primary obstacle to many workshop goals' and as 'relativist and deeply marketplace oriented' in ways that cultivate consumers in the self-help industry rather than making for better writers (2005: 10). She argues that the academic setting gives us options for refocusing students' assumptions and attention. Stephanie Vanderslice and Kelly Ritter make some similar points – ways 'to develop a culture of readers' in the classroom (2011: 39) – in *Teaching Creative Writing to Undergraduates*.

One way we refocus students' attention and assumptions is to build writerly reading into our courses and introduce questions that require students to think about the text rather than about themselves, about how the text works rather than whether they like it or how challenging it was.

Suzanne Greenberg: Questions matter. We don't always have time in class to discuss every published piece we read, so students sometimes respond in writing as well. I give guidelines for their responses, so they don't end up writing, *I liked this* or *This was boring*. Without directive questions, students default to thumbs-up or -down. What did you as a writer get out of this poem, story, essay or novel? What did the writer try that you might like to try in your own writing? What sentences or moments moved you in some way? The questions I ask are designed to analyze the craft and also link what's gleaned to the writing experience of the student.

Brent Royster: A course designed to foster writerly reading might be concerned first with the components, then with the whole. I'm reminded of the Donald Justice (Gioia & Logan, 1998) passage that likens a poem to a spider's web: 'touch it at any part and the whole structure responds' (1998: 27). By reading as writers, we come to understand the interconnectedness of a writer's choices.

In writerly reading we start with the nuts and bolts, or, to riff on Justice's metaphor, we continue with the skein and the dew. We ask, how is this configured? What are its parts? What choices did the artist make in seaming these seems to be? We might marvel at the construction, and we might even become a bit envious. But in plucking the taut harp strings of the web, we hear its music, and we slowly learn its tune. We analyze and parse and question and reconstruct a poem until it resonates and even sings its own sense. Writerly reading in this way allows us to take on the poem, story, play or essay and to know the piece in its parts in order to understand, or absorb, the whole. To know it by heart, in this way.

Susan Hubbard: In workshop-based courses, participants' stories are the primary texts. We have opportunities to learn how to identify and address problems that extend beyond any given manuscript and to raise questions involving issues of culture and identity. Accordingly, supplemental texts in my courses vary, from published stories with similar plots, settings or characterizations, to visual art forms and music that share some of those elements, to interviews with artists whose aesthetics conform or contrast with those of the story being workshopped.

My classes invite students to move beyond the conventional workshop story, described by Stephen King as 'show-offy rather than entertaining, self-important rather than interesting, guarded and self-conscious rather than gloriously open, and worst of all, written for editors and teachers rather than for readers' (2007: 6). I'd rather read stories that take risks. Writerly reading tends to encourage writers to take risks.

Sandy Feinstein: The order of course assignments – including reading – and discussions plays a role in fostering risk taking. Before we get to the creative projects in a course, my students have read in multiple genres and have written journals and exercises. In my contribution to *Power and Identity in the Creative Writing Classroom*, I talk about the importance of reading to address the limited language of many students 'by which to make their feelings sound genuine and mean something to someone other than their friends' (2005: 192). I also suggest that there should be a limit to talking and that, especially in a workshop-style classroom, it is important to consider the balance of class time spent reading, writing, and talking (2005: 199). Journals are one way to re-envision a sort of talking as a sort of writing.

Anna Leahy: Though they are much more, as you suggest, journals are a practical way to hold students accountable for their reading. Vanderslice and Ritter, in *Teaching Creative Writing to Undergraduates*, discuss briefly the pop quiz, which is simple to administer but is an intermittent and fleeting experience for students. Instead, Vanderslice and Ritter advocate that 'reading responses, journals, or talking points, which encourage students to engage with the text more deeply, making their own connections or posing their own questions, may also help students better develop the habits of a writerly reader' (2011: 41). They offer pointers for grading such activities quickly and also suggest that students 'read their responses to the class on a rotating basis' (2011: 41). Journals can embody several habits and practices – close reading, critical thinking across texts, sentence-level writing, oral performance, listening – all at once.

Sandy Feinstein: Because of that multifaceted engagement, journals can serve as post-reading and pre-writing steps. My journal assignments on the reading focus on key terms, namely poetic and prose techniques, such as motifs or metaphors that structure works. Student responses also help me anticipate problems and plan lessons, which can mean changing direction from my original intended emphasis. Journal entries shape the discussion in the next class period, too, so students have a ready arsenal of words from which to draw when they come to class.

Suzanne Greenberg: I tend to pull exercises out of work we're reading, which is a different approach than journals but functions as post-reading and pre-writing. Though we don't usually imitate entire structures, my students sometimes do that when we're reading pieces with unusual repetitions, sectioning, or paragraphing. Most of the time, however, individual lines serve as instigation for exercises.

In one of my creative nonfiction classes, for example, we read essays from *The Moth*, the best of which model how to write personal stories in ways that surprise and engage readers. 'Good News Versus Bad' by Erin Barker is an essay in which a child finds out from her father that her mother is pregnant by another man. I used a line from the essay as a starting point for my students: 'Don't ever go to the Cold Stone Creamery with my dad' (2013: 202). Each student had to write a version: *Don't ever go to BLANK with my BLANK.*

Anna Leahy: I use imitation, sometimes to organize a whole semester when the class is connected to the visiting poets' series, sometimes as a one-off exercise. Even when I don't teach imitation, discussing the work of others early in the semester prepares for workshop discussions, as we develop language and approaches together with those examples or models in mind.

Stephanie Vanderslice suggests even more explicit workshop preparation in 'The Lynchpin in the Workshop': 'workshopping a published piece before students begin to respond to one another's work' (2012: 117). I find it difficult to do a mock workshop on a published piece, but I do encourage students, as Vanderslice suggests as an alternative, to 'analyse published work not in the traditional literary sense but with an eye towards interrogating technique' (2012: 117). Students consider what choices the writer made and what alternatives might exist, which is akin to workshopping. Like Vanderslice, I want students to think about 'how what they have learned critiquing a particular author or text will now inform their own work' (2012: 117). Especially for beginning students, this kind of reading critique becomes preparation for workshop discussion, and it, like all we're discussing here, becomes more than the sum of its parts and accomplishes multiple pedagogical goals at once.

Brent Royster: Reading the work of models as well as peers helps inform the daily practice. Gary Snyder's poem 'Axe Handles' references Lu Ji's *Wen Fu* in which the speaker fashions an axe-handle with an axe by studying the shape of yet another axe handle: 'the model is indeed near at hand,' Snyder writes, with what must be muffled laughter (1983: 6). Writers at all levels can learn the craft by first watching the craft performed and then emulating it.

In most of my writing classes, I have encouraged imitation and memorization. Contrary to popular belief, reading and imitating and memorization do not inevitably lead to plagiarism. Quite the contrary, once a student obtains the mouth-feel of established work, he or she can begin to experiment with other configurations and constructions, with the goal in mind of creating something new.

Anna Leahy: Yes, how does one create something original when it's all been done before? Or does understanding what exists already give rise to new iterations, iterations writers couldn't conceive without the context that reading provides?

Susan Hubbard: In my 'History of Prose Style' class, participants read, analyze and imitate texts that may include Sufi tales, folk tales, fairy tales, detective stories, ironic-twist stories, modern allegories and fantasies, in order to trace the evolution of the structure, content, and style of the short story. Our examination of those genres begins with close readings but also embraces critical and cultural reception of the texts today and at their time of initial publication. Writerly reading looks at the roles of writers and of readers within respective cultures.

When we read Kate Chopin's 'Désirée's Baby,' we ponder why certain words, such as 'quadroon,' 'pyre' and 'pall' were more commonly used in the antebellum South than in our contemporary culture; that conversation leads to a consideration of the roles race and gender played in late 19th-century Louisiana and discussion about the extent to which those roles persist in contemporary Florida. Half the students in the most recent iteration of this course wrote the first three pages of stories replicating the style and theme of 'Désirée's Baby,' and the other half performed close readings and analyses of peers' work. Many students said they found imitating other works a valuable means of reassessing and revising their own writing styles.

Anna Leahy: When I conduct in-class exercises, I also leave time for reading aloud. Students complete the same exercise, use the same guidelines, or imitate the same excerpt, but then they hear the variations, the different choices and voices. Hearing others' work, especially an imitation based on a text we've all read, allows them to discern immediately a range of choices and become more aware of decisions they make as they write, decisions that give voice. While clichés among the pieces become readily evident as we hear them repeated, imitation exercises breed surprising variety, as students strive to distinguish their individual voices in the mix.

Brent Royster: In class, reading with the ear is very helpful for writers at all levels. Those of us who write professionally will oftentimes read our own work aloud. Why hear a text aloud? To recognize the artistry and to understand the sense and music of the work and, when it is our own work we hear, to make it better.

Suzanne Greenberg: In the graduate fiction workshop, I choose work that I think will speak in some way to what the students are working on in their own fiction. This approach can inspire close reading since student writers actively want to learn from published writers. For example, if several students are working on linked short stories, I may assign *Babe in Paradise* by Marisa Silver (2002), in which the character of Babe pops up several times, or Junot Diaz' *Drown* (1997), with the recurring Yunior. Dylan Landis' *Normal People Don't Live Like This* (2009) demonstrates how to write a novel told in stories. Model texts become guides without being prescriptive.

Sandy Feinstein: Because I primarily teach literature classes, reading is presumed; the primary and secondary relationship of reading and writing is reversed. The nature of these courses – Arthurian, fantasy – argues that reading is imperative for learning how to write in multiple genres. Teaching J.R.R. Tolkien and C.S. Lewis in the context of fantasy includes discussing the authors' scholarly lives and the reading that made possible their canonical novels. Students see the connections for themselves because they have usually read the authors' novels many times before taking my courses; consequently, they tend to become more willing to accept starting a fantasy course with *Sir Orfeo* (in Middle English no less) if not Spenser's *Faerie Queene* (a much harder sell). For creative writing students, recognizing the connections across texts and genres – our literary traditions, our literary conventions – is important, and not only for providing insight into their favorite works when seen in a new context.

Recognizing new connections opens up fresh possibilities for their own creative efforts. Old works are buried treasures offering riches to reverse the production of copy-cat fashions, what David Hollander opined was 'competent students writing competent prose, crafting competent stories modeled after the stories they see published in the major trade magazines and placed front and center in their local bookstore atrium.' As he has said, 'Their teachers (my peers) extol the same competent, well-crafted stories, written by the same set of writers lionized by booksellers across the country. The students, in short, are becoming what they've been taught to become' (2006: 21–22). Reading in earlier literature and forms, in short, offers new possibilities for originality, perhaps even inspiration.

Therefore, I lay the foundation of my courses with early literature. Then, the students each propose a work to teach, which typically leans toward 20th- and 21st-century works. In re-viewing, re-reading, or re-seeing the works they have chosen, which tend to be favorite works they assume they know well, it is they who suddenly realize something about the works that got them into the class in the first place. I am not referring to recognition of all the allusions and the satisfaction in that recognition – though there is that – but a deeper understanding of the tropes and conventions that transform, for example, their understanding of Monty Python or, rather, its structure and what it parodies in form as well as content, including various motifs, the use of repetition, alliteration, etc.

The teaching project immediately precedes the creative project in this class. So they are making the case for reading, for themselves and each other, as preparation for the creative projects.

Suzanne Greenberg: Reading as preparation makes sense in creative writing, and such preparation is often quite individual. Steeped in literature courses, my students in the second-year MFA readings course often have to be reminded that I'm not looking for the meaning in the books we're reading. I'm looking to see what the books mean to them, for that deeper understanding. Discovering books that speak to us as writers, wherever we are in our careers, is like finding soul mates even if we never meet the writers themselves and, most likely, never will.

Susan Hubbard: Unfortunately, frequent, diligent reading may not improve our writing. As Neil McCaw notes in an essay for *New Writing:* 'Close reading in isolation (even of a literary classic) seems hopelessly ill-suited to the task of helping students understand how their reading will help them to become better (let alone published) writers' (2011/2015: 5) He goes further to argue, '[...] implying that a familiarity with the words and form of canonical works will necessarily improve a student's ability and discriminatory powers is little more than a comforting myth. It glosses over the fact that the benefits of reading for writers depends [sic] on precisely what sort of reading we are actually talking about. Such benefits are not inevitable and universal' (2011/2015: 5).

McCaw does not recommend abandoning close reading but, instead, redesigning it as a practice he describes as 'imaginative and dynamic, multi-layered and also (equally importantly) enjoyable for its own sake. It should be a process of creative exploration, often without tangible, directly related writing outcomes, wherein texts are considered in all their glory and grubbiness: as they are constructed, as they are interpreted, as they allow themselves to be imagined. And the introduction of numerous knowledges (social, cultural, political) is a key element of this' (2011/2015: 8).

Anna Leahy: We all are suggesting how we read dynamically. We've talked about reading as a way to focus into a text, as about style and techniques, but you're suggesting, via McCaw, that reading is a way out, too, out to the world in which we write and in which our writing exists.

Susan Hubbard: I agree with McCaw that using concepts from fields such as gender studies, literary history, sociolinguistics, sociology, English studies, philosophy, theology and scientific studies can greatly enrich appreciation and understanding of creative work. I would add music and visual arts – including painting, sculpture, photography, film, television and digital media – to the list. When close reading provokes questions that lead readers to conduct research in other fields, the results often enrich their own writing as well.

Suzanne Greenberg: Some of my students get this notion of the largesse of reading; some haven't yet; some never will. If I introduce a student to one essay, story or novel that she or he thinks about later or to one writer she or he can't wait to read more of, this is, finally, the best I can hope to do. That sort of introduction may be the most important thing I can offer students.

Whether they're reading each other's work or published pieces, reading teaches students to have greater empathy and compassion. Complex characters can move students out of a good-or-bad, right-or-wrong mindset. Writerly reading lets in ambiguity. Characters are complex. Real people are complex. When we read closely, we become in many ways more fully human.

Anna Leahy: In 2013, *Science* published a study that indicates reading literary fiction increases our ability to understand others' states of mind, which is essential for humans to interact as a society (Kidd & Castano, 2013). In other words, literary fiction heightens our empathy. Though the study is limited and has its critics, literature immerses our imaginations with characters and settings. By making particular kinds of cognitive leaps between literature and life – among language, thinking and feeling – humans distinguish themselves from other creatures and are connected with each other. Lisa Zunshine draws from cognitive science to assert, in her book *Why We Read Fiction*, '[F]iction engages, teases, and pushes to its tentative limits our mind-reading capacity' (2006: 4). In addition, when reading novels, we keep track of who said, thought and desired what, and we track these mental states of characters over time (2006: 5).

Suzanne Greenberg: In *Bird by Bird* Anne Lamott writes, 'Books help us understand who we are and how to behave. They show us what community and friendship mean; they show us how to live and die' (1994: 15).

Anna Leahy: Lamott's view is a beautiful way to think about reading and situates it as our pedagogical responsibility. The word *read* is related to the word *riddle* and harkens back, in the Old English, to notions of advice, guidance, and putting things in order. Indeed, reading can guide our courses and offer our students guidance as writers. Reading can guide writing. Reading, ultimately, orders and re-orders the world on and off the page. Writing, by extension, is a creation of new ways of ordering and re-ordering language, thought, the world.

References

Barker, E. (2013) Good news versus bad. *The Moth* (pp. 201–205). New York: Hatchette Books.

Bausch, R. 'Letter to a Young Writer.' National Endowment for the Arts. See http://www.nea.gov/national/homecoming/essays/bausch.html (accessed 13 May 2016).

Booth, S. (1994) Close reading without readings. In R. McDonald (ed.) *Shakespeare Reread: The Texts in New Contexts* (pp. 42–55). Ithaca: Cornell University Press.

Chopin, K. (1995) Désirée's baby. In E.S. Rabkin (ed.) *Stories: An Anthology and an Introduction* (pp. 240–244). New York: Harper Collins.

Copland, A. (2011) *What to Listen for in Music.* New York: Signet.

Diaz, J. (1997) *Drown.* New York: Riverhead.

Doctorow, E.L. (28 June 2004, replayed 22 July 2015) Interview with Susan Stamberg. 'Intersections: E.L. Doctorow on rhythm and writing.' *NPR Morning Edition.*

Feinstein, S. (2005) Writing in the shadows: Topics, models, and audiences that focus on language. In A. Leahy (ed.) *Power and Identity in the Creative Writing Classroom* (pp. 192–202). Clevedon: Multilingual Matters.

Gioia, D. and Logan, W. (eds) (1998) *Certain Solitudes: On the Poetry of Donald Justice.* Fayetteville, AR: University of Arkansas Press.

Goodman, R. (2008) *The Soul of Creative Writing.* New Brunswick, NJ: Transaction Publishers.

Hollander, D. (2006) Imperative: Finding community outside academia. *Poets and Writers* 3.1 (Jan/Feb): 21–22.

Kidd, D.C. and Castano, E. (2013) Reading literary fiction improves theory of mind. *Science* 342, 6156 (18 October), 377–380.

King, S. (2007) Introduction. In S. King (ed.) *The Best American Short Stories, 2007.* New York: Houghton Mifflin.

Kuhl, N. (2005) Personal therapeutic writing vs. literary writing. In A. Leahy (ed.) *Power and Identity in the Creative Writing Classroom* (pp. 3–12). Clevedon: Multilingual Matters.

Lamott, A. (1994) *Bird by Bird: Some Instructions on Writing and Life.* New York: Anchor Books.

Landis, D. (2009) *Normal People Don't Live Like This.* New York: Persea.

Leahy, A. (2012) The importance of reading for all of us. *The Huffington Post.* 24 June 2012. See http://www.huffingtonpost.com/anna-leahy/the-importance-of-reading_b_1623078.html.

Leahy, A. (2015) In it for the long haul: The pedagogy of perseverance. In D. Berg and L.A. May (eds) *Creative Composition: Inspiration and Techniques for Writing Instruction*. Bristol: Multilingual Matters.

Maxwell, G. (2012) *On Poetry*. London: Oberon.

McCaw, N. (2011/2015) Close reading, writing and culture. *New Writing: The International Journal for the Practice and Theory of Creative Writing* 8 (1), 25–34. 3 March 2011. 6 May 2015.

Perl, S. and Schwartz, M. (2006) *Writing True: The Art and Craft of Creative Nonfiction*. Boston: Cengage.

Prose, F. (2007) *Reading Like a Writer*. New York: Harper Perennial.

Ratcliffe, S. (2010) *Reading the Unseen: (Offstage) Hamlet*. Denver: Counterpath.

Ratcliffe, S. (1988) *[where late the sweet]Birds Sang*. Oakland: O Books.

Silver, M. (2002) *Babe in Paradise*. New York: W.W Norton.

Snyder, G. (1983) *Axe Handles: Poems*. San Francisco: North Point Press.

Vanderslice, S. (2012) The lynchpin of the workshop: Student critique and reflection. *Teaching Creative Writing* (pp. 116–120). New York: Palgrave.

Vanderslice, S. and Ritter, K. (2011) *Teaching Creative Writing to Undergraduates: A Practical Guide and Sourcebook*. Southlake, TX: Fountainhead.

Vonnegut, K. (1990) *Fates Worse than Death: An Autobiographical Collage of the 1980s*. New York: J.P. Putnam's.

Zunshine, L. (2006) *Why We Read Fiction: Theory of Mind and the Novel*. Columbus, OH: The Ohio State University Press.

Part 3
Programs

5 Text(ure), Modeling, Collage: Creative Writing and the Visual Arts

Anna Leahy, Lia Halloran and Claudine Jaenichen

Several articles on collaboration across artistic fields have appeared in *New Writing*. Shauna Busto Gilligan and Karen Lee Street, in an essay called 'Critical reflection on creative collaborations: imagining the image and wording the work,' assert, 'It is through collaboration and the sharing of information and craft – at events such as community workshops and academic conferences – that as artists we can expand our art (whether it is art of the word or image) and critically reflect on what we are trying to do through further creations' (Gilligan & Street, 2011). For those of us working in universities, we can connect with other creative disciplines to expand our artistic practices and, even more so, our approaches to teaching these artistic practices. Similarly, Phillip Gross and Wyn Mason, in their essay 'Surface tensions: framing the flow of a poetry–film collaboration,' assert: 'Collaboration, working across art forms and media in particular, offers a window into creative process. [...] Collaborators across forms cannot presume a common language; they have to make their work apparent to each other' (Gross and Mason). 'Text(ure), Modeling, Collage' explores the intersections and differences among creative writing, graphic design and visual art, in terms of artistic practice and pedagogy.

Claudine Jaenichen: We don't often make time for these conversations across artistic fields. As Karri Holley explains in *Understanding Interdisciplinary Challenges and Opportunities in Higher Education,* academic institutions often isolate faculty both physically and intellectually (2009: 18). A creative writer may not have occasion to bump into a visual artist across town or across campus to talk about how rigorous our practice is, how our fields share similar kinds of problem solving that build intuition, or how revision works across artistic endeavours. This interdisciplinary conversation essay is designed to circumvent our usual isolation, cultivate pedagogical allies, and develop new perspectives that invigorate teaching in both creative writing and the visual arts.

Lia Halloran: What would happen if artists and writers sat down together on a regular basis to talk about their creative projects and their teaching? We could make some conclusions about overlap among our disciplines and how we can borrow from each other. What if artists at a university tapped musicians to discuss the physicality of their practices? What if poets, theatre professors, and musical professionals discussed voice techniques? What if fiction writers, painters, and historians explored together how narrative employs time and place?

Anna Leahy: Surely, we'd find intersections. The term and concept of *studio*, for instance, emerges as crucial for the three of us. A space in which art is produced or performed through interaction both with the artistic medium – words on a page, paint from brush to canvas, a computer mouse and screen – and also as we share that space with other artists.

The Association of Writers and Writing Programs (AWP) *Director's Handbook* defines three types of graduate creative writing programs, each with a different balance between studio and other pedagogical approaches. The common focus is each student's writing, and those programs that label themselves primarily as studio programs 'most closely parallel studio programs in music, dance, and the visual arts. Most of the degree work is done in workshops, independent writing projects or tutorials, and thesis preparation' (2011: 7).

Lia Halloran: In art making, the studio is not only a physical space of production but encourages students to research and experiment to develop a studio practice that is cultivated in the classroom. The genesis of an undergraduate art education begins with students partaking in group critiques and dialogues to articulate verbally what they are exploring visually, while upper-division coursework develops into more creative and individualized projects and one-on-one critiques. These early stages are essential for a student to begin to set up a studio space of his or her own that will eventually be an outward expression not only of the work being produced but also as a physical informant of the concepts explored in the artist's work.

Claudine Jaenichen: In graphic design, the term studio is applied differently during one's educational experience than it is in professional practice. Courses required for majors are labeled as studio courses and reflect similar objectives as creative writing and studio art.

Lower-division courses combine design and studio art students who share physical space in painting, drawing, and sculpture foundation courses. As design students enter upper-division courses, they are introduced to digital media and technique. The studio space and structure change to reflect this new technological medium. The undergraduate studio course provides a location where students not only interact with materials and develop content for their work but also provides a transcendent space where students begin placing work in historical and contemporary contexts and where considerations for cultural, social and semiotic implications are initiated. These design studio courses include a component of making work as well as research, theory, seminar and critiques. Explorations, experimentation and defining one's creative originality continue outside the classroom and will develop in parallel to other studio courses threaded into the curriculum.

Anna Leahy: Creative writing as a field doesn't break down the undergraduate curriculum that neatly, though a given programme or professor often gives attention to specific goals for students at different stages. According to *The Director's Handbook*, 'Whereas the general goal for a graduate program in creative writing is to nurture and expedite the development of a literary artist, the goal for an undergraduate program is mainly to develop a well-rounded student in the liberal arts and humanities, a student who develops a general expertise in literature, in critical reading, and in persuasive writing' (2011: 35). These categories of expertise reflect areas of study in English departments that parallel those in art departments, including art history and theory.

Undergraduates in art and design, then, are very aware of how they are becoming artists. Though programs vary, creative writing promotes generalism – well-roundedness – for undergraduates. Many write in more than one genre, many programs include multiple genres in the introductory course, and most programs have hefty literature requirements.

Lia Halloran: College Art Association (CAA) also has separate standards for undergraduate and MFA programs and distinguishes between the BA, which has a liberal arts context akin to what AWP advocates, and the BFA, which includes greater focus in studio art and art history. Very similar to creative writing, the trajectory of learning outcomes toward a career for a visual artist is much more mystifying in terms of how one becomes an actual practicing artist, in large part because it is unlikely one will get a salary for making artwork upon graduation, as opposed to the clearer trajectory of graphic design. Many art majors go on to very creative careers, art making or otherwise, but benefit from this same well-rounded education.

Anna Leahy: AWP makes little distinction between the BA and BFA, which is worthy of further investigation in which art might be a model, but does distinguish the MFA from the undergraduate program in significant ways. The MFA is a professional and terminal degree.

Lia Halloran: At the graduate level, MFA students in studio art inhabit a studio for two to three years. They do not treat the studio as an exhibition space but, rather, use it as a physical space to make, collect, look at, research and glean from influences and inspirations to create a body of work that culminates in a cohesive exhibition. The one-on-one critique interactions students have with professors and critics is the common model for most MFA programmes and also serves as an introduction to the interaction that professional artists have in studio visits with gallerists, writers, curators and collectors after the completion of their education.

Claudine Jaenichen: It is not common for graphic designers to pursue an MFA unless they are interested in academia or research. The majority of students who graduate from undergraduate programs will enter the work force right away. Graphic designers who do pursue the MFA will use their studio as a space for discussions and critique.

The term *studio* is much more fluid and organic in design education than in professional practice. The studio in professional practice becomes more rigid and reflects the physical place of business in design. The majority of design studios are small business hubs where designers, account executives, clients and project managers share a space.

Anna Leahy: Visual art practices suggest that creative writers might give greater attention to these distinctions and relationships between practice as a student and practice as a professional. Of course, we see a connection between developing a writing practice as a student and continuing to read and write over a lifetime; it's all on the same continuum.

At the same time, creative writing teachers readily admit that most of our students, even our MFA students, will not go on to publish books. The visual arts, especially in graphic design, see a more overt connection between what happens in an academic program and the career the student goes on to have. Even if my students don't go on to publish poetry collections, what careers am I preparing them for?

All three of us ask our students to develop creative ways of seeing, thinking about and articulating the world. These skills and habits of mind are useful in and of themselves and in a variety of pursuits our students may have. Creative writing plays an important role in forming literary citizens, and we need to articulate the relationship between what we are doing in our programs and classrooms and what our alums will do in their careers and their larger lives.

Claudine Jaenichen: Graphic design has both an accreditation association, National Association of Schools of Art and Design (NASAD), and also a professional organization, the American Institute of Graphic Arts (AIGA), suggesting the two distinct arenas: inside the academy and the so-called real world or profession. Also, the rarity of an undergraduate BFA student pursuing a graduate degree suggests the strong preparatory approach to professional application over research in graphic design, whether at the undergraduate or graduate level.

Lia Halloran: This relationship between education and career is an important difference among fields in the arts. The path toward professionalism in the field of visual art shares a similarity to creative writing, where many art students go on to be involved with the arts through galleries, museums, curatorial positions and even as critics, but only a very small percentage will become exhibiting artists. Especially over the last decade, an increasing trend I've noticed in galleries is that almost all younger exhibiting contemporary artists have MFA degrees. It's rare for emerging artists to not be linked with an MFA program and, therefore, a specific pedagogy associated with the art market and gallery or the museum collective of a specific city.

Perhaps the MFA gives a physical space in which to encounter critiques and professors in the same format in which a professional artist meets with galleries, museums and curators, whereas a graphic design student can get a job and essentially be mentored in a professional environment in the early stages of a career.

Anna Leahy: In the arts, there exists a long tradition of the mentor–apprentice relationship. Though we are teachers inside educational institutions, the process of critique – workshopping, in the case of creative writing – upon which we base our pedagogy, draws from that tradition. The one-on-one attention a student artist or writer receives puts that student in the role of apprentice. Of course, teaching and mentoring aren't the same thing, and we're not working with all our students day to day as, say, a stonecutter and his apprentices would have toiled together to build a church in yesteryear. Yet, through workshopping, individual conferences and informal advising interaction, our academic programs mimic that sort of good counsel.

In fact, academic programs seem especially good places for the arts – visual or written – to flourish because they serve as hubs where creative people can congregate with experts and with relative validation for what we do. As Nancy Andreasen notes in *The Creating Brain*, '[C]reative people are likely to be more productive and more original if surrounded by other creative people. This too produces an environment in which the creative brain is stimulated to form novel connections and novel ideas' (2005: 129). Our job is to create an environment that stimulates the minds of creative people and to nudge, advise and critique there.

Lia Halloran: While the studio apprenticeship model is not relevant any longer, it is common for students in MFA programs to become studio assistants for the professors with whom they work in graduate school. This kind of practical hands-on learning is different from the conceptual and theory-based artmaking found in most MFA programmes. This environment allows for continued mentorship and a space for young artists to develop their own studio practice while being able to take part in many aspects of the art and gallery world that are not addressed in academia. Many students who graduate from an MFA program look for guidance on how to get gallery representation and to polish the technical aspects of their work that are conceptually flushed out in school.

Claudine Jaenichen: Printers and print shops were the first to do the jobs of what we know as graphic design today. To practice as a printer, one needed to seek an apprenticeship with a printer willing to mentor. The printer would gain extra help in exchange for his knowledge, room and board. In its early years, as graphic design broke away from the printing sector and became its own sector in creative development, learning the skills of graphic design reflected a similar mentor-apprentice relationship.

This tradition still underpins a major segment in graphic design education. For example, internships at design agencies are required and students complete 120 hours at an off-campus design agency in exchange for academic credit. Both full- and part-time teachers are expected to be current practicing designers in order to pass on relevant knowledge of the field in the classroom. Several chapters of the professional association, AIGA, offer a seven-month mentorship program with volunteer professional designers beginning at the high-school level.

Importantly, the faculty-to-student ratio is kept relatively small, usually 1-to-18 (depending on various goals and constraints), in order to manage a level of individual commitment to each student's development.

Anna Leahy: Creative writing also sees a small class size as part of the connection between education and the larger practice. AWP recommends 15 students at most for workshops, with 12 as ideal. While many programs encourage internships and some students seek them out, creative writing degrees rarely require that practical work, so there isn't the direct connection of our students to a workplace environment or market.

Several years ago, AWP changed its name from the Association of Writing Programs to the Association of Writers and Writing Programs. That recognizes the two arenas – education and profession – and welcomes writers from outside the academy. The field, at least symbolically, makes a distinction that could be helpful in articulating differences between student and professional and, at the same time, implies an important connection. Recognition of this connection in program curricula and requirements should be considered, especially as students and parents ask about applicability of arts degrees in the so-called real world.

Claudine Jaenichen: In 2010, AIGA held a design educators' conference titled 'New contexts/New practices' and organised by the North Carolina State graphic design faculty. The conference included six topics: changing conditions, shifting paradigms, social economies, design research, interdisciplinarity and designing for experience. Emphasis is placed on the speed in which design is changing, but design education is slower to respond and prepare students for real-world applications and expectations.

Lia Halloran: The College Art Association (CAA) represents artists and art programs in the academy. Just as AWP states for the MFA in creative writing, the CAA defines the MFA as the terminal degree. There is a clear goal for 'professional competency in the visual arts and contemporary practices. To earn an MFA, a practicing artist must exhibit the highest level of accomplishment through the generation of a body of work. The work needs to demonstrate the ability to conceptualize and communicate effectively by employing visual language to interpret ideas' (College Art Association, 2008). CAA suggests minimum required credits, coursework in art history and visual culture and a final exhibition. In some ways, it offers clear and rigorous guidelines; it takes what we do seriously so that others (like university administrators) will too.

But there's also an overt recognition that programs vary widely. Many of the requirements of MFA programs today are accompanied by the completion of a substantial written thesis in addition to the MFA thesis exhibition in a gallery. This requires the combination of art theory, art history, writing and the work developed in the studio practice.

Anna Leahy: Those guidelines sound like the best of both worlds: student and apprentice. That combination of theoretical and practical is also rationale for housing the arts in universities.

Claudine Jaenichen: NASAD, graphic design's academic accreditation arm, determines the standards and guidelines for graphic design undergraduate and graduate programs. NASAD's purpose and philosophy is summarized as follows:

> Art and design are professions requiring talent, knowledge, skill, and dedication. Employment depends almost entirely on demonstrated competence. Success is based primarily on work rather than on credentials. Experience tells us that art and design, though dependent on talent, inspiration, and creativity, require much more to function as a significant spiritual and educational force. Talent without skills, inspiration without knowledge, and creativity without technique can account for little but lost potential. The primary purpose of schools of art and design is to help individual students turn talent, inspiration, creativity, and dedication into significant potential for service to the development of art and design culture in its multiple dimensions. (NASAD)

It is interesting to note the differences in how design education is framed between the two graphic design organisations. NASAD places emphasis on talent, creativity and technique, whereas the professional organization, AIGA, places priorities on preparing professionals for social and cultural problem solving, design research, advancement in technology and interdisciplinarity. Design theory, visual literacy, visual histories, formal critiques and design discourse are threaded through the undergraduate program. Classroom projects help develop macro methods of research and process (e.g. participatory methods, benchmarking, etc.) and micro methods of research (e.g. image research, client objective, etc.) that reflect the concerns stated by the AIGA educators conference.

Lia Halloran: In conceptual investigations of research and development, perhaps it is at the initial brainstorming stage that our three disciplines share the point when students are being the most creative. The above statement by NASAD holds very true to visual arts as well: 'creativity without technique can account for little but lost potential.' All three disciplines – creative writing, studio arts and graphic design – are concerned with creativity as an essential, magical component to the wellness and success of a student's learning. We are continually asking ourselves how we can best foster and encourage these traits while instilling competent technical skills that will lead to a confident and creative student.

This is a difficult balance. Too much technique and rigour can lead to an over-practicing, a performance of creativity. Not introducing enough skills results in a lot of energy and ideas with no way to make something substantial of that.

Claudine Jaenichen: This idea of over-practising is a constant challenge in developing content for courses. Students easily over-prioritize learning software as a way to compensate for the much harder skill of developing conceptual thinking. The result of over-practicing in graphic design is a project that appears polished and finished but with no substantial idea. This conclusion may also manifest because of back-to-back rigorous scheduling and a multitude of constraints.

Anna Leahy: That difficult balance – of talent, energy, ideas, skills, practice – seems central for all of us. Investigation of creativity by cognitive scientists points to talent not playing nearly as large a role as we've traditionally thought (Andresen; Flaherty). While we can't teach talent per se, we can model and guide motivation and skills, which ideally go hand-in-hand, one fuelling the other. Energy and ideas are tricky to teach, but we create environments that spark and nourish curiosity, serendipity and a variety of other less tangible habits that we think of as inspiration or talent.

Classroom Assessment Techniques lists writing skills, think for self and analytic skills as the top three teaching goals for English, where creative writing programs are often housed. In fact, across the humanities, we want students to think for themselves (without classes becoming some free-for-all). Our top goals in creative writing, despite its usual disciplinary home in English departments, may be closer to the priorities of the arts: aesthetic appreciation, creativity and think for self (Angelo & Cross, 1993: 368).

It's important to note the differences, too, among our disciplines. Writing skills are central to creative writing (we have writing in the name of the field, after all).

Claudine Jaenichen: Writing is especially relevant in graphic design. Lower- and upper-division courses include a seminar and writing component. Students are expected not only to formalize their own work analytically but also to analyze the work of others using established formal vocabulary shared in design and art. A writing program begins sophomore year that stays consistent throughout the requirements of the graphic design program. Every project requires a written statement that includes: (1) stating the problem and addressing constraints, requirements and research methods of the project; (2) explaining the concept and how formal decisions (e.g. typography, colour, choice of imagery, visual composition, etc.) support the idea; (3) describing decisions behind formal elements; and (4) providing how their influences and decisions affect the position of their work in a context of contemporary and/or historical influences.

Lia Halloran: In a studio program, writing is used to pinpoint conceptual rigor and theoretical discourse outside the work, not necessarily within it. For foundation courses, writing is not as important as students are encouraged to amass technical proficiencies and formal aspects of creating visual work, while using group critiques to develop skills to define in language what they are seeing visually within the work. This ability to read a work formally, solely based on looking at it without outside information, is an entry point, which then develops from critique into writing. Dave Hickey, in his book *Air Guitar* on art theory and art criticism, states,

> Colleagues of mine will tell you that people despise critiques because they fear our power. But I know better. People despise critiques because people despise weakness, and criticism is the weakest thing you can do in writing. It is the written equivalent of air guitar – flurries of the silent, sympathetic gestures with nothing at their heart but the memory of the music. It produces no knowledge, states no facts, and never stands alone. It neither saves the things we love (as we would wish them saved) nor ruins the things we hate. (Hickey, 1997: 163)

In upper-division courses and exhibitions, artist statements help to define intent of the subject matter and technical execution and place the work within a historical and contemporary context.

Anna Leahy: These written statements sound like the reflective essays I ask my students to include in their portfolios. The graphic design and studio art models propose that students articulate their process in relation to learning and/or audience. In creative writing workshop discussions, the author often remains silent so as to not explain the work before others discuss its effects. We often ignore the author's intentions, assuming that she will recognize when an intended effect diverges from the actual effect on readers (and be able to decide which should be encouraged through revision). The author could use a written statement to document constraints and decisions, and such a statement could be done before and/or after workshopping. That way, the student becomes aware of gaps between intention and effect and can rethink decisions, perhaps letting go of triggering intentions in favour of something more original sparked by readers.

Whether in creative writing or in art, written statements make students more aware of their learning. Awareness can be a time-saver in the long run of a writing career.

Lia Halloran: Similar in studio critiques, it's common for the instructor to have the student whose work is being critiqued remain quiet while the class discusses the work, which is important feedback to see if the artist's intentions in the work are visually translated. In art museums as well, there is an impulse to use language as a guide when we do not understand a work – we look for the wall label to illuminate the meaning. In any learning environment, written statements can be useful for accountability of one's thoughts or impulses that help to define parameters and goals in a project. Even articulating simple things, such as defining materiality to link with specific concepts or artistic influences, would be helpful for the direction of the work.

Yet there is great value when a student follows some sort of lead that is outside language, outside of description, in the physical act of making. When students are neither performing creativity, nor relying on direction, they are creators. There is such a rich history of artists describing meaning – finding language – months or years later; it was almost through subconscious direction that a great breakthrough occurred.

The South African artist William Kentridge, who uses drawing and film together in his work, speaks about art as an active event when the artists must be open and confident with the physical making to move forward along the trajectory and see new things about the work: 'It's a physical process, new images and ideas suggest themselves' (Kentridge 1999, 2009). I find my studio art students seem more inspired and take new directions in their work through reading about art rather than writing about art.

Anna Leahy: I hadn't thought of it quite that way, but it makes sense that reading about writing pushes students in new directions more than writing about writing. Graywolf has a smart, wide-ranging series called *The Art of – The Art of Recklessness, The Art of Syntax, The Art of Attention, The Art of Daring, The Art of Description,* all about poetry, and others in the series about other genres (see https://www.graywolfpress.org/books/nonfiction/on-writing for the full *'The Art of...'* series).

Creative writers resist over-articulation of intent and process, too. Poet Larissa Szporluk and I, in another chapter of this book, acknowledge the importance of imitation (which requires reading) and the usefulness of writing exercises that encourage invention and, as Szporluk says, 'the marriage of two previously disconnected things' (p. 45). But even invention can be tied to intention, to solving the problem the exercise poses or to a preconceived purpose. Ultimately, we want to end up in what Szporluk calls *deep imagination*. Poet Jane Hirshfield puts it this way: 'a kind of fullness that overspills into everything. One breath taken completely; one poem, fully written, fully read – in such a moment, anything can happen' (1997: 32).

Claudine Jaenichen: In the field of typography, writing as a technique and application to content is addressed. Designers are required to write headlines, taglines, slogans, mission statements, body copy, etc. and are introduced to concepts that include tone-of-voice, writing structure, hierarchy, narratives and editing. Donald Norman provides an appropriate comparison to design and writing in *Writing as Design, Design as Writing*. As with writing, design has a reader. Design is read. Design communicates usually with definitive intention. 'A good designer and a good writer have to share certain characteristics, among the most important being "empathy"' (1993: 175–186).

Anna Leahy: We acknowledge the role of empathy in creative writing, too. In a *Poets & Writers* article (2005), Jane Ciabattari mentions it as one of the life-long skills creative writing students develop. Wallace Stegner talks of 'empathy, a capacity to enter into another mind without dominating it' (2002: 52). Lisa Zunshine, most notably in *Why We Read* (2006), is one of several literary theorists who argue that empathy is central to literature. The pretense of art has real effects of feeling.

Lia Halloran: Absolutely true! Designers are constantly assigned the task of having the visuals for the words say something about how we feel without the meaning of the word.

A great example is the work of Ed Ruscha; he invented fonts for painted words as a pictorial landscape to speak about how we interpret and ingest meaning. One of my favourite works by Ruscha, which I first saw at the Los Angeles County Museum when I was a student, is the word *Adios* painted as a puddle of spilled beans and bean juice. I loved the confusion of the viewer: registering the image of the beans before language, or perhaps the other way around.

Ruscha worked in an advertising agency after completing his education at Chouinard Art Institute (now California Institute of the Arts) in 1960, and, as a painting student there, he was in the midst of post-abstract-expressionism influences from New York and the early dawning of pop art, and also a more graphic approach to art with artists like Jasper Johns. His eventual studio practice straddled both worlds of design and art and became something new.

Anna Leahy: Our disciplines may be even more closely aligned than I'd imagined. Our goals aren't about knowing, or memorising factual information, though that kind of study can be foundational. These skills we value most for creative writers, visual artists and graphic designers must be built over time, through practice, and by the sort of straddling the Ruscha example demonstrates. Our fields invite that wonderful confusion or disorientation as aspects of originality and as part of our practice and process.

Lia Halloran: Our discussion of all these goals and skills points to the artistic process. Historically, the idea of a studio visit was valued not only because on any one occasion you might see new work or more work that the artist has created but also because you would be privy to the process, as if given a sneak peek to decipher the creative steps that one took toward creating an artwork.

For students, this focus on process may start by having been guided to think about their physical space as they stand in front of an easel, how they organize a palette, where they keep their brushes beside them and many other seemingly trivial moves that, over time and practice, will develop into a rigorous and dedicated studio practice. It is through exploring and developing a physical space to work that many conceptual issues get explored in art. While there are many conceptual crossovers between design and creative writing, undoubtedly art is the most physical practice and, therefore, the space in which the act of creating becomes intrinsically linked to the finished piece. The studio is the physical manifestation of the artistic process.

Anna Leahy: A focus on process clearly links our disciplines and, importantly, distinguishes our teaching from those of many other disciplines. Our pedagogy embodies practice, and we want students to cultivate habits of mind and, as you suggest, body.

The concept of *studio* in art and graphic design, then, is equivalent to the concept of workshop in creative writing. A workshop, in commonplace parlance, is a physical space, but in creative writing pedagogy, it is larger than that. Rather than referring to the place in which the student writes in isolation, the workshop is the classroom of writers, the act of sharing and critique, the passing of habits and vocabulary from teacher to students and the nudge into revision. By experiencing the workshop, students internalise the deeper processes of our work as poets, fiction writers, essayists or playwrights.

We use writing assignments of imitation and invention as ways to invite creative habits of mind. The first few times a student writes a sonnet, for instance, the result is likely to be hit and miss, but the task requires creative problem solving and focus on certain aspects of language. The focus on form may also free up subconscious play with areas of content because an artist can't possibly keep every choice at the tip of the tongue (or fingers) at the same time. When fledgling sonneteers share and discuss their attempts, they become more aware of their decisions and surprised at the variety that emerges within seemingly narrow constraints. The workshop is a process through which we not only practice writing but also become aware of our development.

Claudine Jaenichen: In other words, our disciplines share an attention to the interrelationship of form and content and also of practice and awareness, though the straddling or balance varies across disciplines.

Content of graphic design projects is diverse and is placed within social, commercial, trans-cross-multi-and/or-inter-disciplinary, cross-cultural and/ or political contexts. Students are required to take responsibility in the impact and footprint of the work they create. *Impact* refers to how visual and textual messaging is received by the viewer and how meaning is transferred in the context and ideology into which the work is being placed. This also includes the more literal impact of choice of surrounding materials and production processes, such as in printing and packaging.

A target audience is also provided at the beginning of a project in order to justify and evaluate student choices in visual and verbal language. For example, a political campaign project might be assigned with a pre-defined audience of people who are 18–25 years old with a gross income of $30,000–35,000 per year and who have never voted in past elections. The research, approach, placement, and effect of creative decisions would be significantly different than the same project with an audience twice as old with twice the income and who have claimed a political party for several years. These constraints, or parameters of the target audience, were reflected in the design campaigns during the 2008 presidential election between Barack Obama and John McCain, who defined their target audiences very differently.

Lia Halloran: Audience is a fantastic question for studio artists because, while one of the very first stages of a design project is to identify the client or target audience, this aspect is rarely defined in studio art. If we can think of design as a visual democracy, we can think of art as a visual hierarchy in which the artist chooses how much to explain (in the work or peripherally). While context is always important, specific sign and symbols need to be decoded in some work for a viewer to be inspired and challenged by a piece of art.

Many successful artists today address conceptual universalities, but, importantly, these arise from some personal narrative. The audience isn't as clear in contemporary art. Shepard Fairy was quite well-known for years as the street artist in San Francisco making the street posters of Andre the Giant; I doubt he had the intentions of developing a visual style to target young Democrats in a presidential election. His work that made him well known was not even intended for a gallery or for financial gain. For a long time, his audience was himself and his universe of peers in the know and only inadvertently every lucky San Franciscan that came upon his work on BART or walking down the street. The Democratic Party successfully used his visual style to target back the audience from which the style had emerged in the first place.

Anna Leahy: These intersections – between the personal and the universal, between accessibility and the need to be decoded, among different disciplines or areas of endeavor – point to creative writing and the arts as inherently interdisciplinary. While poets have written poems about poetry, our subject matter can come from history, science, personal experience and so on.

That's why I find Steven Johnson's book *Where Good Ideas Come From* such a good reference point for thinking about creative writing pedagogy and about the usefulness of the academy for the arts. He writes, '[E]ncouragement does not necessarily lead to creativity. Collisions do – the collisions that happen when different fields of expertise converge in some shared physical or intellectual space' (2010: 163). Of course, neither he nor I dismiss encouragement. The point is that the academy in the United States serves the same role as the pub in Ireland during the last century or the coffee shop during the Enlightenment in Europe. As teachers, we orchestrate a shared physical and intellectual space in which creativity can flourish.

Lia Halloran: This circles back on the idea of studio as a social construction where creativity is fostered by more creativity – and not necessarily in one's discipline. Some of the greatest artwork and writing of the early 20th century came out of small salons where writers, thinkers and visual creators came together to share, learn, and grow from each other. One of the most fantastic and famous examples is the salon held by Gertrude Stein and her brother Leo Stein as they started to collect art where everyone from Picasso, Matisse, Rousseau and writers Max Jacob and Guillaume Apollinaire frequented. Their salon became the place people came to see the cutting-edge artwork and talk about it, which not only helped to propel these artists into fame but also became the place and process through which the artists themselves developed ideas by interacting with writers and thinkers outside their own disciplines. (There was an exceptional exhibition held at the San Francisco Museum of Modern Art that shows the collection, highlighting the importance of the salon to elevate many careers into fame.) I wonder if it would be beneficial in our classrooms, as they become more interdisciplinary, to take on the model of a salon and to practice creativity through interaction.

That notion that poets have written poems about poetry but that most poems focus their subjects toward outside experiences rings true for art as well. The most interesting or engaging art pieces historically have an interaction with something outside the discipline of art as a subject of its own work and are not simply self-reflective. If this is the trend for successful designers and writers, then encouraging interdisciplinary as a pedagogical model seems crucial to students' success.

Claudine Jaenichen: In graphic design, the nature of the client-designer relationship exposes the profession to levels and lengths of various disciplines. In one eight-hour day, a designer can work on projects ranging from healthcare and aviation to candy and toy products. Projects are client driven, which dictates the content a designer researches and works in. Some may argue that, by this nature, graphic design is interdisciplinary, but I beg to differ. My proposal of interdisciplinarity is the exchange of activity and thinking between disciplines – emphasis on exchange. For example, students are required to obtain the skill set of conducting basic ethnographies, a skill in building empathy and perspective outside their own experiences. In a medicine design project, students invite people who use over-the-counter medicines into the design process as decision makers. The exchange is between audience and designer, where the activity as user and designer equally affects the creative outcome. In typography, students consider the work of concrete and kinetic poetry and the role of typography, page composition and authorship intersections more intimately.

Anna Leahy: Our conversation is an invitation to simultaneously blur the lines between our disciplines and more clearly articulate those boundaries. In *Academic Instincts,* Marjorie Garber astutely points out, 'The inevitable consequence of interdisciplinarity may not be the end of the scholarly world as we know it but the acknowledgment that our knowledge is always partial, rather than total' (2003: 79-80). Creative writers and artists seem attuned to this partial-ness and willing to explore collisions among ideas.

Lia Halloran: Even if these collaborations do not immediately produce a product – whether an article, a musical composition, or a piece of artwork – the creative capital gained from these discussions would be undoubtedly monumental. This intersection is process, and, while creative process may be performed or expressed differently in various disciplines, sharing these creative steps would be enriching.

I teach a course called 'The Intersection of Art and Science' with NASA's Jet Propulsion Laboratory. My desire to teach this class was to pair science and art next to each other not so that we could see similarities or differences but, instead, to see where each discipline could learn from the other through observation and discussion of creative process. When we spoke to the engineers who designed and built the Mars Rovers, the students could understand that each step was about problem solving. How do you put a machine on the surface of another planet where we don't know the atmosphere, the contents of the soil, whether there is extreme heating and cooling, and a countless list of other unpredictable variables? All normal operating environments are out the window. You have to think outside of the box; if you don't, you're probably not going to get very far, not to Mars anyway. My students could relate to this situation because the engineers were making something that has never existed in the world before. This is true for writing, design and art: our desire to create something that has never existed before, that which creatively pushes the boundaries, inspires and surprises us.

Anna Leahy: Robert Frost famously wrote, 'No surprise for the writer, no surprise for the reader' (1972: 394). Creative writers and artists must surprise ourselves in order to make something that has not existed in the world before.

Claudine Jaenichen: In part, in order to explore that kind of surprise, Lia and I discussed teaching a team-taught course with a third faculty in a different discipline entitled 'Up.' The course could be taught in multiple disciplines with possible contributions from art, science, history, psychology and theology. As a conceptual course that merges three disciplines into one classroom, it would explore all things unbounded by the earth. Topics would include looking at how things move in air, images that point us upward (conceptually, physically, and spiritually), go over the history and future of flight on the earth and space, look at the anatomy of birds, understand the physics behind airplanes, explore the dynamic structures of clouds and the fears of flying and perhaps even conclude with students taking part in a discovery flight. Project outcomes would be defined by the exchange of disciplines, and team-teaching would nurture at least three areas into actively looking at and discussing their perspectives.

Lia Halloran: Taking one subject that has inspired multiple disciplines would offer students a new perspective of researching one's creative subject matter. Perhaps some of the first steps to encouraging our students' creativity are exploring the process of various creative disciplines and, through these early stages, making a case they are linked together. And, let's face it, what student wouldn't be thrilled to take a course that moves them outside the gravitational boundaries and offers flying lessons at the end of the semester?

Anna Leahy: This course is why we must talk across academic departments and disciplines. In having this conversation, we discovered common interests. My chapbook called *Turns about a Point* (Leahy, 2006) draws together poems about the concept of flight, and Lia has been working toward her private pilot's license. A course like Up could include reading of literature about flight, perhaps Alain de Botton's essay 'On travelling places,' astronaut Michael Collins's *Carrying the Fire*, Helen Humphreys's short novel *Leaving Earth*, Margaret Lazarus Dean's novel *The Time It Takes to Fall* or the poems that *Air & Space* published online for National Poetry Month. There's a marvellous online collection of true stories called *Airplane Reading* – 'a kind of storytelling that can animate, reflect on, and rejuvenate the experience of flight' – that's continually expanding; students could submit their writing there for possible publication.

After publishing this essay in *New Writing*, I became the third team-teacher in this proposed course, and we've been awarded an institutional grant to run the course in the honors program, with each of us earning full credit for a course. Students in such a course will also consider how we use language and metaphor. Why is *up* as an idea generally a good thing? What does it mean to cheer someone up (or to feel down in the dumps)? In aviation museums, why are aircraft hung from the ceiling in an upright position that shows viewers its underside? What does it mean to be upside-down? It also might be fruitful to study words and phrases for *up* across different languages. It's a really exciting opportunity for me as a teacher, and I'm glad to be included, even if cost and liability prevent end-of-semester flying lessons.

Lia Halloran: It is clear how valuable these interactions can be as we prepare our students to be interdisciplinary creators in the 21st century. It's not easy to gain intuitional support for these kinds of co-taught courses and other interactions that will give our students the fuel for graduate school and unique professional directions.

Anna Leahy: This conversation essay laid the groundwork for and made the case for the team-taught course in the grant proposal. We were able to work through our ideas in conversation, and we demonstrated that something had already come out of our collaboration. Our creative work, scholarship and teaching are intertwined in this collaboration.

Claudine Jaenichen: Conversations like ours open up possibilities for ourselves as creative artists and as teachers and, therefore, open up possibilities for our students – and for our institutions. We each do our work differently, of course. Those differences make the intersections all the more exciting.

Anna Leahy: Poet Robert Frost wrote, 'Scholars get theirs [their knowledge] with conscientious thoroughness along projected lines of logic; poets theirs through cavalierly and as it happens in and out of books. They stick to nothing deliberately, but let what will stick to them like burrs where they walk in the fields' (1972: 395). So a creative writer, a studio artist and a graphic designer have just meandered through a field together, pointing out and discussing flora and fauna as we went. As we continue to explore the distinctions among our separate fields, we will likely find reasons – unexpected burrs that have clung to us – to use these intersections within our teaching together and separately.

References

Airplane Reading. See http://airplanereading.org/.

Andreasen, N. (2005) *The Creating Brain: The Neuroscience of Genius.* New York: Dana Press.

Angelo, T.A. and Cross K.P. (1993) *Classroom Assessment Techniques* (2nd edn). San Francisco, CA: Jossey-Bass.

Association of Writers and Writing Programs (2011) *AWP Director's Handbook: Guidelines, Policies, and Information for Creative Writing Programs.* See https://www.awpwriter.org/guide/hallmarks_quality (accessed 13 May 2016).

Ciabattari, J. (2005) A revolution of sensibility. *Poets & Writers* January/February, 69–72.

College Art Association (2008) MFA Standards. See http://www.collegeart.org/guidelines/mfa.

Collins, M. (2009) *Carrying the Fire.* New York: Farrar, Straus and Giroux.

Dean, M.L. (2007) *The Time It Takes To Fall.* New York: Simon & Schuster.

de Botton, A. (2002) *The Art of Travel.* New York: Random House.

Flaherty, A (2004) *The Midnight Disease: The Drive to Write, Writer's Block, and the Creative Brain.* New York: Houghton Mifflin.

'Flight Lines.' 2009. *Air & Space Magazine,* April. See http://www.airspacemag.com/flight-today/poetry-april.html.

Frost, R. (1972) The figure a poem makes. In E.C. Lathem and L. Thompson (eds) *Poetry & Prose* (pp. 393–396). New York: Holt, Rinehart and Wilson.

Garber, M. (2003) *Academic Instincts* (pp. 79–80). Princeton, NJ: Princeton University Press.

Gilligan, S.B. and Street, K.L. (2011) Critical reflection on creative collaborations: Imagining the image and wording the work. *New Writing* 8 (1), 43–58.

Gross, P. and Mason, W. (2013) Surface tensions: Framing the flow of a poetry-film collaboration. *New Writing,* July 24, 1–13.

Hickey, D. (1997) *Air Guitar: Essays on Art and Democracy.* Los Angeles, CA: Art Issues Press.

Hirshfield, J. (1997) *Nine Gates: Entering the Mind of Poetry.* New York: HarperCollins.

88   Part 3: Programs

Holley, K.A. (2009) *Understanding Interdisciplinary Challenges and Opportunities in Higher Education.* Hoboken, NJ: Wiley Periodicals.
Humphreys, H. (2000) *Leaving Earth.* New York: Picador.
Johnson, S. (2010) *Where Good Ideas Come From.* New York: Penguin.
Kentridge, W. (1999) *Documentary: Drawing the Passing.* Director: Reinhard Wulf, Studio: David Krut Publishing.
Kentridge, W. (2009) *Five Themes,* March 14–May 31, SFMOMA, San Francisco, CA.
Leahy, A. (2006) *Turns about a Point.* Georgetown, KY: Finishing Line Press.
Leahy, A. and Szporluk, L. (2010) Good counsel: A conversation about poetry writing, the imagination, and teaching. *Mid-American Review* 30, 57–69.
NASAD (National Association of Schools of Art and Design) See http://nasad.arts-accredit.org/index.jsp?page=Standards-Handbook.
Norman, D. (1993) *Turn Signals are the Facial Expressions of Automobiles* (pp. 175–186). New York: Basic Books.
San Francisco Museum of Modern Art (May 21–September 6 2011) The Steins Collect: Matisse, Picasso, and the Parisian Avant-Garde. See https://www.sfmoma.org/press/release/landmark-sfmoma-exhibition-showcases-the-art-and-/.
Stegner, W. (2002) *On Teaching and Writing Fiction.* New York: Penguin.
Zunshine, L. (2006) *Why We Read Fiction: Theory of Mind and the Novel.* Columbus, OH: The Ohio State UP.

6 More Than the Sum of Our Parts: Variety in Graduate Programs

Anna Leahy, Leslie Pietrzyk, Mary Swander and Amy Sage Webb

A quick search in AWP's *Guide to Writing Programs* reveals that 360 member institutions include graduate programs, whether MA, MFA or PhD. Creative writing as a field has moved beyond the days when every MFA program can be assumed to have roughly the same curriculum, approach and goals to vary only in perceived reputation. Expansion has bred variety, not merely an increase in the number of programs. 'More than the sum of our parts' is a celebration of the variety among graduate programs. It's exciting to explore what it means to have both residential and low-residency programs, programs with a specific area of focus and challenges to assumptions about what might be required. Because this variety among creative writing programs is likely to grow, especially as each program negotiates resistance and accommodation within and from outside its hallways, the authors include some suggestions for future innovation as well.

Anna Leahy: In the introduction to *Creative Writing and Education,* Graeme Harper points out that creative writing is an odd fit for universities: 'Creative writing is not always assisted by these contemporary institutional structures and functions, wherever these might be in the world, because these structures and functions relate to relatively fixed time frames (at the macro level for such things as completion of college degree and at the micro level for such things as completion of work to be assessed) and the actions of creative writing most often do not, and because creative writing practice and understanding are highly individualized and our contemporary educational institutions are not' (2015: 1). Indeed, how do we best mentor burgeoning novelists over 15-week semesters? How do we individualize instruction and feedback while teaching a class of a dozen students?

By situating creative writing in the academy, we accept certain structures and constraints. The variety of MFA programs, however, suggests that opportunities and constraints vary from institution to institution. Niche programs and newly configured courses seem to challenge those set structures even as they work within them.

Leslie Pietrzyk: Logically, prospective graduate students focus on applying to the so-called best program, with the definition of *best* perhaps based on meaningless or outdated lists floating around the internet or on happenstance comments from professors who knew the lay of the land better a decade or two ago. A niche should indicate to the student what kind of place the program is. A niche might be an alternative structure like low-residency, a topical focus for a program or specialized coursework within what we think of as the traditional framework. These characteristics speak differently to different students. Not everyone learns in the same way; not everyone has the same needs. The variety of MFA programs encourages students to self-select and apply to the programs where they have the best chance for success. Different programs will be exactly the best program for different students.

Mary Swander: At Iowa State University, we consciously wanted to be different, different than we had been and different from other programs. Iowa State University had an MA program with an emphasis in creative writing, which served the English Department well for about 20 years, but most of the creative writing students and faculty longed for more focused study with a terminal, more professional MFA degree. In the end, our MA students had difficulty getting jobs – even teaching composition at community colleges – without a terminal advanced degree. We faced a practical and ethical dilemma with the MA.

Anna Leahy: I was one of those MA students back in the day. It served me well, especially because I had a teaching assistantship and because I was able to work both in poetry and in fiction. But I went on to an MFA program.

Amy Sage Webb: Cross-genre study is an area of strength for the MA, and the program at Emporia State University sounds somewhat like the MA experience that existed at Iowa State University.

Leslie Pietrzyk: Indeed, the MFA tends to be more narrowly focused than the MA. The program in which I teach doesn't allow for a cross-genre option.

While it complicates curricular logistics and could compromise depth of study, cross-genre work might make for a more rounded experience and offers intriguing possibilities.

Anna Leahy: Interestingly, at the MFA program at the University of Maryland, when I was there, the fiction and poetry workshops ran on the same day at the same time. When I questioned this, I was told that most students were not prepared to write in both genres – and now, as someone who has taught a few unprepared students, I understand that thinking.

The PhD program at Ohio University, on the other hand, required every creative writing student to take a workshop in a second genre. More than making graduate students experts in a second genre, taking workshops in more than one genre prepares them, especially in the absence of a creative writing pedagogy course (which I wish I'd had), to teach the multi-genre introductory course that is relatively common in undergraduate programs.

Mary Swander: Creative writing programs weren't always divided into genre, though. That evolved because the instructors found it easier to teach a poetry workshop or a fiction workshop. Stephen Wilbers' book *The Iowa Writers Workshop* traces the development of the single-genre workshops at Iowa. There are old photographs included in that text that show famous fiction writers like Flannery O'Connor sitting next to the likes of poet Robert Lowell in the same classroom. The Iowa Writers Workshop began admitting students only in one genre. They didn't want beginning fiction writers – i.e. poets – in the same class as advanced fiction writers and vice versa. I was admitted to both the poetry and the fiction workshops there, so I could take courses in both genres, but most fellow students could not.

Most poets read widely and are very familiar with fiction. Fiction writers, in contrast, venture less often into the world of poetry. Poets benefit from knowing fictional techniques and from studying longer forms like the novel. Fiction writers benefit from understanding figures of speech and getting a sense of the compression of meaning found in the special language of poetry. A quick glance at the AWP Job List shows that academic jobs often demand the ability to teach a second genre, at least at the introductory level.

Anna Leahy: For me as a poet over the long haul, one of the most important degree requirements for the MA I earned, but one that doesn't seem common in MFA programs, was two courses in linguistics. The MA allowed for broader study that influenced my writing and my teaching.

Amy Sage Webb: Also uncommon is the three-year program with required area coverage and comprehensive exams. That preparation has helped me more than anything in the types of teaching I've done and in broadening my curiosity and creativity as a writer and scholar.

In addition, such a program required a critical foreword with a creative thesis manuscript. Thus, I not only wrote fiction, but I also contextualized it within an academic discourse. In this process, I discovered feminist sociolinguistics, which opened a new way of integrating my studies then and thereafter. After some coursework in rhetoric, linguistics or literary criticism, students become more at ease in identifying fruitful questions for exploring what they read and what they write. They also develop a critical language beyond anecdote for talking about writing. This moves the profession beyond the cult-of-the-author concept.

Mary Swander: The original requirement at Iowa State University was fluency in a second language. That worked until students started coming to us without ever having studied a language as an undergraduate, so the department let students opt for two courses in linguistics. That study of linguistics sensitizes a writer to language and formalizes the choices one makes.

Now we're in another dilemma. Current students not only don't have a foreign language but also don't know grammar well. As undergraduate education shifts, so do most graduate programs.

Anna Leahy: Programs change over time, and what we once considered the basics might now be considered innovative. I wrote an essay for *Pedagogy* called 'Grammar matters' because exploring grammar has become a bigger part of my teaching than it was 15 years ago. Why not brush up on diagramming sentences as a way of seeing a poem, in conjunction with reading, for instance, the chapter on syntax and line in Robert Pinsky's *The Sounds of Poetry?*

Amy Sage Webb: I sometimes give students sentences like the opening of William Faulkner's 'Dry September' or the opening of James Joyce's 'The Dead' and ask them to diagram them on the dry-erase wall of our lounge just to see the syntax laid out like organic chemistry. As creative writers, we appreciate other writers' styles, but we too rarely examine language construction closely. Writers tend to rely upon grammar as a copyediting skill, but not as frequently a source of aesthetics.

Anna Leahy: I've also been talking with my literature colleagues about what they're teaching. In residential programs, students often have significant literature course requirements, and there are often more MFA than literature students in those classes, but I don't get the sense that we're coordinating very well as faculty.

Mary Swander: The original literature requirements at Iowa State University arose from the English Department's desire to put the proverbial butts in seats in those areas that were undersubscribed, so those requirements had little to do with the shaping of writers.

Anna Leahy: With the English major down nationwide in both numbers and especially percentage over the last several decades – the report by the National Center for Educational Statistics is telling – enrollment in literature may drive some decisions about curricular requirements. Still, reading is part of the writer's study and growth.

Leslie Pietrzyk: In our low-residency MFA program, which does not have literature course requirements, students are responsible for a reading list of 8–12 books each semester. Sometimes the mentor will assign these directly, but, most often, the list comes through a process of exploration and negotiation between the mentor and the student, with texts chosen specifically to advance both the student's self-assessed writing goals and the needs the professor identifies. For example, if a student tells me she's interested in writing linked stories about a girl coming of age, and I, having read her work, believe she could benefit from creating a more distinct voice, the reading list would contain authors who accomplish those goals – say, Grace Paley's (2007) stories, *Ellen Foster* by Kaye Gibbons (1997), *The Brief Wondrous Life of Oscar Wao* by Junot Diaz (2007), *How the Garcia Girls Lost Their Accent* by Julia Alvarez (1992) and Tim O'Brien's (1998) *The Things They Carried*. Each selection on the reading list directly informs – while also provoking – the student's particular writing interests and needs. Every book requires a separate response paper, so our MFA is reading-intensive, with works spanning the ages, with perhaps a slight skewing to the 20th and 21st centuries. Additionally, that reading list also includes relevant craft books, which reinforce the ideas brought forward in workshops and craft lectures during the writing period and the mentoring portion of the semester.

Anna Leahy: That description of how reading functions in a low-residency MFA program suggests striving for both breadth and depth, for both shared aims and individual attention.

Leslie Pietrzyk: In my ideal world, MFA programs would be three years, not the traditional two. What's the rush? (Of course, money is partly the rush.)

When else will any of our students have the time during which their creative work is as valued and appreciated?

That extra time – a third year is a 50% increase – might allow for in-depth reading and practice in more than one genre. The PhD program, because it is longer, might allow easily for this kind of work, but it is also a very different academic pedigree. Many fiction writers and poets turn to writing creative nonfiction at some point, for instance, so examining that genre would help untangle some of the ethical dilemmas one faces when making the move into telling the truth, even if one tells it slant. Perhaps we could throw in some literary journalism for all – reviews, interviews, and such. The whole range of what writers write over a career.

Mary Swander: Ours is a three-year MFA program, and many of our students write in more than one genre because the topical attention takes the focus off genre, to some extent. I've taught graduate courses on craft, and I've taught courses that include different genres, in large part because I publish in different genres myself. I've also supervised graduate student fieldwork, from studying herbs in the mountains of Spain to working on a small local CSA vegetable farm. Our students even take courses with an environmental bent in other disciplines, such as the sciences, environmental studies, landscape architecture, sustainable agriculture, history, sociology and more. The three-year program, completely reconceived, has allowed for a different way of thinking about a program and a writing life.

Anna Leahy: With the rise of the MFA and also now the PhD and with increased variety among these terminal degree programs – low-residency and residential structures, two- and three-year options, different curricular plans – proliferating in the mix, I wonder whether the MA is being squeezed out.

Amy Sage Webb: Or perhaps, with the proliferation of MFA programs, the traditional master's degree is now niche. Emporia State University's graduate program is an MA, not an MFA program. Some students seek apprenticeship to graduate-level reading and critical writing and exposure to a range of graduate-level study to identify areas of interest and focus.

Importantly, our MA does not align all that well with the AWP hall-marks in a number of areas because the goals are different than for the typi-cal MFA. For instance, our program does not have its own philosophy but, rather, operates under the strategic plan of the university: 'uncommon educa-tion for the common good.' So, there is extensive literary study, as would be expected in an MA program, and also attentiveness to revision, strong thesis advising and strong mentorship, as would be expected in an MFA program. Our uncommon education includes vocational study options and focuses on learner-centered teaching and applied learning. The consistency and frequency of course offerings in an MA program is not going to compare with the variety of creative-writing-specific seminars and workshops in an MFA, though.

Mary Swander: We might have gone on as we had, with an MA program akin to the one you're describing at Emporia State University. But our non-terminal degree in creative writing was very vulnerable at a university of science and technology being squeezed with university budget cuts. The MFA in Creative Writing and Environment responded to that changed institutional context.

To survive as a program, we needed a terminal degree that fit into the mission and vision of our land-grant university. While the university's mission says much of what many institutional mission statements say – 'student-centered education, global collaboration, and transformational basic and applied research' – the vision statement says, 'Iowa State University will lead the world in advancing the land-grant ideals of putting science, technology, and human creativity to work' and goes on to mention the US departments of agriculture and energy in particular. Also, we needed to distinguish ourselves from the University of Iowa's famous writing program. State universities are often under pressure to avoid replicating degree programs available at other universities in the state, and we didn't want to directly compete with the most well-known MFA program in the country.

Amy Sage Webb: Answering the redundancy question is the necessity that has given birth to a lot of the niche innovation. The business ethos driving education pits institutions against each other in open market competition for dwindling resources. To survive, we each must define our markets and demonstrate how our so-called product – our program – aligns with the needs of that market. Moreover, we must continually identify new markets and demonstrate growth and innovation. The culture of this endless striving in higher education today is at odds with creative and critical work of quality, which requires breadth, depth, time for thinking and time for dialogue.

That said, as the number of creative writing programs has exploded, the competition among them has brought some real gains. Institutions and faculty are talking with each other and students about where they want to focus, then building programs that go about their concerns in different ways.

In her preface to the important 1996 book, *The Ecocriticism Reader: Landmarks in Literary Ecology,* Cheryll Glotfelty notes:

> If your knowledge of the outside world were limited to what you could infer from the major publications of the literary profession, you would quickly discern that race, class, and gender were the hot topics of the late twentieth century, but you would never suspect that the earth's life support systems were under stress. Indeed, you might never know that there was an earth at all (1996: xvi).

Her observations about this omission in literary professions rings true for both the writing and literary-critical portions of the humanities equation. The Iowa State University Creative Writing and Environment program is one that addresses this omission.

Demands to diversify (fire!) the canon are old. The new diversity of creative writing programs we are seeing now strikes me as the best answer academia has developed in a long time to consciously and deliberately foster a greater diversity of writers and writing topics.

Anna Leahy: Constraints, then, create opportunity; pressure creates explosion. That state oversight seems to be one reason why Ohio University developed a PhD program instead of an MFA. Ohio State University already had a thriving MFA. Ohio University's program is still one of only 48 PhD programs worldwide, according to the *AWP Guide to Writing Programs.*

Mary Swander: In the early 1990s, we had an external review. The report stated that we had a strong creative writing program and urged us to set up a PhD program with a creative dissertation, really a literature PhD with a few writing workshops and a book of poetry, fiction or nonfiction instead of an academic dissertation. At the time, the literature area did not offer enough graduate courses – just two a semester – to support a PhD. So we moved to an MFA in Creative Writing and the Environment. The politics of a department, university, and state factor strongly in the creation of writing programs.

Amy Sage Webb: The oversight of Boards of Regents and accrediting agencies creates a real pressure on programs to shape themselves around enrollment. It has benefitted some programs to pitch a wider tent rather than to specialize at too granular a level. While we lose some of the benefits of specialization, the security of strength in numbers is such an overwhelming benefit that it forces us to develop other adaptive strategies and collaborations. Some programs, including the one in which I teach, place creative writing within literary and cultural studies and create literary citizenship and applied learning experiences that are open to all the tracks in the department. For example, a children's poetry anthology project with local schools starts out with creative writers but gains ballast as a true literary citizenship project through collaboration. You don't think of the feminist rhetoric scholar and the speculative fiction writer and the TESOL specialist and the Medievalist coming together in a lot of places, but that type of cross-pollination has been fruitful for us.

Mary Swander: We decided to work with and emphasize the environment as we reconceived our program as an MFA because many of us had backgrounds and personal interests in the area. More importantly, the emphasis allowed the students to draw on the great interdisciplinary expertise on campus.

Anna Leahy: What we're seeing then, in the wake of rapid growth of graduate programs in creative writing over the last three decades, is that one size doesn't fit all. Each program resides within a distinct institutional and geographical setting, and each combination of faculty offers different strengths and quirks. Instead of seeing factors like geographical location, institutional culture, and faculty expertise as limiting, we might be able to use them to our advantage.

Amy Sage Webb: Programs are continually trying to identify niches of students whom they serve and to develop tracks or curricula to serve those students. Some programs, like Seton Hill University's low-residency MFA in Writing Popular Fiction, serve a niche market because it's entirely focused on genre fiction. Our MA program gains about half its students from undergraduate English majors, many of whom want to teach. Emporia State University began as the Kansas State Teachers College and is still widely known for teacher preparation. Knowing that, we put attention into pedagogy and approached genres as gateways where teachers and students fall in love with literature and learn creative writing.

Leslie Pietrzyk: Many, though not all, students come to the Converse College program with an interest in regional, Southern literature and are pleased to find a graduate program in which several members of the faculty, both permanent and visiting, are writing in multi-layered interpretations of Southern tradition. What faculty write and know can overtly or subtly shape a program and draw certain types of students.

Amy Sage Webb: This really begs the question about whether we build programs around what faculty know and do or whether faculty shape themselves around the students they serve. How much, I wonder, is our staffing and pedagogy adapting to a new programmatic and student landscape? We are talking about programs having changed, but can our understandings of ourselves as faculty be understood with the concept of niche too?

Anna Leahy: Niche and variety go hand in hand, then. Having taught at several different types of institutions over the years, including a community college, an open enrollment and a selective public university, and private colleges, I've seen how different constraints – faculty expertise, student demographics, institutional missions and budgets, and so on – interact to make for programs of different shapes, sizes, and specializations. Who I am and how I tell my career story has adjusted as my professional context has changed. When I was teaching at Missouri Western State University, I wrote about the need for generalists. My current institutional context defines me as interdisciplinary, though my teaching is almost always in my primary area of specialization.

Leslie Pietrzyk: The low-residency program's individualized attention and focus as well as its self-directed nature (admittedly a disaster for the wrong type of person who lacks organizational skills) heightens this attention to honing a role. By investing in the composition of the individual reading list and setting forth a signed contract for the semester writing plan, the student's experience mirrors the greater reality of the writing world, where no one will be eagerly awaiting that next short story. The so-called helicopter parents may be creating a generation of passive students who expect material to be presented to them, and the low-residency model pushes against that expectation. The low-res student is a direct partner in the educational experience, and the program adapts as the student evolves.

Anna Leahy: Goddard University launched its low-residency program in 1963, so, though low-residency MFA programs are perceived as newcomers or alternatives, that type of program was part of the landscape before the big proliferation of MFA programs. Now, the *AWP Guide to Writing Programs* lists more than 40 low-residency MFA programs. Certain approaches of the low-residency programs were born out of the inherent constraints of time and distance, but residency MFA programs might look to borrow some of the best practices – especially those that encourage responsibility, intensity and focus – of low-residency programs.

Leslie Pietrzyk: The stereotype of the low-residency student, of course, is someone older, but that needs to be re-examined; many of our students come to us right out of college or a year or two out. Low-residency is a deviation from the traditional MFA model and radically influences the landscape and challenges the traditional educational model.

Anna Leahy: The traditional model is probably an ideal that never existed. There exist many ways to design a program, many ways to teach, learn and practice our discipline. That's probably long been the case, but we're in a position to benefit from the variety now.

Amy Sage Webb: As arduous as outcomes-based assessment is for education, one of the most exciting changes happening now as a result of it is the focus on student learning rather than on product. There's much more attention to apprenticeship to craft and personal growth in writing programs now and less focus on publication as the goal. Publishing has become more accessible, and the purveyors of wisdom about writing are no longer holding the keys to the literary kingdom (if they ever were). There's a greater sense of collaboration and entering into the life of the artist in these programs. Marketing descriptions of creative writing programs today no longer focus entirely on credentials of faculty but, instead, emphasize the literary community these programs offer to their students and alumni.

Leslie Pietrzyk: Converse College is a women's college, a particular type of community. The MFA program is not limited to female applicants, however, and draws students from across the country. I wonder what an all-female MFA program – both faculty and students – might be like. Or historically black colleges and universities might develop a graduate creative writing program that focuses entirely on teaching writers of color. The arts organization VONA has found success in its mission: 'to develop emerging writers of color through programs and workshops taught by established writers of color.' Like most arts organizations, its mission includes 'artistic excellence'; but 'social justice' and community empowerment carry equal weight.

I'm not saying we should all divide ourselves up into groups and sub-groups. I see problems with over-compartmentalizing the field. But might it be interesting to have that choice?

Amy Sage Webb: At Antioch University, I work primarily with students in a low-residency post-MFA certification program focused on teaching that provides pedagogical training and professionalization activities and places MFA-degreed individuals into supervised teaching placements where they live. The goal is, in this competitive market, to help these students enter academic careers. Most MFA programs are not really preparing students for academic positions, even though the terminal degree qualifies graduates for those positions. Even if they don't enter academic professions, this certificate program offers students a glimpse into some of the big picture concepts and on-the-ground work and issues that are part of academic jobs today.

Anna Leahy: Low-residency MFA programs, of course, don't have teaching assistants, and residential programs don't have enough assistantships to go around, with some students earning degrees completely on their own dimes and without a background in pedagogy. I've come to question whether it's ethical for us to put all our assistantship eggs into the teaching basket, when the academic job market is terrible and the adjunct life shouldn't be a long-term plan for someone who seeks or needs a full time salary.

I've been working with colleagues to develop opportunities that might prepare our students for careers other than teaching. While we have several full fellowships that include a stipend and tuition remission, some scholarships for partial tuition remission, and a few adjunct teaching positions for current graduate students, we're also now using student worker funding to develop assistantships jointly with the alumni magazine, the Dean of Students Office, the Office of Undergraduate Research and Creative Activity and other entities on campus. This new assistantship program takes advantage of the entrepreneurial spirit at our university and encourages students to acquire and build skills that can help them land jobs. Editorial or nonprofit work may be more relevant to writers than is teaching.

Mary Swander: Our students who most easily get jobs upon graduation are not the students who have had the traditional teaching assistantships, teaching two classes per semester of composition. Some of our students get assistantships in communications in other departments. Other students, those with computer skills, have had assistantships in distance learning. Several who are bilingual and well-travelled have had assistantships in the study abroad office.

We are frank about the job prospects in academe. Nonetheless, our students become employed as professors and also as editors, science writers, park rangers, technical support workers, web designers, communications specialists and more.

Anna Leahy: That's a necessary shift in the wake of the economic downturn in 2008, hikes in tuition, changes in student loan policies and the increasing reliance on adjunct teaching.

Several post-MFA fellowships, at places like Stanford University and the University of Wisconsin, have existed for a while. The post-MFA certificate, like the one at Antioch University, could really catch on now. While not always dependent on completion of the MFA, certificate programs exist at several universities in professional writing, editing, and publishing. The American Medical Writers Association runs certificate programs as well, and several universities run similar programs, sometimes through their continuing education offices. Johns Hopkins University, after recent reconfiguring of an existing program, runs a five-course online certificate program in science writing. Dollars to donuts, we'll see more of these non-degree or post-degree options with narrower curricula and fewer course requirements, which might offer add-ons to or even substitutions for the MFA.

Mary Swander: As a freelance writer, I found it very difficult to write all day for someone else, then write creatively for myself at night. My own writing went much better when I had my own business as a massage therapist. People laugh at me, but I think one of the best jobs for a writer is a tax preparer. You work four months of the year, make a good amount of money, then, if you live frugally, you have the rest of the year to write. Young writers can now be more much entrepreneurial. It's not perfect, but the Affordable Care Act has even made it possible to start your own business without the risk of going without health insurance.

Amy Sage Webb: None of us, including students, should assume that the world we inherited will be the one we inhabit going forward. Writing professions and the means to enter them are radically changing. Niche programs can give students opportunities to develop the types of innovations that will create new jobs. I would like to see more graduate coursework and especially post-graduate programs focusing on entrepreneurship, on media studies, on rhetoric and advocacy, on community building, on medical writing. Graduates need to be able to make new jobs and new markets for their arts. The MFA, in all its variety, can be part of that.

In addition, if we don't help students to explore speculative fiction and genre studies, we aren't answering a cultural need. Once we let go of some of the staid notions of the MFA, the degree becomes more useful for more writers to pursue areas of their passion and interest, areas for which there are more readers than there are for so-called literary fiction. How about writing the body, self-image and body studies, writing the self? Writing grief is another possibility. Writing family histories – complete with genealogy – is another. Niche writers have a lot to gain by studying craft and literary studies but may not wish to produce the same kinds of literature usually associated with the MFA. They will help to transform the genres.

Leslie Pietrzyk: The program at Converse has recently implemented tracks in young adult fiction and environmental writing.

Mary Swander: More programs with a focus on editing and publishing are undoubtedly in the works. I'd also like to see programs focused on community or global outreach, travel writing, social justice issues or languages.

Anna Leahy: Creative writing is one of the most dynamic, responsive and innovative areas of graduate education. Even when we do not rethink whole programs, we might still rethink the components of a curriculum. For instance, Chapman University's MFA program aligns pretty well with the *AWP Guidelines & Hallmarks* for programs. Recently, we've wondered aloud how we can use the curriculum in more innovative ways and to explore relationships between writer and author, between a writing life and a career, between an individual's art and the larger culture. Those conversations can lead to change in attitude and in catalog copy.

Amy Sage Webb: Of course, the traditional model can work well, if we remain thoughtful about how we're working with it. For instance, it's not just about having a visiting writers series. It's a question of what that series will enable students in the program to do as literary citizens. Let's take an unflinching look at some of the mainstays of writing programs and ask ourselves how those elements need to evolve.

Anna Leahy: Yes, it's not only *what* we do but *how* we do it. I'm assigning book reviews more often, in part to get students reading contemporary poetry more widely and reading individually as well as with their peers. I've started requiring that graduate students submit their reviews for publication because I want to help them build a writing life beyond the classroom. What if there were a whole course devoted to reviewing?

Leslie Pietrzyk: Low-residency programs almost always include visiting agents and editors as part and parcel, often with pitch sessions or one-on-one conferences about student work-in-progress. I didn't get this sort of information or experience as part of my residential MFA, but it might have helped me understand earlier the business side of being a writer. The realities can seem harsh to the students, but they graduate with a sense of how the publishing world works and with a few contacts. Opening a query letter with *I met you when you visited my low-residency MFA program* will keep an agent reading to the second paragraph. Additionally, there is also career interest; following the presentation by an agent, someone always asks, *How can I become an agent?*

Mary Swander: It's one thing to rethink an aspect of a program, but, as Amy suggests, niche on the whole-program level is not for everyone or for every institution. You'll need interested faculty and support from your department and college. Often, before coming to Iowa State University, our students have been in the Peace Corps, lived on Native American reservations or done some other kind of travel, research or service work. Many have gone on to earn PhD degrees from other departments in the university, including the sciences and agriculture. The future looks interdisciplinary.

Amy Sage Webb: In most programs, though, we make a choice to focus rather exclusively on craft and student development, which has real benefits but comes at a cost in terms of what happens after the degrees are earned. It is absolutely necessary that we give students the knowledge and skills they will need to be advocates for arts or to build and sustain arts in their communities.

Mary Swander: Exactly. Our students teach creative writing in the prisons, in the high schools, in nursing homes, in the schools in Trinidad and Tobago and for people with disabilities. They are actively involved in local arts councils and in environmental causes. I've taken them to do creative projects at the Iowa Department of the Blind and the Iowa School for the Deaf. They teach challenged youth and home-schooled youth.

Anna Leahy: In her book *The Write Crowd*, Lori A. May writes, 'Literary citizenship takes the power of the individual and puts it to use in fostering, sustaining, and engaging with the literary community for the benefit of others' (2015: 6). Though the MFA benefits many individual writers, MFA programs are part of the larger literary community and arts culture. When we are cognizant of that intersection and interaction, we begin to expand programmatic, curricular and pedagogical possibilities. While the center holds, the variety across graduate programs in creative writing is healthy for the larger culture and the future of the arts as well as for the variety of students our programs serve and a more inclusive future.

References

Alvarez, J. (1992) *How the Garcia Girls Lost Their Accents*. New York: Plume.
Association of Writers and Writing Programs (AWP). *AWP Guide to Writing Programs*. Association of Writers and Writing Programs. See https://www.awpwriter.org/guide/guide_writing_programs (accessed 13 May 2016).
AWP. *AWP Guidelines & Hallmarks*. See https://www.awpwriter.org/guide/hallmarks_quality.
AWP. *AWP Job List* (2015) See https://www.awpwriter.org/careers/job_list (accessed 15 November 2015).

Converse College MFA. See http://www.converse.edu/admissions/graduate/masters-of-fine-arts-in-creative-writing-mfa/.

Diaz, J. (2007) *The Brief Wondrous Life of Oscar Wao.* New York: Riverhead.

Gibbons, K. (1997) *Ellen Foster.* New York: Vintage.

Glotfelty, C. (1996) Preface. In C. Glotfelty and H. Fromm (eds) *The Ecocriticism Reader: Landmarks in Literary Ecology* (p. xvi). Athens: University of Georgia Press.

Graduate Catalog 2014–2015. Chapman University. See http://www.chapman.edu/catalog/oc/current/gr/.

Harper, G. (ed.) (2015) *Creative Writing and Education.* Bristol: Multilingual Matters.

Leahy, A. (2005) Grammar matters. *Pedagogy* 5.2 (Spring), 304–308.

Leahy, A. (2001) Who's on first? Generalism, multitasking, and playing ball,. *Journal of the Midwest Modern Language Association* 34.3 (Fall), 38–53.

May, L.A. (2015) *The Write Crowd: Literary Citizenship and the Writing Life.* New York: Bloomsbury.

MFA in Creative Writing and Environment. Iowa State University. See http://www.engl.iastate.edu/creative-writing/mfa-program-in-creative-writing-and-environment/.

National Center for Educational Statistics (2015) Table 322.10: Bachelor's degrees conferred by post-secondary institutions. See https://nces.ed.gov/programs/digest/d14/tables/dt14_322.10.asp (accessed 13 October 2015).

O'Brien, T. (1998) *The Things They Carried.* New York: Broadway.

Paley, G. (2007) *The Collected Stories.* New York: Farrar, Straus, and Giroux.

Post-MFA Certificate in the Teaching of Creative Writing. Antioch University. See http://www.antiochla.edu/academics/mfa-creative-writing/post-mfa-teaching-creative-writing/.

Strategic Plan 2010–2015. Iowa State University. See http://www.president.iastate.edu/sp.

Strategic Plan 2015–2025. Emporia State University. See http://www.emporia.edu/president/strategicplan/strategic-plan.html.

VONA (n.d.) Mission & Values. See http://www.voicesatvona.org/mission (accessed 20 November 2015).

Wilbers, S. (1980) *The Iowa Writers' Workshop.* University of Iowa Press.

7 The Bold and the Beautiful: Rethinking Undergraduate Models

Katharine Haake, Anna Leahy and Argie Manolis

Over the last 10 years, a great deal has been written about the under-graduate creative writing program, and a good portion of that forms the New Writing Viewpoints series. In this chapter, Katharine Haake, Anna Leahy and Argie Manolis begin with one of the models posed in *Power and Identity in the Creative Writing Classroom*, service-learning, and go on to explore other possibilities that are not the usual fare of creative writing programs, including connections with graduate programs and extremely open-ended projects. In addition, this chapter discusses institutional environments that shape programs and some types of constraints that limit faculty's ability to change a curriculum or program. In doing so, the authors challenge common lore, the dominant focus on craft, and the Hallmarks suggested by the Association of Writers and Writing Programs.

Argie Manolis: In *Power and Identity in the Creative Writing Classroom*, I wrote about an introductory creative writing class designed around an outreach project. That project emerged because, as an MFA candidate at Arizona State University, I participated in an internship at an Alzheimer's unit in a nursing home. I hung out with residents, recorded what they said, and crafted their words into poems. The project transformed how I understood myself as a writer and as a teacher; it changed my priority and my pedagogy from there on out. Later, at the University of Minnesota, Morris, the dean asked me to write a grant to grow service-learning beyond a handful of classes. Fifteen years later, my students are involved in the original service-learning project that led me to this career.

Anna Leahy: That contribution to our earlier book led me to dip my toe into service-learning, too. In an advanced composition class, I had each student interview a grandparent and tell that person's story (or part of it), and, when students preferred not to interview a grandparent or didn't have a grandparent to interview, I set them up with a social hour at a local nursing home. My pedagogical goal at the time was to figure out how to help students become effective, confident interviewers. In hindsight, I realize that I thought very narrowly, trying only to bring a smidge of service-learning into my existing course, rather than considering how to re-envision my course and thinking through service-learning. I was thinking about it but not rethinking. The latter, of course, was the point of your essay, but I wasn't ready to take that on.

Katharine Haake: California State University Northridge, where I teach, is very big on service-learning, with a university-wide center that provides faculty training and mentoring, logistical support and a range of grant opportunities. Partly as a result, we have a couple of upper-level 1- and 2-unit creative writing classes built around a focused service-learning component. Some students have taught workshops at our on-campus high school and elsewhere – one at a home for pregnant teens and another, previously homeless herself, at a women's homeless shelter. And our playwright, Rick Mitchell, involves students in community theater projects. But the time commitment – including extensive paperwork – is prohibitive, so I have never sponsored students off-campus myself.

Anna Leahy: I have a colleague, Jan Osborn, who has developed a community outreach project in which MFA students work with the at-risk students at the high school just a block from the edge of our university campus. They meet after school once every week during the spring semester to write and discuss writing, attend readings by visiting writers on our campus and give a final reading themselves. It's a somewhat quiet effort and a yeoman's task.

What if these sorts of experiences – a range of innovative ideas, including service-learning – became centerpieces in creative writing programs?

Argie Manolis: These efforts are rarely centerpieces, of course. The Association of Writers and Writing Programs (AWP) Hallmarks seem to construct the center for our discipline. I appreciate many principles in those Hallmarks: competence in multiple genres, a second language, and reading contemporary work from a variety of cultural backgrounds and perspectives.

Tiered workshops and a focus on revision are important for the development of craft, of course.

While internships and service-learning opportunities are included in the Hallmarks, their framing concerns me. As currently articulated, service-learning experiences 'promote and celebrate literacy, literature, writing, and reading in communities,' rather than providing students with an opportunity to be of use as writers or to engage in reciprocal relationships with community members that will benefit the community as a whole. Internships are framed as opportunities to funnel students into literary careers rather than engage with mentors outside academia. These opportunities can be much richer. We can think bigger in our programs.

Anna Leahy: These opportunities might be, in practice, both selfish and altruistic at the same time. Those extremes intrigue me. What's in it for me as a writer – how will this experience help me become a better writer, more successful, or perhaps a better person generally? What's in it for others – for readers, for culture, for the world? Building undergraduate programs and courses such as service-learning balances our selfishness and our altruism as writers, as teachers, as students – as members of larger communities.

Katharine Haake: There are other ways in which service is intrinsic to our work. I teach at a large, urban campus with a diverse population, and very few of our students will go on to careers related to writing, with many more returning to their home communities to live and work. If their creative writing study prepares them to become informed, inquisitive and engaged participants in those communities, maybe the service comes later, but it will last longer.

Such preparation occurs both inside and outside the classroom. As program director, I participated in an ambitious advising program sponsored by the College of Humanities in which I met with every creative writing student at least twice – when they declared their major and when they applied for graduation. The goal was to support all students, especially first-generation ones (we have many), in such critical college literacy practices as appropriate course selection, effective sequencing, institutional savvy, self-advocacy and so on – skills that are transferable and can prove useful far beyond college. But probably a more important benefit of the program was that students had an opportunity to tell their stories. Listening to these stories, I could help them frame – and solve problems – they might not even know they had.

Anna Leahy: As important as advising is, that work is treated as service, which is often the least heavily weighed part of workload in the faculty review process. At some institutions, faculty spend a lot of time mentoring the most ambitious, talented students, the struggling students and everyone in between. At other institutions, most academic advising is left to a university-wide center and, when an issue arises, to department chairs and program directors.

If we look at the roots of the term *advising*, though – giving counsel – we can understand that it's a way to help students see what they're doing and what the future might hold so that they can make informed choices even when the decision seems small or routine. It's a way to guide them toward reflection, to show them possibilities. We should do this as part of undergraduate programs, but it takes time and expertise.

Katharine Haake: That advising program – once promoted as a model university-wide – was casualty of the financial crisis. Partly as a result, enrollment is declining, and the students end up with transcripts – and the college experiences to go with them – that don't make much sense. I do a lot of what we used to call 'advising on the run' – just stopping in the halls to chat, or chatting while you walk – and it's surprising how welcome this seems. But you can't talk to everyone without a system to support it.

Argie Manolis: I agree that advising is key to a positive undergraduate experience, regardless of one's major. At the University of Minnesota, Morris, there's an expectation that faculty advisors provide ongoing guidance to students – connecting them to other campus resources, providing input on job searches and graduate school planning. It's an incredibly time-consuming commitment.

Anna Leahy: The curriculum isn't merely catalog copy; it shapes our pedagogy, goals and class dynamics. Advising helps students negotiate all of this and tailor their experiences.

Katharine Haake: We've been trying to revise our curriculum for the 30 years I've been here, without much success. And yet everything is also completely different. Our faculty, like our students, are diverse, and so much depends on who's teaching what that what may look in catalog copy like a stodgy old curriculum has become, in practice, a vibrantly current one.

Still, one thing that has long distinguished CSUN's creative writing curriculum from the AWP Hallmarks is a required genre theories course for creative writers that was in place when I arrived. Although some people do teach it as a craft course and others as an aesthetics course, I've always used it to teach theory as a framework within which students can frame the kind of culturally, historically, and aesthetically informed poetics that Rachel Blau Du Plessis says 'gives us permission to continue' (1990: 156).

Anna Leahy: Many programs do not overhaul or revise the curriculum regularly. Change involves work and risk. One aspect we recently rethought at Chapman University is the balance of creative writing and other requirements, especially literature, so that our program is distinguished as a BFA. Anecdotally, our students very much want to earn a BFA, not a BA, and the university is supportive of BFA programs and the implications of creativity on campus. The AWP Hallmarks don't make clear distinctions between the two versions of undergraduate programs, but a fine arts degree implies certain features and approaches and should connect the program to others in art, music, dance and film.

Argie Manolis: Connecting creative writing to other art forms is incredibly important, but I've found that it's more difficult to embed such experiences into the curriculum than it ought to be. Team-taught classes are one way to create connections among artistic disciplines. I was lucky enough to co-teach a class about creative process with a dancer and painter, a study-abroad class about aging with a psychologist and a class about social change with an historian – but, in all these cases, the classes were either honors or summer offerings, not embedded in the curriculum or taught regularly.

Anna Leahy: At my previous institution, the required first-year course was team taught so that it supported interdisciplinarity as well as the usual first-year course goals of critical thinking, retention and so on. I taught Photography and Writing with an art historian, which led to scholarly collaborations with her as well. This coming year, a visual artist, a graphic designer and I (see chapter with Halloran and Jaenichen) have been awarded a co-teaching grant for an honor's course on the concept of *up*. Teaching with faculty in art is a tremendous opportunity for me to continue to hone my pedagogy, but team-teaching is a resource issues.

Katharine Haake: There are other ways of cross-fertilization that are not so expensive. At CSUN, we teach a variety of hybrid classes that bring literature and creative writing students together in generative ways. And graduate students and undergraduates also come together in 500-level classes, which take place in the space between graduate (600-level) and advanced undergraduate (400-level) classes, in another generative mix.

Anna Leahy: But it's also important to make distinction between degree levels. Our new required course called Aspects of a Writer at the MFA level is one way that program is distinguished from the BFA. While it introduces important concepts and the business of writing, the most important result is that it creates connection and community among the students and faculty. As I write this, we have begun to discuss developing an undergraduate equivalent, probably in the junior year, which would, among other goals, connect students with the Office of Fellowships and Scholarships, Career Services and the internship coordinator as well as covering the business of publishing and cultivating a writing life.

Katharine Haake: That sounds like a great course. Our required core course in the MA program is an introduction to the discipline, which I wrote it in the 1990s (and have discussed it in *What Our Speech Disrupts*). It's been an incredibly important course, helping students explore what it means – and what it takes – to be a working writer in this world. But that's at the graduate level.

And our graduate program is in crisis because another casualty of the economic crisis has been our MA thesis, which we have currently replaced with a multi-genre capstone class.

Anna Leahy: A capstone course can offer great opportunities for undergraduates and often fits into program assessment plans. I don't think all faculty, however, are equipped to teach a multi-genre course or mentor students with writing projects in various genres. A multi-genre capstone allows for breadth and encourages interaction. But not all programs are working with the same resources, constraints and cultures.

Katharine Haake: Well the capstone really is a challenge. Initially, we were all reluctant to do a multi-genre workshop, especially at the graduate level, but circumstances led me to do precisely that last spring, and the class was a surprising success. We made a print-on-demand course anthology and staged an off-campus reading.

Argie Manolis: Limitations in funding and staffing often shape our decisions. Spelling out too much in guidelines for our whole field, as the AWP Hallmarks do to some extent, can be problematic for small institutions like mine. But more importantly, spelling out too much might limit our students' ability to create their own imaginative worlds. If we encourage students, they are likely to create entirely new genres in our lifetimes and to make writing relevant to the political and social landscape in new ways. I want our students to write the literature that will reflect the real world, not the professionalized version of the writing world that our predecessors created. We all need to think beyond the existing traditional model, even as we take advantage of its benefits.

Katharine Haake: I love that idea of our students creating new genres. They are really such a powerful voice.

We all seem to be suggesting that our programs challenge the Hallmarks by virtue of the very nature of our institutions. Those Hallmarks reflect a presumed ideal as a financially secure and likely homogeneous institution where, not unlike the model workshop, people with similar minds and/or objectives come together with shared assumptions about the nature of our enterprise. But most of our situations don't really look like that.

Anna Leahy: Still, having models or an ideal can be helpful. I teach at one of those relatively well-funded, though medium-sized, private institutions. We are all too aware of race and class, though, sadly, in the lack of some types of diversity among our students and faculty. The cultural or social divisions – and the increasingly pronounced hierarchy based on economics – in higher education are stark and, I fear, worsening, despite diversity and inclusion projects on many campuses. Any undergraduate education, no matter the major, should help students grapple with cultural issues and interact with a variety of people and ideas.

Katharine Haake: Many creative writing students in the United States attend large public institutions. Chronically underfunded and often urban, these institutions serve ethnically and culturally diverse populations from poor and working-class communities. The students work, often full time; they're multilingual, with English not being their first, or most fluent, language; they struggle with such real-world problems as health care, transportation (a huge issue in Los Angeles) and, increasingly, immigration status. And as much as I hate to say this, almost all have been poorly served by the public schools. As far as creative writing goes, effective reading and writing practices correlate well with the critical and cultural literacy skills necessary for success in the larger world, and it makes sense to frame our teaching in such a way that the skills we foster are transferable ones.

Anna Leahy: What we seem to be suggesting is a creative writing education that is not the idealized model confined inside ivory tower. Creative writing, after all, should be part and parcel of the world in which we live and want to live.

Argie Manolis: I teach at a small, public liberal arts college in rural Minnesota. The college draws students from the region who are primarily first generation and relatively poor, as well as students from larger urban centers interested in small class sizes and individualized attention. We also provide a tuition waiver for Native American students, so we are quite diverse.

Students come to classes at my institution needing to heal from very real trauma or feeling embarrassed about their privilege. They come from farms to which they'll be returning over the weekend to help milk the cows because their father is sick, from parents who are addicts, from funerals of friends who killed themselves. They come from over-privileged helicopter parents who policed everything they said and did. They come concerned about police shootings and Nepal and recent votes in the state legislature.

My teaching philosophy is based on the premise that students need to use writing as a means for self-discovery, with the purpose of enacting social change, as much as they need to learn craft. I don't believe these goals can be achieved separately.

Anna Leahy: These goals – self-discovery, enacting of social change, the study of craft, the practice of writing – are likely all necessary. We tend to latch onto one goal – usually craft – and we tell ourselves that's good enough. Faculty don't often want to be unsettled. As we feel demands beyond the classroom increase, as many of us have in the wake of the recent economic downturn or, in my case, at a growing institution, we may long to relax into simpler work lives.

Katharine Haake: I used to share a similar teaching philosophy about the personal value of writing, but over time, I've found myself turning outward again. Creative writing students need to learn about the history of their discipline to understand what it looks like in the world today, never mind what it can become. I suppose my ideal undergraduate program would not be one in creative writing at all, but in English studies, and would introduce all students to the various writing, literary and critical and cultural studies–based work that we do. So that's typically how I approach my classes however I can.

Anna Leahy: Your approach could be taken up by our literature colleagues as well. Creative writing majors who have literature requirements are more likely than literature majors to get a broader mix of approaches to what English studies is or can be.

A few years ago, our department tossed around the idea of a first-year course that would introduce all English majors to the variety of specialties housed in the department: literature, creative writing, journalism, rhetorical studies, maybe even film studies and cultural studies. With so many stakeholders, as we are called in these situations, the department didn't even get to the stage of drafting a proposal. In some ways, the discussion helped us talk about what united us, but, in other ways, we were staking out territory. The status quo is easier for personnel management, scheduling and immediate workload, and faculty sometimes resist innovation so as to keep risk of failure low, even though some of us are trying to instill just the opposite in our students. And, of course, we each have a primary expertise – for me, that's the craft of poetry – and it's our obligation to use and share that expertise, which is, in a way, a resource.

Argie Manolis: The blend of craft-based instruction with service-learning – and the multiple goals they invite – drives my pedagogy. After four weeks of preparation in my course, students begin to engage with elders and craft poems from their words with careful attention to line and stanza breaks and titles. We rework these poems with different breaks and titles and discuss the varying effects, how small choices can make a big difference in how a piece is read. We talk about theme and how where we begin and end a poem or story matters a lot. Students then reflect on how these lessons are applicable to language they have crafted themselves.

My classes include workshops, revision and reading a range of contemporary pieces. They also involve a semester-long conversation about why writing matters – to each individual, to our regional community and to the broader society. We read and talk about how writing can enhance healing and social justice. We grapple with our own reasons for writing. We engage in service-learning as part of this grappling. Craft learning and service-learning both serve the emerging writer.

Anna Leahy: It takes a lot of effort to get these innovations – even one or two courses – up and running. Such projects or curricular changes can't be accomplished by one person and often require support from administrators.

Katharine Haake: You are right – it's a lot of work, and there are countless obstacles.

A good thing that came out of one of my own failed attempts at such revision was a selected topics course in creative writing. Since I couldn't transform the whole curriculum, I decided that a course in which faculty could experiment according to their own work and interests might produce incremental change. And, in fact, it has.

Some topics have included hybrid narrative forms, interstitial writing, experimental performance and the long poem. While I teach a variety of topics, the first one I offered was on transnational writing, a focus that continues to inform all my teaching. I began with one primary objective – to encourage students to look beyond the self and expand their ideas about what might count as writing and a writing life in a globalized world culture, although many more benefits have emerged. First, the texts themselves are new and unfamiliar; this really changes the way they see what's possible on the page. The idea that a writer can function as an important political or intellectual force in a culture is equally surprising and provocative. The effect has been so powerful that I'm teaching new texts in translation in all my classes.

Anna Leahy: We also have a junior-level special topics course that's required of BFA students. It's been taught as Southern California writing, with a hefty reading list, and as *avant garde* writing. It's a way to pilot new ideas as well as fit topics and aesthetic approaches into the curriculum. As a shell course, it allows for flexibility in staffing and resists territorialism. It's a course with multiple goals and multiple benefits, so requiring that every student in our major take the special topics course seems important to the shape of the undergraduate program.

Argie Manolis: Multiple goals should shape our programs and our pedagogy. For my teaching, there is an 'intention to benefit the provider and recipient equally' and 'equal focus to both the service being provided and the learning that is occurring,' (1996: 6) as Andrew Furco notes in his ground-breaking article 'Service-Learning: A Balanced Approach to Experiential Education' that defined how service-learning was different than other community-based approaches.

My courses end with a completely open-ended project. The assignment begins, 'Write something that you consider to be brave. E-mail me a proposal, explain how what you want to do is related to creative writing, then go do it.'

Anna Leahy: That sort of assignment might appear lazy to outsiders. In practice, it's a bold pedagogical move that sets the bar high for students. Students are often unsettled by a lack of imposed focus and guidelines. The assignment could also unsettle some professors, who may be used to seeing portfolios that contain versions of writing they've already seen.

The unknown keeps everyone on their toes and creates an ambitious environment.

Argie Manolis: Some students write more pieces in the genres we've studied, so that's more traditional pedagogy, and that's okay. Others fail miserably because they aimed too high – importantly that's okay, too. Still others create amazing artifacts – word-and-drawing sidewalk art, photo-and-poem collages, short choose-your-own-adventure films, albums of original songs based on the pieces they wrote earlier.

Anna Leahy: Grading failure is tough, and awareness by the student may be one of the few ways to credit the student for incorporating useful missteps and sometimes big flops into their writing practice. If a student makes a huge misstep and is unaware of it, that's a real failure. But if a student is aware that something is amiss, has a sense of what happened and what might be done differently in the future and conveys learning, that awareness might be more important in the long run than the student who has no idea how he or she managed to write a good poem. Awareness may be one of the most important reasons to study creative writing in an academic program, and refection is certainly key in my pedagogy.

Argie Manolis: I assess these projects based on what each student aimed to do, what he or she did, and how that student reflects on the process at the end. The goal is to apply what they've learned outside the constraints of genre and subject matter, of space and time.

Anna Leahy: Reflection – articulating one's awareness – has become very important to my pedagogy and to my grading of a final portfolio. If I guide students to an understanding that failure is necessary and fleeting, that's a great accomplishment in my teaching life.

Argie Manolis: It would be impossible for me to teach a creative writing course if my grading did not focus on evaluating students' reflections. I also have the opportunity to observe my students interacting with elders and provide some feedback to them about how they are bringing their writerly selves into the world. Experience is awareness too. At the end of the semester, elders and their families gather to share coffee and cake with us. Students read at least one of the poems that each resident spoke. We make a book of poems and student reflections for each family. Over the years, I've been asked to read these poems at funerals and even at the bedsides of dying people, so I know they have made an impact in the community.

Katharine Haake: This idea of experience is part of the open-ended continuum, which I, too, embrace, as principled and also disciplined, not to mention fun and, in some instances, what my students might call mind-blowing.

To help them figure out, for example, what it might mean to figure out what you want to be about or do or even be in a piece of writing, I often ask them to make something with their hands they don't know how to make. There's only one rule – that they have to use material they already have on hand or can scavenge or find, a kind of bricolage, I say. Over the years, I have received, among other surprises, an illuminated manuscript, a quilt that still hangs in my office, a working Saussure-o-scope, a wide range of collages and sculptures and a pair of narrative shoes (see Haake, 2000: Chapter 3). And last semester, the ever-inventive and irrepressible Gina Srmabekian made a giant three-dimensional labyrinth that stretched out some 26 feet and glowed in the dark.

What happens in these projects relates directly to writing because it takes students in to the place where writing takes place without the distraction of language. They also learn that making something is hard, that first ideas are seldom the best ideas and that they are most successful when they give themselves over to a trial-and-error problem-solving process by letting go of intention and engage in a series of intuitive leaps. They learn, and routinely report, that all this is just like writing, which, of course, is precisely the point.

Argie Manolis: Truth be told, not all my students love service-learning, the design-your-own final project or my ongoing big-picture discussion. At least half of the class evaluations note a desire to spend more class time workshopping. I resist the urge to respond by aligning my course more closely with a traditional workshop. I have a file folder of cards former students have sent me, usually several years after graduating, about the impact the project and class had on them, right next to the file of thank-you notes from elders' family members. I choose to measure student impact through that file folder instead of the student evaluations.

Anna Leahy: Given your approach, the contents of that folder measure well the course's effectiveness. Studies continually point out the flaws in student evaluations, including gender bias, so much so that the topic has been covered in *Slate* and *The Washington Post. Inside Higher Ed* (Flaherty, 2015) summarized a recent AAUP study as pointing to problems such as poor student response rates, undue weight in personnel decisions and 'a creep of the kinds of personal comments seen on teacher rating websites into formal evaluations.' Also, many standardized forms that institutions use to measure a particular course's effectiveness aren't well matched to the field's goals and methodologies nor to the instructor's pedagogical approach. *Classroom Assessment Techniques* (Angelo & Cross, 1993) includes a valuable section on the differing teaching goals among disciplines (1993: 368), and thinking for oneself, for instance, is one of the trickier goals to evaluate. Service-learning is likely much better represented by your folder than a generic rubric.

Still, many institutions value student evaluations as part of annual faculty evaluation as well as the tenure review process. In fact, the guidelines our college developed to hone the university tenure and promotion criteria ask that any course average below a certain number should be explained. With that level of pressure to conform to student expectations, a faculty member may at least hesitate to try new assignments, let alone radically re-envision a course in what might be innovative and rewarding ways like service-learning or extremely open-ended assignments. Adjuncts and pre-tenure faculty may be especially hesitant try new things when they are in the process of developing their pedagogy and styles, even when they have inklings that there may exist better or different ways to build students' skills.

Katharine Haake: There's a lot of support at CSUN for individual pedagogical innovation, which is both supported by grants and valued in the faculty review process. But larger-scale innovation has proven more elusive. Some years ago, I spearheaded a proposal in creative writing to enrich our curriculum and improve faculty morale by addressing address intractable workload issues.

CSUN is part of a vast 27-campus system, all bound by the same contract and a very rigid 24 weighted teaching units requirement for all full-time faculty, which amounts to a 4/4 teaching load. Our idea was to create a series of one-unit labs that could be linked to extant courses, effectively turning 3-unit courses into 4-unit ones. The labs themselves were to have been designed to provide for enhanced instruction in areas of perceived need: reading, writing and critical and cultural studies.

Anna Leahy: Our department proposed the addition of a fourth credit for all upper-level courses. This fourth credit could work in a variety of ways similar to the notion of a lab credit. One faculty planned weekly work with an archive of *avant garde* poetry; another planned to shift discussion of readings to online discussions, freeing up class time for developing student's own research and writing projects. But the university-wide committee that oversees undergraduate programs didn't approve the plan. My sense is that the committee viewed it as a way to get out of work, and they expressed concern that the idea would appeal more widely and create a logistical nightmare of courses with varying credits and faculty with varying workloads (both of which the university already has).

We tend to complain about the lack of skills we think our students should be learning in other people's classes, so why not add a lab credit or a fourth credit? Why not blend or sync up courses across specializations? I am often flummoxed at how difficult such attempts can be.

Katharine Haake: Here, too, even though our lab proposal was rejected as an unfair advantage for creative writing, which had proposed the trial run. But the logistical problems are real. Even if scheduling could have been solved, we'd have ended up with a two-tier system, with part-time faculty stuck in the 3-unit general education classes. The more I got into it, the more complex – and less appealing – it became.

Argie Manolis: We are embedded in academic culture and higher education institutions. We must prove to administrators that creative writing is a field worthy of serious study and tenure-track positions, and we compete with other departments for limited funding. All of this is necessary because, as institutions, we have to beg for resources from politicians and others in a climate where over-standardization of higher education is the norm. We also have to prove ourselves to parents of prospective students, who want to know whether their children will be employable after college, not to mention to the students themselves, who have a wide range of generationally specific criteria for what will make a good college experience, including whether they'll be able to pay back their loans.

Katharine Haake: The typical undergraduate program still adopts graduate pre-professional paradigms, but a writing career really is an option for only the tiniest percentage of our students, increasingly even at the graduate level. The most important thing I do may be to help students develop autonomous and sustainable reading and writing practices for lifelong engagement not just with the literary arts, but also with their families, their careers, their communities and the larger world. We used to call this a liberal arts education.

Anna Leahy: Interestingly, in response to the sometimes overwhelming disparagement of the liberal arts, the liberal arts education has been touted recently in mainstream media such as *USA Today* and *Forbes.* CNN commentator Fareed Zakaria has written a whole book called *In Defense of a Liberal Education.* There, he summarizes the current sad state of the liberal arts: 'A classic liberal education has few defenders. Conservatives fume that it is, well, too liberal (though the term has no partisan meaning). Liberals worry that it is too elitist. Students wonder what they will do with a degree [...]. And parents worry that it will cost them their life savings' (2015: 16). He goes on to discuss the sharp declines in majors like English and philosophy since the 1970s, the explosion of the business major and recent state-level efforts to reduce funding liberal arts programs. The current narrative, a big shift from my own thinking as an undergraduate, is that a college education should lead directly to a specific type of job.

Katharine Haake: But it's at least partly our responsibility to challenge that narrative, or at least help students frame it more clearly. I had one son who majored in creative writing (a big surprise to me) and is now a banker, and another who majored in environmental studies and, after two years of unemployment, is in graduate school. Katherine Bell's 2008 Harvard Business review blog post, 'The MFA is the new MBA,' can be helpful, along with the rest of the web chatter it produced.

Argie Manolis: After a while, we internalize the narratives we're forced to provide for others. But the truth is, these narratives have very little to do with why we write or teach. Besides that, students' undergraduate majors usually have little to do with their career paths. Given how rapidly the job market is changing, should we be preparing students for specific careers at the undergraduate level at all?

Yes, but not by teaching technical skills. Students should graduate as critical and imaginative thinkers, collaborators and leaders and, most importantly, responsible and responsive citizens in a complex and continually changing world. Creative writing is a critical tool for developing a voice, compassion, perspective and connection with others.

Anna Leahy: That's also what CEOs say, according several articles in the last few years in *Forbes. The Huffington Post, Fast Company*, CNBC and *Inside Higher Ed.* I fear that the middle managers who do the hiring, however, don't view job applicants quite the same way as CEOs and we do. I've become more cognizant that my students need to be aware of the skills they're building and be able to talk about them. But it's not easy for any of us to put into words exactly what we've learned to do as creative writers.

Katharine Haake: A long time ago, when I was still resisting small group pedagogies, Wendy Bishop advised me to trust that students would learn *something* in their groups and that even if it wasn't what I wanted, it would be of value. This probably applies to everything we do in our classes. We may cling to the illusion of control, but you never know. Just as in their small groups, what students take away from our classes might not be what we want – it might surprise us, and it might take years. But as Wendy would say, it will be something, and it will have value.

Anna Leahy: Wendy Bishop modeled what she taught in her classes that were 'writing-intensive zones.' In fact, she even ends her essay there with that self-awareness: 'I reminded myself that I was in my writing-intensive, evaluation-free zone, and I got to work on a riskier version, a re-creation of a classroom that teachers and the writers they teach can use' (2005: 119). Bishop was very ill when she wrote that, but, even then, she trusted the process and held people accountable, whether dealing with colleagues like me, with students or with herself.

In our assessment-oriented, data-driven world inside the academy, it's dangerous to admit that we can't control student learning but are, rather, carefully orchestrating an environment in which students are likely to learn something – maybe what we intend but maybe something we can't predict – and then will carry that learning into their lives over the long haul. If creative writing faculty – presumably innovative and imaginative people – don't try something new, who will?

Argie Manolis: Creative writing is a way to relate to and make sense of the world. We desperately need writer-physicians and writer-social workers and writer-non-profit directors and writer-parents and writer-politicians. I don't just mean political science majors who took one creative writing class to fulfill a general education requirement. I mean skilled writers who have thought deeply about how writing relates to what they are doing both for a job and in their communities. We limit ourselves and our undergraduate programs when we don't remember this, when we fail to imagine what a difference this makes to our lives and our futures.

Note

Artwork photographed and shared with permission of Gina Srmabekian.

References

Angelo, T.A. and Cross, K.P. (1993) *Classroom Assessment Techniques* (2nd edn). San Francisco, CA: Jossey-Bass.

AWP Guidelines & Hallmarks. See https://www.awpwriter.org/guide/hallmarks_quality (accessed 13 May 2016).

Bell, K. (2008) The MFA is the new MBA. *Harvard Business Review*, 14 April 2008. See https://hbr.org/2008/04/the-mfa-is-the-new-mba.

Bishop, W. (2005) Contracts, radical revision, portfolios, and the risks of writing. *Power and Identity in the Creative Writing Classroom: The Authority Project* (pp. 109–120). Clevedon: Multilingual Matters.

DuPlessis, R.B. (1990) *The Pink Guitar: Writing as Feminist Practice*. New York: Routledge.

Flaherty, C. (2015) Flawed evaluations. *Inside Higher Ed*, 10 June 2015. See https://www.insidehighered.com/news/2015/06/10/aaup-committee-survey-data-raise-questions-effectiveness-student-teaching.

Furco, A. (1996) Service-learning: A balanced approach to experiential education. In B. Taylor and Corporation for National Service (eds) *Expanding Boundaries: Serving and Learning* (pp. 2–6). Washington, DC: Corporation for National Service.

Haake, K. (2000) *What Our Speech Disrupts: Feminism and Creative Writing Studies*. Urbana, Illinois: NCTE.

Manolis, A. (2005) Writing the community: Service-learning in creative writing. *Power and Identity in the Creative Writing Classroom: The Authority Project* (pp. 141–151). Clevedon: Multilingual Matters.

Zakaria, F. (2015) *In Defense of a Liberal Education*. New York: Simon & Schuster.

8 The Program Beyond the Program

James P. Blaylock, Douglas R. Dechow, Anna Leahy and Jan Osborn

While professors are expected to write and publish and are paid to teach, many of us also build creative writing programs that extend beyond the curriculum to extracurricular programming such as reading series, literary journals and presses and community outreach. 'The Program Beyond the Program' is a case study of sorts in which four faculty at Chapman University – a fiction writer, a poet, a composition-rhetoric faculty and a librarian and digital humanist – work independently and together to build programming. The program beyond the program matches expectations of the Hallmarks suggested by the Association of Writers and Writing Programs, fits the institutional opportunities and constraints, and pushes students beyond what they already know and can do. This chapter also explores commonsense concepts that challenge institutional territorialism: when individuals share ideas, each individual starts only with his or her own ideas but comes away with a whole host of ideas.

Jim Blaylock: I currently direct the MFA program at Chapman University and have directed both the BFA and the MFA programs here for the past 12 years. I only recently secured course reallocation to support this position. Over the past several years, the full-time creative writing faculty has grown from three members (two tenured, one not) to seven members, all tenured. We've added a creative nonfiction element to the program and a poetry program with a dedicated poetry journal and reading series. We've also joined the larger community of university writing programs by becoming active members of the Association of Writers and Writing Programs (AWP) and making changes in the program that are in line with AWP Hallmarks. In fact, we've cited AWP Hallmarks when negotiating teaching loads and course reallocation. We've also added extracurricular activities: readings, guest authors and other events.

Anna Leahy: We've made some important changes to the MFA curriculum, too, including adding an introductory class called Aspects of a Writer, which hosts guest lecturers and creative writing faculty, and creating a thesis process that's more in line with other graduate programs. We've recently overhauled the BFA curriculum, too, building in more creative writing and adding a practical facet that includes journalism, digital humanities and related options. Importantly, we're building other features of the MFA program, like a variety of assistantships. How do we best help our students cultivate writerly or literary lives and prepare them to sustain themselves in careers? That's a question we're trying to answer here; it's a question that drives far more discussion in this field now than it did 10 years ago.

Jan Osborn: That question is part of my thinking as well, even though I'm faculty in composition-rhetoric, not creative writing. I'm the director of the Chapman University/Orange High School Literacies Partnership, which brings together our MFA students and Orange High School students for after-school seminars in creative writing and for the spring reading series hosted by the John Fowles Center for Creative Writing. I also co-direct the Orange County Literary Society Collaborative. In that role, I work to bring together students from three area community colleges, as well as Chapman University students, for luncheons and talks in a community-based reading series. These projects intersect with the AWP Hallmarks Community Outreach feature: 'establish a strong, positive presence in the local community' and go beyond inviting the community to lecture series to working with high school and community college students in conjunction with visiting writers.

These community outreach projects are part of my work in rhetorical studies. While '[s]ocially engaged scholarship can be a euphemism for social justice work or direct intervention into inequitable and exploitative systems' (McConnell, 2012: 168), it is an integral part of the rhetorical tradition, which began with questions of social and civic engagement.

Douglas Dechow: I'm the Digital Humanities and Sciences Librarian, which doesn't imply much connection with the creative writing programs. In that capacity, however, I'm the liaison between Leatherby Libraries and the Department of English, so I have a lot of interaction with the faculty in the MFA and BFA programs. In fact, I posed the idea for that new introductory MFA course – Aspects of a Writer – during informal interaction, which is often an amorphous but important part of our professional lives as academics.

Managing events and programs has become an important part of my job. In 'Freedom Without Walls: One Model for Interdisciplinarity on Campus' (Gallagher *et al.*, 2011), we argue that the university's library is an ideal partner for collaborative projects and events. As is discussed in that article, event planning may:

> [R]equire a detailed understanding of pragmatic aspects of university operations. Numerous offices might be involved in a large project: university calendaring and scheduling, media services, catering, facilities management, residence life, alumni relations, university advancement, and publications, to name a few. Librarians may have experience working with such administrative units that individual faculty do not. (2011: 136)

The primary example discussed in the paper is about partnerships between libraries and language departments, specifically German, but the argument is equally apt for creative writing programs (and a poetry reading was part of that project). In part, libraries can serve in this role because we often see ourselves as the intellectual heart and soul of the university. Programming is already a significant activity in most academic libraries, and we are often able to prioritize resources and personnel to support events.

Anna Leahy: These projects fit the mission of the library at many institutions, and libraries are connectors. 'Connectors – nodes with an anomalously large number of links – are present in very diverse complex systems, ranging from the economy to the cell' (Barabási, 2002: 56). As Kevin Bacon is to Hollywood (2002: 60–62), the library – and the good librarian – is to the academic institution: a hub. 'Indeed, with links to an unusually large number of nodes, hubs create short paths between any two nodes in the system. [...] From the perspective of the hubs the world is very tiny' (2002: 64). The hub that is the library can make projects more manageable.

Finding a way to make a difference to more participants in our projects and events is important to long-term success for the creative writing program, the library and the university. When our projects or events make a difference, we build momentum and meaning. The traditional academic model may be one of silos and territory, but we're rethinking of ourselves as hubs and as putting things into motion to see what happens. 'Emergent behaviors, like games, are all about living within the boundaries defined by rules, but also using that space to create something greater than the sum of its parts' (Johnson, 2001: 181). We each make our individual decisions, plan our particular events, but, as Steven Johnson points out about cities in his book *Emergence*, conscious decisions 'also contribute to the macrodevelopment that we have almost no way of comprehending' (2001: 99) as the scale gets larger, as we create a program larger than the program, as we continue to make academia and creative writing within it.

Jan Osborn: Exactly. My work with the CU/OHS Literacies Partnership is an opportunity to engage graduate students in the university's creative writing program with high school students eager for creating writing experiences. This partnership works to further the literacies of students at our neighborhood school – Orange High School, which, according to recent demographic information, serves 85% Hispanic/Latino, 7% White, 3% Vietnamese, and 2% Black youth in a student body of 1895. Of Orange High School students, 87.3% are considered 'socio-economically disadvantaged' according to the Federal Government; therefore, Orange High is a school-wide Title I high school, designated to support the academic achievement of the students most 'at risk.' The English Language Development Program serves nearly one-third of the students there, and results of the STAR testing – 44% of the students scored at Proficient or Advanced and 56% as Not Proficient – indicate that literacies opportunities are essential (2013–2014 School Accountability Report Card).

These students represent a starkly different demographic than Chapman University's students, and bringing these two communities together is an opportunity for both populations to learn from one another and an ethical responsibility on the part of the university, which has diversity as a focus. While Hispanic college enrollment more than tripled between 1996 and 2012, the data indicate disturbing completion rates, possibly attributed to 'the fact that Hispanics are less likely than whites to enroll in a four-year college, attend a selective college and enroll full-time' (Krogstad & Fry, 2014). With a university just a block away, this is a reality we can address. The projects in which I invest my energies and scholarship are as much about addressing societal needs as they are about building academic programs; in fact, I hope they link the two, linking rhetorical scholarship with a larger societal picture, linking the terms *rhetorical, community outreach* and *political.*

Anna Leahy: Ideally, many projects we take on should work toward multiple goals. In a list of writing tips reposted at *The Atlantic* (Popova, 2012), Kurt Vonnegut says, 'A sentence must do one of two things – reveal character or advance the action.' Like a scene in a novel, our projects might do more than one thing. We need to have purpose and create effects; we need to build character and take action.

We should look for ways as writers and as teachers to get the most – not only for ourselves but also for our students, institutions and communities – out of the time and effort we invest. The rest of Vonnegut's list includes other tidbits that might be adapted as well. He suggests not wasting a stranger's time and giving readers an understanding of why they're spending time with your work. In making sure that we don't waste others' time, that we create something meaningful, we avoid wasting our own time as well. The ethos of writing can be connected to an ethos of an academic program.

Jan Osborn: At this point, however, these roles, central to my identity as an educator, do not fit into my job in terms of time. They are important community outreach projects, but I have not yet institutionalized this work in a way that is valued by the university beyond a service component, and service is, by far, weighted least heavily in our faculty review processes. I need to better frame these community outreach projects as engaged scholarship; this conversation is one way of doing that.

Anna Leahy: Creative writing is undoubtedly perceived as a less traditionally academic discipline than rhetorical studies. Certainly, we're expected to publish regularly and teach well, but we don't neatly fit the traditional model for an academic career. That can make it difficult to make a case for ourselves if we use only traditional academic models, but it opens up opportunities if we admit we can't live entirely by those rules and forsake our own. Creative writers, therefore, may have more ability to define our careers and goals for ourselves than do our scholarly colleagues.

In addition, I've felt much more able to take risks since earning tenure. I sense a sort of post-tenure trust – earning tenure is earning that trust – that I am making a sound decision. That relative job security and respect allows me freedom to explore, and that's when I became much more involved in program building.

Jim Blaylock: As someone who taught for over 30 years without tenure and without particularly caring about tenure, I was surprised at the rapid alteration in the way I was perceived after tenure, although I hadn't changed in any noticeable way, nor had my duties. I was suddenly appearing on radar screens that I'd managed to fly under in the past. There are good reasons to care about tenure, one of which is that the university expects me to publish and provides me with time, research funds and general encouragement. At the same time, my duties as a university citizen expanded, and (as is true for all writer-teachers) it's a constant battle to get the writing done. I'd call that an uptown problem however: I can't imagine a better job.

Anna Leahy: While a few academics may be able to lean back and rest their feet on their desks, my experience and observation indicate that the demands both for publishing and for service increase after tenure. In fact, our review criteria make it clear that associate professors are to bear the brunt of institutional service, even as we are expected to continue to make a name for ourselves in the wider field and are rewarded most for publication. That's a good problem to have, of course, but it remains a struggle to balance what counts most and what matters most – to me and to those who will review my accomplishments for the next promotion. As a group, the four of us work to prioritize what matters and make the argument that it counts a lot too.

Douglas Dechow: We each have primary job responsibilities, and those who review us expect certain types of accomplishments that have nothing to do with building events, extracurricular projects or out-of-class opportunities for students. That means time – my own personal time, my writing time – is a conundrum. There's never enough time to do all of the events that could be done, and there's more to the job than events. You've got to choose the projects that matter most to you as well as to the university.

Ultimately, I fall back on my primary role – that as an academic – to help me choose what to pursue. I privilege those events that might also lead to a publication. I've been pretty successful using this as a decision metric. In addition to the 'Freedom Without Walls' article, I served as the editor of a festschrift (Dechow & Struppa, 2015) that resulted from a conference I organized. Of course, this chapter closes the loop on the Chapman University Pub(lishing) Crawl that Jim and I organize. It's important to remember that publications live on a CV long after the momentary career glow yielded by a successful event fades away.

Anna Leahy: Making choices is crucial, and using service toward publication goals is a great idea. Being willing to say no is also crucial to building the strongest possible program with the resources available. I built Tabula Poetica – starting with a reading series funded by the English department – because there was a lack of poetry consistently going on here. In hindsight, I realize that developing a program that focuses entirely on poetry allows me to turn down – or not even be approached about – opportunities unrelated to that focus. Still, in conversations with my dean and my chair, I agreed, the year after I had tenure, to say *Yes!* to all things poetry for the first two years of the project to see what could happen. In return, they agreed to consider course reallocation.

Jim Blaylock: One way we manage these extracurricular projects is through collaboration. The four of us are often working with each other and others on campus to make these events and projects happen. As a writer of fiction, I've successfully collaborated with only one other writer. Although I'd be happy to collaborate further with that writer, I can't imagine collaborating with anyone else. Creative writers tend to do their writing in isolation, even if they discuss drafts with others. As a teacher, on the other hand, I've found collaboration to be absolutely necessary. Steven Johnson, in *Where Good Ideas Come From,* writes, 'Ideas rise in crowds, as Poincaré said. They rise [...] where connection is valued more than protection' (2010: 245). In my writing, I'm extremely protective. In my service, connection works. My fellow faculty members have skills that I simply don't have.

Many of us are willing to put prodigious amounts of time and effort into extracurricular projects, which allows good things to happen that wouldn't happen if each of us works alone. Because I'm jealous of my time, I'm unhappy with bureaucracy, with slow-moving committees, with anything that becomes an impediment to getting things done. That's why I choose collaborators – or agree to collaborate – only when I have a high regard for a project and also am certain that the collaboration will enhance and simplify the process rather than the opposite.

Anna Leahy: This whole book is based on that two-fold premise about collaboration. As I was orchestrating these conversations within a deadline, I wondered whether it might have been easier to do a single-author book. But if I'd done that, some of the good things – ideas, examples, perspectives – wouldn't have happened here. Collaboration can require extra effort even when it saves time overall or can require extra time even when it minimizes the effort expended by each individual. And the balance isn't easy to predict.

Douglas Dechow: An important thing to keep in mind, though, is that one can't always choose all of one's collaborators. Some of the people that we rely on for events and programs are in place because of the university's organizational structure. With this in mind, when building an event planning team, I make sure that I have someone upon whom I can rely with regard to navigating and orchestrating myriad university units that are required to hold an event: scheduling, catering, facilities, media services, marketing, to name a few. It's important to develop a team of people who understand events and event planning.

Jan Osborn: Collaboration is at the heart of both the CU/OHS Literacies Partnership and the Orange County Literacy Society Collaborative. The Literacies Partnership is a *partnership* for a reason; it is important that public schools and universities collaborate to share resources and opportunities.

This partnership represents a long-term commitment – founded in 1998 – to participate in community literacies, to consider what we might help one another accomplish in terms of educating our students. Likewise, the OC Literary Society Collaborative is based on shared resources and opportunities.

These sorts of projects can be considered community-based participatory research, in that equal partners combine their collective knowledge and take action together to improve the community. While the term is more commonly applied to community health projects, literacy can be an important part of a community's well being. The community organization link in this collaborative has been an important component. The larger community has much to offer the academic community, strengthening relationships between the academic, the social, the political.

Anna Leahy: We should probably use those terms – *partnership* and *collaborative* – when we describe our projects.

For me, the collaborative project needs to make a meaningful difference in my career, my students' writing lives, the university's prestige or the larger literary community. I'm looking for opportunities that meet at least two of those criteria, preferably all of them. A project also needs to have enough support that I can reasonably expect it to succeed. AWP recommends that an MFA director have one or two full-time administrative assistants, but our program doesn't have a dedicated staff position. The level of staff support is part of the equation that determines how much we can take on and how well our ambitions will pan out.

My dean calls me a frill-necked lizard, by which he means (I hope) that I make something relatively small, simple or nondescript appear big, beautiful and meaningful. It's good to make the most of what we have or can piece together, especially when university resources are sparse for the arts and humanities. Poetry is never going to be the top priority on campus. So part of that building involves working with others to make a project more than the sum of its parts. Working with other academic departments, the library and the dean of students and crediting them, too, for the success of the Tabula Poetica reading series makes that project bigger. The frill is real, not an add-on; the frill becomes integral to the true form.

Jan Osborn: It's also important to consider location and duration. Sometimes, one-off projects meet certain goals quickly and make a splash. Ongoing projects, though, have lasting, deepening effects and create sustained growth.

The literacies collaboration works by establishing close ties with the faculty at the high school and by maintaining long-term relationships with the students. I chose this collaboration because of the proximity of the high school to our university and because of my own background in public school education. Students from the local high school can come to the university and can begin to think of themselves as fitting into a college environment. The exchange works in both directions, university students interacting with young people from often radically different socio-economic and linguistic backgrounds, challenging their understanding of merit and academic excellence. We continue to learn about one another in meaningful ways.

Anna Leahy: Meaningful projects have some reach and some momentum and longevity.

Many programs host readings. I felt strongly that the series needed to include both a talk and a reading by each visiting poet, and the talks have been varied and vibrant and have created an amazing, wide-ranging video series. These projects that we're discussing can be thought of as akin to genres, again applying our discipline's models within the context of an academic institution. Steven Johnson writes in *Where Good Ideas Come From*, 'Genres supply a set of implicit rules that have enough coherence that traditionalists can safely play inside them, and more adventurous artist can confound our expectations by playing *with* them. Genres are the platforms and paradigms of the creative world' (2010: 191). So, we know what a reading series is, but how can we adapt that genre?

Jim Blaylock: In a way, the visitors we bring to campus are also our partners. Several years ago, I brought agents, editors and publishing writers to campus to chat with students about potential career opportunities for writers in what I called the Pub(lishing) Crawl. I have also, on occasion, organized readings or found guest speakers, as do other members of the creative writing faculty. We have some set, ongoing projects and remain adept at accommodating one-off options.

Anna Leahy: I appreciate that we are open to one-off opportunities here. Last spring, when I don't usually host events, the Chancellor contacted me to say that the Israeli Consulate was paying for a group of poets to visit Southern California. If Tabula Poetica could host, the Chancellor would pick up the remaining travel expenses. With partners, I built a jam-packed day. The best event – the most well-attended and most profound for the students – was the least likely: a question-and-answer session with general education classes in English. These students wouldn't have attended a poetry event if it hadn't been built into their classes, yet they learned a lot about creative thinking, and the poets were at their most candid. That success depended on buy-in from the professors of those classes; they trusted, and it paid off.

I've used most of my final exam periods for a student reading that counts toward their grades and is open to the public, a balance between curriculum and community engagement. Other disciplines might take a page from our playbook with simple ideas like these.

Jim Blaylock: We're always looking for ways to connect classwork with the community and the larger life of our students now and in the future. Because students lauded its first iteration, the Pub(lishing) Crawl now occurs every spring, when seniors are very much thinking about their futures and all students are facing summer schedules. Five speakers – or sometimes panels of speakers – chat about how they made use of their creative writing degree or otherwise developed a career as a writer, agent or editor. Participants range from early-career writers or editors to seasoned, successful professionals. Recent speakers included Karen Joy Fowler, novelist and winner of the Pen Faulkner Award; Martin Dugard, bestselling nonfiction writer; Ellen Datlow, award-winning short fiction editor; poet Kim Addonizio; and the editor of Black Hill Press, which has published novellas by three different Chapman University alums. The idea is for our students – and anyone else who wants to attend – to become aware of ways to pursue a writing life beyond the university.

Douglas Dechow: I see Pub(lishing) Crawl, which began in 2011 and became a collaborative effort between the Department of English and the Leatherby Libraries in 2012, as striking a balance for students between what's immediately in front of them and what awaits them after graduation. By that, I mean that we understand that the students' own writing is the thing that should be paramount for them. At the same time, we want them to be able to see what life as a mature – or at least maturing – writer could be like as well as what kinds of jobs writers might hold to pay the bills.

The event has morphed into two parts: (1) a program of speakers/panels and (2) a post-program reception and book signing. One unusual feature of the event is the book raffle. The reception and book signing begins with a raffle of each presenter's book, which the library provides. The local Barnes & Noble has books for sale as well. The extra excitement of raffle prizes, the chance to socialize with presenters and the ability to leave with a signed copy of a book has enlivened this project.

Anna Leahy: I'm thinking of our readers hearing what we're saying: parties with raffles! As a professor, there's pressure to focus on learning outcomes, and, of course, we want to foster creative and intellectual accomplishment, but there exists a social, interactive component to being a writer or artist that we shouldn't set aside. Traditional academic disciplines might learn something from the arts – we're engaging our whole selves in what we do, and we're having fun. We're learning from each other, not only in terms of our commonalities and shared aesthetics or practices but also in terms of our differences and beyond so-called student learning outcomes.

Douglas Dechow: As is often said, there's no one way to write a book. The same is true for being a writer; there's no one way to do it. Pub(lishing) Crawl gives the students a sense of the kinds of people with whom they will interact in their careers – agents, publishers and editors – and some of the career options that are open to them. We've had a poet who is a librarian talk about her experiences, and I've talked with MFA students about how librarianship can complement the writing life, as both are connected to literature, research and audience. This year, Pub(lishing) Crawl had a lengthy panel about the hows and whys of being an adjunct professor. Few MFA programs seem to be having in-depth discussions about adjunct teaching and how an individual might make the most of it without making it a long-term lifestyle.

Jim Blaylock: We've made a concerted effort over the past several years, in the wake of the national economic crisis, to make the MFA more attractive to students. In the past we've lost top-notch students to universities that offer more opportunities for full funding or that offer the opportunity to teach classes. We've made progress in both of those areas, although there's a great deal more work to be done – most often tedious work. There have been successes, however. We've partnered with the rhetoric and composition faculty to add four graduate teaching assistantships for students-as-adjuncts. Those students are required to first take a class in teaching composition and then to take a teaching practicum during the semester that they teach. We've also added assistantships (via university student worker funds), making it possible for graduate students to do meaningful work with *Chapman Magazine*, the Dean of Students Office and the Office of Undergraduate Research and Creative Activity.

Jan Osborn: The MA and MFA students who have participated as instructors/mentors in the Literacies Partnership are also getting valuable experiences for future careers. They often speak to the time and energy it takes to participate as well as the sense of meaning and a deepened understanding of the realities of students living in low-socioeconomic communities. So while the partnership inspires some to pursue teaching in secondary schools (a past student coordinator went on to Teach for America in Chicago), others realize that if they want to continue their creative writing focus, teaching is not a good trajectory. The work helps them question the realities of teaching and how teaching in secondary schools (full-time) or as adjunct faculty in colleges (part-time) has an impact on their goals as writers. There is no one correct answer to these questions, but an opportunity for graduate students to be in an instructor position certainly affords them a platform from which to consider their options.

Even more than this career focus, participation in the Partnership reinforces the idea that there are political dimensions to education, that what may seem like a given – a level playing field, if you will – has tremendous disparities that often go undetected by those within and outside the university. For that reason, the partnership affects the graduate students as more than future educators but as citizens of a country dedicated – at least in public discourse – to equal education and democracy.

Anna Leahy: Our students are citizens of culture, too; they are producers and consumers of that culture. The most exciting collaborative project for me professionally has been *TAB: The Journal of Poetry & Poetics*. As editor, I work with graphic designer Claudine Jaenichen; we've consciously nurtured a poetry project – and an artistic collaboration – that explores the reading experience, the materiality of print and digital, the interplay of text and image. But I've struggled to figure out how to make it valuable for students, especially as Claudine and I were experimenting as artists and editors and figuring out both the software for the electronic issues and the rhythm of the publishing cycle. In order to be worthwhile, this project needs to matter to students.

Over the past year, I've taken time in my poetry-writing classes to train MFA students both as readers for the journal's submissions and as book reviewers. Editorial work gives students real-world experience for future editorial jobs and also allows them to see what happens on the other side of the desk when they submit their poems for publication. I'm always looking for ways that one task or assignment can have at least two consequential rewards, rewards for me professionally and for our students.

Jan Osborn: That's similar to my approach. There are benefits to students *both* at the university and at the high school in working with creative writing beyond the curriculum. Because of the standardization of the high school curriculum, creative writing has been limited, and now, with Common Core, opportunities to read fiction and poetry are limited even further. Writing in high school is now focused much more on informational texts, on functional writing and test scores. Students are hungry for creative outlets, for opportunities to learn about themselves and the writing community beyond these functional parameters. The university can provide such outlets.

Anna Leahy: If high school students aren't reading literature, let alone writing poems and stories, they'll come to college – to our programs – without those interests and abilities. To not have been introduced, to not have the chance to cultivate interest – that's the beginning of a widespread cultural drought for the future.

Jan Osborn: For university students, it's important to see how their interests, talents, and passions matter beyond themselves. Particularly for those at a campus with little socio-economic diversity, the opportunity to work with students from diverse ethnic, language and socio-economic backgrounds is a growth experience. The MFA students come to realize that the high school students have much to say, that they are living complicated lives, are intelligent and creative, but often lack educational opportunities that the university students take for granted. The rewards that emerge from this one project are multiple within and across the individuals involved.

That said, because the focus of the program is on bringing underserved high school students to the university campus, I am continually challenged by logistics – scheduling rooms for workshops and other events, communicating with high school students when I do not work at their school, communicating clearly with parents from diverse language backgrounds. The challenges and the learning for me are continuous. This takes me back to the issue of how the academy can better support the relationship between the academic and the political, between scholarship and the social and between community-engaged scholarship and tenure and promotion. These are essential questions that must be addressed if the 'program beyond the program' is to remain a reality in higher education.

Douglas Dechow: Logistics appear mundane only to those who don't deal with them. I've developed a system for planning and executing events and other projects. We need to make sure we aren't continuously reinventing an existing wheel, even as details shift.

In learning how to do things better, I tend to focus on the premise that the planning and holding of events is always about the people – not the people in the crowd or the people doing the presentations, but the team of people who organize the event. There aren't enough detail-oriented people in the world to go around, so when you find them in a university setting, they're often overworked. You've got to find these people, cultivate professional relationships with them and have their backs going forward.

Jim Blaylock: Of course, the people in the audience and the presenters do matter as well. I learned long ago – both as a writer doing readings and as a professor encouraging students to attend events – to expect a fairly meager turnout at readings and literary events unless one of the participants has superstar status. Anything that one can do to promote the event had better be done: flyers, classroom visits, the promise of extra credit or food, food being especially persuasive with the college crowd. Such things will increase attendance, although the increase is often disproportionately small compared to the effort that goes into promotion.

Anna Leahy: Food definitely boosts attendance and fosters community, and some of our students may seek out events because they cannot afford all their meals every day. I've fiddled with times, written newspaper articles, invited the university president to introduce the Pulitzer Prize winners we've hosted – all this boosts attendance.

When I launched the Tabula Poetica series, I built it into my classes; that has been key. That's meant scheduling two or three poetry writing classes on the same day so that those students can attend the talk or the reading during class and be encouraged to attend the other. But it isn't always easy to negotiate the university and department scheduling processes. Sometimes I'm able to cajole other faculty into bringing a class to a particular event, but not all faculty see these opportunities as important. Some professors allow students to earn extra credit by attending. Students need to be nudged, and they have expressed gratitude when they've been required or encouraged to attend these events. We should remember that students don't know what they don't know; it's our responsibility to help them create interest and appreciation in themselves. No matter the headcount, as long as I'm putting the visiting poet in direct contact with those students studying poetry that semester, I've done a good thing.

Jim Blaylock: There's virtue in lowering one's expectations. Raymond Carver, in his essay 'A Storyteller's Shoptalk,' wrote the following: 'Isak Dinesen said that she wrote a little every day, without hope and without despair.' Writing and teaching have much in common, and approaching both without hope and without despair works surprisingly well.

The curriculum has – or ought to have – to do with craft, whereas a writer's life ideally has to do at least partly with connections to other writers. Extracurricular activities help us engage with that community, to be a writer among writers and readers. We, faculty and students both, understand that we're not laboring alone, that the community of writers has a rich past and will have a rich future, that we can make connections with writers and readers and with people in publishing and that the successes of others can make our own success more possible. Sometimes those connections pay off literally, but it's more often that they help sustain us in our otherwise lonesome pursuits.

Anna Leahy: All these projects, then, are about the long game. Administrators and accreditors might call these projects high-impact educational practices or active learning, for they constitute the sort of phenomenon that increases student engagement according to numerous studies. Cindy Kilgo *et al.* conclude, 'Two high-impact practices in particular – active and collaborative learning and undergraduate research – were especially beneficial to students' (2015: 519–521). The program-beyond-the-program represents active and collaborative learning, and Kilgo *et al.* assert that such experiences make a more significant difference in learning than writing-intensive courses themselves.

Presumably, when students are more engaged, they learn more and learn more deeply. In other words, what we're doing when we host events, do community outreach, and offer students real-world experiences is immersing our students rather than depending entirely on the curriculum for their learning. Completing a degree in creative writing should mean more than checking off course requirements, and teaching in a program should involve more than checking boxes on a rubric of student learning outcomes. In building a program beyond the curriculum, we create conditions in which students can thrive as writers and as human beings. We set interests and habits in motion and trust that the result will matter over the long haul of a career and a life.

References

2013–2014 School Accountability Report Card for Orange High School. See http://www. orangeusd.k12.ca.us/sarc/ (accessed 13 May 2016).

Association of Writers & Writing Programs (2015) AWP Hallmarks of a Successful Creative Writing Program. See https://www.awpwriter.org/guide/directors_hand book_hallmarks_of_a_successful_mfa_program_in_creative_writing (accessed 10 June 2015).

Barabási, A.-L. (2002) *Linked: The New Science of Networks.* Cambridge, MA: Perseus.

Carver, R. (1983) A storyteller's shoptalk. *New York Times,* 15 February 1983. See www. nytimes.com/books/01/01/21/specials/carver-shoptalk.html (accessed 25 November 2015).

Dechow, D.R. and Struppa, D.C. (eds) (2015) *Intertwingled: The Work and Influence of Ted Nelson: Ted Nelson Festschrift.* London: Springer.

Gallagher, K., Dechow, D. and Leahy, A. (2011) Freedom without walls: One model for interdisciplinarity on campus. *Die Unterrichtspraxis/Teaching German* 134.

'Guidelines and Hallmarks.' Association of Writers and Writing Programs. See https:// www.awpwriter.org/guide/hallmarks_quality.

John Fowles Center for Creative Writing. Chapman University. See http://www.chap man.edu/wilkinson/research-centers/john-fowles-center/staff.aspx.

Johnson, S. (2001) *Emergence: The Connected Lives of Ants, Brains, Cities, and Software*. New York: Scribner.

Johnson, S. (2010) *Where Good Ideas Come From*. New York: Riverhead.

Kilgo, C.A., Sheets, J.K.E. and Pascarella, E.T. (2015) The link between high-impact practices and student learning: Some longitudinal evidence. *Higher Education: The International Journal of Higher Education and Educational Planning* 69, no. 4 (April 1, 2015): 509–525. *ERIC*, EBSCO*host*. See https://www.ebscohost.com/ (accessed November 1, 2015).

Krogstad, J.M. and Fry R. (2014) More Hispanics, blacks enrolling in college, but lag in bachelor's degrees. Fact Tank. Pew Research Center, 24 April 2014. See http://www.pewresearch.org/fact-tank/2014/04/24/more-hispanics-blacks-enrolling-in-college-but-lag-in-bachelors-degrees/ (accessed 10 June 2015).

Kuh, G.D. High-impact educational practices: A brief overview. See https://www.aacu.org/leap/hips.

McConnell, K.F. (2012) The ethical and professional risks of engaged scholarship. *Rhetoric & Public Affairs* 15.1 (Spring): 153–171. See http://www.jstor.org/stable/41955610?seq= 1#page_scan_tab_contents/ [11 June 2015].

Popova, M. (2012) Kurt Vonnegut's 8 tips on how to write a great story. *The Atlantic,* 3 April 2012. See http://www.theatlantic.com/entertainment/archive/2012/04/kurt-vonneguts-8-tips-on-how-to-write-a-great-story/255401/.

Tabula Poetica. The Center for Poetry at Chapman University. Chapman University. See www.chapman.edu/poetry.

Part 4
The Profession

9 Creative Writing (Re)Defined

Dianne Donnelly, Tom C. Hunley, Anna Leahy, Tim Mayers, Dinty W. Moore and Stephanie Vanderslice

As the field of creative writing has grown, it has drawn some harsh criticism, including that of poet Anis Shivani, who called this group of authors 'berserk,' and novelist David Foster Wallace, who sees graduate programs as riddled with 'unhealthiness,' 'resentment' and assembly-line approaches. Rather than positioning creative writing as complementary to the larger national and even international literary culture, Wallace claims in his 'The Fictional Future' (2014) that the MFA degree is caught up in a battle against other communities of writers. Six creative writing professors counter these naysayers in a question-and-answer format by taking a look at what's really going on in our field. These authors address straightforwardly some of the more important, more complex questions critics have raised, and they share their perspectives on students and coursework based on decades of teaching, research and scholarship. To a great extent, this chapter offers talking points we all might adapt for situations in which our discipline or program is criticized.

I. It Can Be Taught

Is there a crisis in literature, as Anis Shivani suggests? And if so, is the rise of creative writing to blame?

Tim Mayers: Those of us with even a cursory knowledge of literary criticism know that literature as a concept, as a canon or as a term has been contested throughout its existence. To assert that a stable notion of literature has persisted throughout the history of writing is a spectacularly ignorant claim. Alexander Pope, for example, penned broadsides against the so-called hacks populating Grub Street. Not only does literature change in meaning over time, but it also is – and has been – the subject of deep disagreement among contemporaries. Yes, of course, literature is in crisis. That's its very nature. And that has little to do with the rise of creative writing in the academy.

Stephanie Vanderslice: Conflating creative writing and literature doesn't serve a useful purpose, especially if the main issue is teaching. Thousands of creative writers – some publishing during their time, some not (Emily Dickinson) – aspire to write work of literary merit that will transcend their own era, or perhaps they merely aspire to a writing life because they are compelled to do so, just as a painter is compelled to paint. Most of these artists have evolved past the desire to simply express themselves. In fact, as studies like Greg Light's 'How Students Understand and Learn Creative Writing in Higher Education' in *Writing in Education* show, realizing that making literary art transcends self-expression is the first step in the writer's development. Like most artists, writers struggle to define their own aesthetic and to find their place within any number of literary traditions.

Anna Leahy: Literature suggests a host of assumptions that only partially capture the writing life – then or now. We have the text *Origin of the Species,* then we have Charles Darwin's claim that his idea of natural selection came to him in a flash, but Steven Johnson points out, in *Where Good Ideas Come From* (2011), that Darwin's notebooks indicate he'd worked it out over almost three decades. In a *New Yorker* article a few years ago, Malcolm Gladwell highlighted that the experimental innovator is at least as important as the precocious genius when we look at artistic talent and production. Creative writing is about doing the work of writing, and the experimental innovator benefits from time, support and guidance.

That's what creative writing classes and programs provide. That's what novelist John Irving said to John Stewart on *The Daily Show,* namely that a creative writing program and his mentor Kurt Vonnegut showed him, 'You do these things better than those things. Why don't you do more of these things and fewer of those?' Irving remains grateful for the time this saved him in his development as a novelist. Not crisis in literature but instead, for some of us, a crux of participation in literature.

Some critics assume that the goal of the workshop is therapy or catharsis and attack the field for prioritizing therapeutic goals over educational or literary goals. What's the role of therapy in creative writing?

Dinty W. Moore: Creative writing as therapy is an easy charge to make because, to be honest, some folks do use it that way. There are, in fact, so-called memoir coaches who have made an industry out of helping people explore past trauma or family tragedy on the page, as a way to touch and understand hidden feelings. You can judge that as you wish, but that is not what happens in any college classroom I've observed, and it is certainly not what happens in our many graduate creative writing programs. Critics of creative writing as an academic pursuit take a small, small part of the whole and attempt to paint the entire enterprise in one, inaccurate color.

Tim Mayers: It would be silly to deny that some students – and some teachers – view writing as therapeutic. But it would be even sillier to box the entire enterprise of creative writing within the bounds of therapy. Many creative writing teachers actively discourage aspiring writers from focusing on the therapeutic or confessional aspects of writing. If you look at recent work like Dianne Donnelly's edited collection *Does the Writing Workshop Still Work?* and Alexandria Peary's and Tom C. Hunley's collection *Creative Writing Pedagogies for the Twenty-First Century*, you'll find plenty of examples. The complaint that the (allegedly) monolithic creative writing workshop promotes self-absorbed writing-as-therapy is a classic rhetorical straw man.

Anna Leahy: Therapy may be a welcome side effect for some writers or in some workshops. Writing to express yourself? Yeah, you and everybody else. Self-expression is inevitable when we write, but that's not the goal of our classes. Creative writing is a different medium than the other ways we express ourselves (e.g. in scholarship, in debate, in dance, etc.), and those differences – the characteristics of poetry, fiction or creative nonfiction – are our focus. That's why creative writers usually talk about craft, revision and how a poem or novel works, not merely what it says or means.

Dianne Donnelly: Anyone who studies a range of creative writing programs or has witnessed the emergence of new theories and practices over the last three decades or has looked at the books we've written (or even at the indices) will have trouble concluding that therapy is the dominant approach. Many of us are exploring the scope of knowledge areas that distinguish the ways in which creative writers read, write and respond differently than writers in other domains. Pointing to therapy, when discussing creative writing, completely dismisses the work of creative writing and its contribution to new knowledge.

How do writers in creative writing programs learn by sitting around talking?

Anna Leahy: In a book called *The Creating Brain*, by Nancy Andreasen (who is a professor of psychology and a former professor of Renaissance literature) argues, 'creative people are likely to be more productive and more original if surrounded by other creative people. This too produces an environment in which the creative brain is stimulated to form novel connections and novel ideas' (2005: 129). A creative writing program is this sort of environment. Students in a workshop learn from writing, which is usually done in isolation, but they also learn from interactions over time, whether that's brainstorming ideas, receiving feedback from the instructor and peers, or offering critiques. In fact, my students comment that they learn how to revise from responding to others' work even more than from direct feedback they receive. This process leads each student toward distinguishing his or her voice. The interactions nudge innovation because, as Andreasen says, 'creative people are individualistic and confident' (2005: 129). They don't want to be just like everybody else.

Tim Mayers: I like to pursue what composition scholar Byron Hawk calls an 'inventive pedagogy.' In most of the workshops in my classes, I do not ask students to consider how the poem or story in question could be made better; instead, I ask them to consider various ways it could be made differently. I encourage people to see more of the possibilities inherent in their own writing and the possibilities inherent in their classmates' writing. The idea is that the more possibilities the writer sees, the more the writer might be able to make an informed decision about how to change the piece in question or, in some cases, whether or not to continue working on it at all.

Tom C. Hunley: In the poem 'Shatterings' from his collection *Here and Now* (2013), Stephen Dunn writes: 'My class is called Whatever I Feel Like/ Talking About. No matter what the subject,/over the years it's been the only course/I've ever taught.' The speaker of Dunn's poem is describing an old-school approach to teaching creative writing that, happily, is on the way out.
     In *Colors of a Different Horse*, one of the dozens of fine books on creative writing pedagogy, Wendy Bishop recalls a graduate workshop in the 1970s in which students sat at the feet of 'a famous white-haired poet' who 'returned no annotated texts, gave no tests, shared no grading standards, kept to no schedule or syllabus, designed no curriculum' (Bishop & Ostrom, 1994: 284). This kind of old-school teaching has proven unproductive and frequently destructive. That's why it's rare to find these days. Many of us are good teachers who interact with our students and their writing and who work hard to encourage their learning. Good teachers don't just do whatever we feel like.

Dinty W. Moore: Good creative writing teachers demand that students isolate specific craft-based strengths or flaws in their critique: Is the chronology confusing? Are the characters under-formed? Is the language flat? Are there inconsistencies in tone, voice, plotting or metaphor? Think like an auto mechanic: in my workshops, we lift the front hood to see into the engine of a story or essay, study the moving parts, determine which parts are properly aligned, which are slipping, which are leaking oil, which are perhaps not needed at all. You learn a lot about writing by studying hundreds of narrative engines.

Stephanie Vanderslice: Some serious studies – again, I'm thinking of Greg Light in particular – show that students move through a series of stages as learning writers, stages that demonstrate they are improving, not as imitators of their teachers, but as artists who have gone beyond self-expression to grapple with serious literary and aesthetic considerations, considerations that result in literary accomplishments. Those of us who have taught creative writing over a long period of time – and the six of us have – can probably attest to this development. We see it in our students.

Why don't creative writing professors explain what they're doing?

Stephanie Vanderslice: We do! Teachers of creative writing are engaged with each other – this conversation is not our first engagement with these issues or each other – and with our students about what we do as teachers in creative writing programs. In the past 10 years or so, there has been a great deal written to share and analyze our approaches. Books in creative writing pedagogy include Katherine Haake's *What Our Speech Disrupts* (2000), MaryAnn Cain's *Revisioning Writer's Talk* (1995) and Carl Vandermeulen's *Negotiating the Personal in Creative Writing* (2011). Of course, all six of us in this conversation have published books about writing and teaching.

Tom C. Hunley: The Association of Writers and Writing Programs issues *The Director's Handbook,* a compendium of guidelines for creative writing programs. And AWP's annual conference occurs every spring. Many of us have presented on and attended panels about teaching. Topics range from teaching the novel to critiquing the workshop to online teaching strategies to using unconventional methods from other fields to K-12 teaching. And that's just a sampling from the first day a few years ago. The conference now draws more than 12,000 attendees. Though not all the panels are about pedagogy, that includes a lot of teachers getting together to examine their teaching.

Dianne Donnelly: Indeed, there's a lot going on in creative writing. Graeme Harper cautions us not to moor our students' learning to one specific island when he suggests that the 'learning of creative writing' by our students 'gains nothing at all from being considered the remit of only one type of learner or one type of teacher' (2006: 1). Many writer-teacher-scholars, like Harper, more accurately describe creative writing as fluid and as an academic discipline that does not stand still for very long. We're always in conversation, always exploring, always sharing ideas in hallways, conferences, journals, books, blogs, pedagogy forums (join our pedagogy forum on Facebook for an engaging example of conversation).

Dinty W. Moore: In law school, students analyze past cases, construct arguments and write opinions, so that eventually they can do these things well enough to practice law. Could they do this outside of law school? Yes, but law school facilitates the process, and the law professor offers guiding thoughts along the way. Writing instruction is no different. The goal is to offer the occasional guiding thought or idea, the craft lesson, a few instructive models and the occasional critical nudge, while all the time encouraging the student to practice writing, practice revising and practice, practice, practice as a means to improvement. It works.

Anna Leahy: If we question creative writing programs, we should indeed question law, medicine, architecture and a host of other programs by which practitioners learn to become participants in their professions. In fact, law professor Stephen Davidoff Solomon wrote an article for the *New York Times* (2013) responding to the criticism that law school is a scam. The parallels are intriguing, and Solomon points to the PhD in English as a worse bet. The job market for lawyers has been particularly low in recent years, and the student loan debt is remarkably high. He argues, 'it is hard not to conclude that many lawyers do not go to law school to be lawyers' and that long-term earnings should be studied instead of salaries in the year or two out of school. The same argument might be applied to judging MFA programs.

I've written before about what Lee Shulman calls 'signature pedagogies' and how engaging and rigorous these fields are. The 'emphasis on students' active participation reduces the most significant impediments to learning in higher education: passivity, invisibility, anonymity, and lack of accountability' (2005: 57). Also, 'These pedagogies create atmospheres of risk taking and foreboding, as well as occasions for exhilaration and excitement' (2005: 57). While Shulman, a leader in pedagogy and former president of the Carnegie Foundation for the Advancement of Teaching, didn't include creative writing in his discussion of signature pedagogies, his definitions make it clear that's what we have going on, especially in MFA programs.

It's not clear why exactly the naysayers glean pleasure in picking on creative writing, but it's relatively clear they're wrong about what's going on.

II. Crisis and Creativity

How is creative writing like other disciplines in universities? And how is it different?

Tim Mayers: Creative writing, like other disciplines, is a way of knowing. Patrick Bizzaro argues that creative writing has an 'epistemology,' or its own distinctive way of encountering language and the world. It is an approach that focuses on how things are put together, always entertaining the possibility that things might be put together *differently*.

Dinty W. Moore: Part of what we're up against in this conversation is the popular notion that creative writing classes consist of celebrated writers lecturing the kids about how exactly it should be done. Anyone who thinks that's what we're all doing in classrooms today is stuck back in the 1960s.

Anna Leahy: Creative writing is a discipline of practice, one that's akin to studio art, in which emerging artists learn about art of the past and the science behind color complementarity and paint components but also grow to understand composition, color and paint characteristics by actually painting. Creative writing shares this prioritizing of practice with medical programs, too, in which book learning is combined with working with patients. During their education, visual artists, doctors and creative writers learn the habits of mind of the field they are entering. For example, in creative writing, the question of *how* a text means – how a story makes meaning, how a poem is put together, how a change alters the effect of the words – is more central than *what* a text means.

Dianne Donnelly: Writers gather anecdotes, bits of conversation, observations, field notes, reflections, research. They synthesize material, flesh out details, make connections, remediate or reshape images and text. These creative processes lead to insights – discoveries that occur through the active practice of writing and problem solving. Scientists proceed through similar creative processes: preparation, incubation, illumination. While the creative processes of creative writers and scientists may proceed along the same lines, the practices of creative writing are not associated with certainty, with exactness, with a formulaic methodology of systematic questioning and replication that is located in the scientific realm. We are aligned with all disciplines that engage in the acts and actions associated with creativity and discovery.

Tom C. Hunley: A biologist studying bacteria through a microscope, a criminologist examining the demographics of homicide offenders and an economist seeking ways to reduce the national debt – all of these share with poets and fiction writers the 'rage for order' that Wallace Stevens spoke of in his poem 'The Idea of Order at Key West' (1990: 97). Like students in other disciplines, our students are entering into a long conversation in which they become immersed so that they can add something of substance.

Writers don't need a degree in creative writing to publish, so why is the academy a good place for creative writing to be fostered?

Tom C. Hunley: Why do health enthusiasts join gyms? Why do religious people gather in churches? A university is one place where writers can be with folks who share their passions and can offer encouragement and support.

Anna Leahy: Creative writing could be considered an aspect of an individual's lifestyle, like gym membership or religious affiliation, and each might be considered more meaningful with regular practice, but exercise, religious belief and writing are not exactly analogous pursuits. It's also unfair to assume that mainstream book publication is the singular goal for creative writing programs. Even if it were, not all students who pursue a major or a career stick with it. In fact, a *Huffington Post* piece (Neason, 2014) points out that the attrition rate of schoolteachers within the first five years is almost 50%. I don't know anyone in my field who asserts that writers need a degree to publish, nor that a degree promises publication. We do talk about and model how those who want a writing life, regardless of publication timelines, can stick with that life.

Dinty W. Moore: The degree is marginally helpful if you want a teaching career, but the true value of an arts degree is that it offers a young artist time and space and a community. Can you do this on your own, perhaps attending a writing center discussion on weekends or workshopping with a local writing group? Sure, you can, and, if it fits your life and goals, you should. Creative writing programs facilitate the process, and graduate programs often offer up a modest living stipend to boot.

Stephanie Vanderslice: The academy is far from perfect – and we argue for ways it might be revised in books like *Rethinking Creative Writing in Higher Education, Establishing Creative Writing Studies as an Academic Discipline* and *(Re)Writing Craft: Composition, Creative Writing and the Future of English Studies* – but it's the best mechanism we have to bring people who care about the subject together to attend to the next generation of writers. Certainly there are writers that emerge outside of it – Dave Eggers and Chuck Pahlaniuk come to mind – but academia provides a fertile soil.

Tim Mayers: I think it's even bigger. Universities and colleges are hubs within this nation's – and the world's – intellectual culture. Creative writers should be immersed in the debates and discoveries in other fields: in philosophy, in theology, in theoretical physics, in neuroscience and artificial intelligence. There's no better place for interaction among different disciplines than a college or university. Poets and fiction writers (at least some of them) also need the community of each other, just as the Shelleys (Mary Wollstonecraft and Percy Bysshe) and Lord Byron did when they headed a literary community in Lake Geneva and Ernest Hemingway and F. Scott Fitzgerald did under Gertrude Stein's tutelage in 1920s Paris. Today's creative writing programs have simply formalized those salons.

What's the difference between an undergraduate degree in creative writing, an MFA and a PhD?

Anna Leahy: I've completed creative writing degrees on all levels, mostly because I craved time to develop, regardless of what I'd end up doing for a living. Programs vary widely, but each degree made sense for who I was at the time and helped me develop. The Association of Writers and Writing Programs' *The Director's Handbook* is a great resource for general principles, including distinctions between undergraduate programs, which tend to be steeped in ideals of a well-rounded liberal education, and graduate programs.

Stephanie Vanderslice: Undergraduate degrees in creative writing are necessarily more taught. They should focus on what beginning writers need to know, a foundation of the elements of writing to engage a reader, how deploy craft to various effects. They also need to dismantle myths that most novice writers bring to college – for example, that writing is easy for so-called real writers, that there's a one-size-fits-all approach to the process – and teach various ways into subject matter. Those who pursue an undergraduate degree may go on for advanced degrees or into any number of creative fields. We should respect that varied desire with a varied undergraduate curriculum, including digital media production, editing, publishing and so on.

MFA students are those who have self-selected to pursue their writing intensely for a period of time (and hopefully afterward) and who want to hasten its development by focusing on writing as an art. Though the MFA is a terminal degree that includes a thesis, those who pursue a PhD (like me) have often decided they want to teach in academia and also specialize in the theory and/or pedagogy of creative writing.

Dianne Donnelly: Differences among programs are influenced also by institutional requirements, objectives and economic realities. Generally, undergraduate programs introduce important writerly and readerly concepts. Even here, there are further program delineations, which consider the ways students acquire knowledge at beginning, intermediate and advanced levels. The introductory course, for instance, often covers more than one genre.

Tim Mayers: Rather than focusing on degree programs, I prefer to focus undergraduate creative writing *courses*. A significant number of such courses exist not as part of any degree program per se, but as options or electives within English majors – or in some cases as parts of larger writing programs that also include technical writing, business writing, journalism, etc. These creative writing courses can accomplish many things, the most important of which is that they give students a glimpse of what it's like to try to *make* fiction and poetry, as opposed to merely deciphering their meanings, as many literature courses do.

What's the relationship between talent, creativity, determination and other qualities of successful creative writers, and what does that have to do with creative writing programs at colleges and universities?

Stephanie Vanderslice: Writer Fred Lebron, speaking at the 2009 Association of Writers and Writing Programs Conference, said, 'Writing is a war of attrition. Don't attrish.' In a world that's rather inhospitable to people who devote their attention to becoming artists, to devoting years of their lives to this process, it's my job to show students how to sustain their writing lives no matter what they end up doing for a living. We talk about this in my classes: What's your plan? How will you keep going as a writer during times when no one cares that you're doing it except you? I've also used books like Austin Kleon's light-hearted *Steal Like an Artist* and *Show Your Work!* to make some of the important points. Writing is a marathon, not a sprint.

Dinty W. Moore: Students bring their own creativity and determination, though these can be nurtured, encouraged and strengthened with a good teacher and serious, committed fellow students. Talent may be inborn, but talent is often just one of the deciding factors. For many working artists, determination makes the difference in the end.

Tim Mayers: Recent books by David Shenk, Malcolm Gladwell and Steven Johnson make the case that talent is far more a matter of relentless practice and preparation – nurtured and supported, especially when people are very young – than an innate quality or gift. Good creative writing programs and teachers make this abundantly clear to aspiring writers. I suspect that many of the writers who went through creative writing programs, but years later claim that these programs can't really teach people anything, have forgotten how their own persistence and determination were sparked in classrooms and professors' offices.

Dianne Donnelly: Doesn't each quality inform the other? In other words, writers who are determined tend to (1) immerse themselves in the practices of writing, (2) develop a reading acumen that reflects a breadth and depth of writing styles, (3) become observers of the world and the human condition, (4) be receptive to images, conversations, experiences, and other possible tangibles and intangibles that might serve as creative triggers or seed incidents for new creative projects and (5) seek answers to what is not known by looking for clues in the world all around them.

Tom C. Hunley: Louis Pasteur put it best when he said, 'In the fields of observation, chance favors only the trained mind' (1854/1954). Unless Arnold Palmer – or probably another golfer, Gary Player – put it best when he said, 'The more I practice, the luckier I get' (Yocom). The world – and creative writing – is full of talented people who never accomplish much. I can't teach anyone to be any more talented than they already are, but I can light a fire under them, I can design a rigorous course of study and model a good work ethic and I can coax each student's best writing out.

Anna Leahy: The verb you use, *coax*, comes from a noun meaning *a fool* or *a simpleton*. How interesting that teaching, then, might be coaxing students out of their foolishness and into complex thinking.

III. Should Mamas Let Their Babies Grow Up To Study Writing?

Why should undergraduate students study creative writing?

Stephanie Vanderslice: You'll find students who've written all their lives, finally thrilled to be studying the subject; students who want to explore their literary, artistic side; and students who think the course is an easy A. The last group is usually disappointed; creative writing courses are much more work than they anticipate. Students who major in creative writing tend to love words, books and the literary arts; they want to do something with that in their lives, perhaps going on in publishing, editing or new media. At the University of Central Arkansas (UCA), like a small but growing number universities I describe in my book *Rethinking Creative Writing*, our focus isn't just on the workshop. It's about helping students make a life in creative fields after they graduate.

Tim Mayers: A small majority of students in my undergraduate courses are English majors yearning for an alternative to the interpretive focus they find in literature classes. These students are not resistant to analysis, but they want to direct analysis toward productive rather than hermeneutic ends.

Dianne Donnelly: Whether students want to write within an interactive environment, experiment with poetic diction or forms or other genres or explore creative literacies, our courses satisfy a broad spectrum of student interests. About the 'graduateness' of our students as writers, Maggie Butt (2001) says, 'They have developed their ability to write well, to express themselves with clarity and vividness in a range of genres; skills which can be applied to writing a good business report, as much as to writing fiction, and satisfaction which comes with any creative activity.' A majority of writers use their skills and strategies to work in other creative industries: advertising, public relations, broadcasting, multimedia and digital content industries, journalism, film, website design, games, animation and more.

Anna Leahy: At my university, the introductory course counts as a general education requirement so students come from all majors and with diverse interests. Business majors make great leaps of imagination; psychology students ask how they can fit a creative writing minor into their plans because they're interested in character; film students want to explore narrative and symbol. And students who major in creative writing aren't one type: introverted or extroverted, hyper-organized or scatter-brained. Mostly, they're enthusiastic about reading and writing and, with some nudging, excited to try new things.

What really happens in undergraduate coursework?

Dianne Donnelly: Based on a survey I did for *Does the Writing Workshop Still Work?* teachers of undergraduate study still rely on the tradition of the workshop. But because the workshop is predicated on critical reading acumen and response skills, the beginning writer is often thrust into these reading and response roles before knowing how to perform them, developing a sense of how to use key terms and vocabulary, the awareness of genre differences or the skills of reading as a writer. That's why, in introductory courses, I focus on invention exercises and in presenting a wide range of literary choices/voices early in the semester, then introduce the workshop after students have gained a better sense of how to read and respond.

Dinty W. Moore: My experience from years of visiting schools as guest teacher is that undergraduate courses are widely varied. Some teachers adapt a standard workshop method supplemented by readings, others use the workshop method only after weeks of reading and discussion to familiarize students with contemporary writing in the genre and some abandon the workshop entirely, saving it for advanced classes. What goes on, in all of these cases, is introducing students to close reading, revision and the questions and concerns an author and editor ask of a work (rather than those a critic might have, something students are likely exposed to in other English classes).

Stephanie Vanderslice: Having studied a wide range of approaches to the undergraduate course, I've found the most successful courses move students slowly from invention (understanding different ways a piece of literary art might be made) to creation (the act of making itself) to critique, with the least emphasis, until advanced courses, on critique. Students need to spend a lot of time in and out of class actually writing, creating the material. This works best when teachers determine what elements of craft on which to focus – say, dialogue or tension – and lead students in writing exercises that help them understand, from the inside out, how those elements are deployed.

Tim Mayers: In the vein Stephanie suggests, my introductory courses are organized mostly around invention exercises. Students start to build poems, stories and novels from specific criteria. One poetry exercise starts with 10 randomly selected words from books students bring to class. These words become end-words of the even-numbered lines in a 20-line poem where each line must fall within a certain syllable range and the total number of end-stopped lines is limited to nine. This (at least temporarily) transforms composition of a first draft into a technical problem that must be solved. For a moment, the desire to write a poem about some abstract theme is moved aside, and the results often surprise and delight the students.

Anna Leahy: Introductory and advanced courses can accomplish different things, but we all are echoing parts of what Larissa Szporluk and I discuss in another chapter of this book that explores stages of the learning process. Any course on campus can be taught poorly, but most of us are incredibly thoughtful about how we teach, and, despite what the naysayers claim, creative writing courses are often challenging and rewarding for students. Mamas should cheer on their poets and their biologists who want to read and write poems. There are certainly worse ways their kids could spend their time.

What really happens in graduate coursework? How is graduate study different than undergraduate study?

Dinty W. Moore: A graduate student in creative writing has presumably come to some understanding of craft and technique. To use the painting metaphor, the student has studied how paint is blended, how different brushes create different textures, the effects of varying thicknesses of paint, the use of perspective and so on. Graduate school is where a student finally tackles the bigger questions: What are my subjects? What is my voice? What questions am I exploring in my writing? This usually culminates in a major project, a book-length work of poetry or prose connected by an idea, theme or concern.

Anna Leahy: I develop a focus for each graduate course, in part because it makes for fruitful conversation when each student engages in work that intersects with that of classmates. One course uses a poetry chapbook (a booklet of 12–20 poems) as the final project so we read published chapbooks and students considered how poems they wrote might be connected by form, theme or something else. One fall, I focused on voice and persona, using the new anthology *A Face to Meet the Faces* (Brown & de la Paz, 2012). Students experimented with writing in the voices of others (and, in doing so, also learn more about their own voice), and we ended with a public reading by students and anthology contributors who visited campus. Such courses offer students sustained study and writing and push them toward book-length work.

Stephanie Vanderslice: Graduate courses help students focus on their material in such a way that they can maximize its potential while at the same time teaching students how to look closely at their own work so that, once they leave the program, they will be able to continue a lifelong process of making art through creation, self-critique and revision. A good graduate program will also help initiate students into what it means to make a professional life as a literary artist. Some bemoan this early professionalization. I believe it's necessary in our flattened publishing world.

References

Andreasen, N. (2005) *The Creating Brain: The Neuroscience of Genius.* New York: Dana P.

Association of Writers and Writing Programs (2012) *The Director's Handbook.* AWP. See https://www.awpwriter.org/application/public/pdf/DirectorsHandbook2012.pdf (accessed 13 May 2016).

Bishop, W. and Ostrom, H. (eds) (1994) *Colors of a Different Horse: Rethinking Creative Writing and Pedagogy.* Urbana, IL: National Council of Teachers of English.

Bizzaro, P. (2004) Research and reflection in English studies: The special case of creative writing. *College English* 66 (3), 294–309.

Brown, S.L. and de la Paz, O. (eds) (2012) *A Face to Meet the Faces: An Anthology of Contemporary Persona Poetry.* Akron, OH: University of Akron Press.

Butt, M. (2001) Creative Writing and Professionalism. Students and Learning Outcomes (Position Paper, Sheffield Hallam University/English Subject Centre). Writing & Media, Middlesex University, London. See http://webcache.googleusercontent.com/search?q=cache:Akn62efXD5MJ:www.english.heacademy.ac.uk/admin/events/fileUploads/MaggieButt.rtf+&cd=3&hl=en&ct=clnk&gl=us.

Cain, M.A. (1995) *Revisioning Writers' Talk: Gender and Culture in Acts of Composing.* Albany, NY: State University of New York Press.

Donnelly, D. (2010) *Does the Writing Workshop Still Work?* Bristol: Multilingual Matters.

Donnelly, D. (2011) *Establishing Creative Writing Studies as an Academic Discipline.* Bristol: Multilingual Matters.

Dunn, S. (2013) Shatterings. *Here and Now.* New York: W.W. Norton & Company.

Gladwell, M. (2008) Late bloomers: Why do we equate genius with precicity? *The New Yorker* 20 October. See http://www.newyorker.com/magazine/2008/10/20/late-bloomers-2.

Gladwell, M. (2011) *Outliers: The Story of Success.* New York: Little, Brown, and Company.

Haake, K. (2000) *What Our Speech Disrupts: Feminism and Creative Writing Studies.* Urbana, IL: National Council of Teachers of English.

Harper, G. (2006) Introduction. In G. Harper (ed.) *Teaching Creative Writing* (pp. 1–7). London: Continuum.

Hawk, B. (2007) *A Counter-History of Composition: Toward Methodologies of Complexity.* Pittsburgh: University of Pittsburgh Press.

Irving, J. (2005) Interview, *The Daily Show with Jon Stewart.* Comedy Central, 17 August 2005. See http://thedailyshow.cc.com/videos/36k9p4/john-irving

Johnson, S. (2011) *Where Good Ideas Come From.* New York: Riverhead.

Kleon, A. (2012) *Steal Like an Artist: 10 Things Nobody Told You About Being Creative*. New York: Workman.

Kleon, A. (2014) *Show Your Work!; 10 Ways to Share Your Creativity and Get Discovered*. New York: Workman.

Lebron, F. (2009) Association of Writers and Writing Programs Conference 2009.

Light, G. How students understand and learn creative writing in higher education. *Writing in Education*. See www.nawe.co.uk.

Mayers, T. (2005) *(Re)writing Craft: Composition, Creative Writing and the Future of English Studies*. Pittsburgh: Pittsburgh University Press.

Meehan, M. Researcher of the Month (April). Research in the Faculty of Arts and Education Deacon University Australia. See http://www.deakin.edu.au/arts-ed/research/profile/mmeehan.php.

Neason, A. (2014) Half of teachers leave the job after five years. Here's what to do about it. *The Huffington Post*. 23 . See http://www.huffingtonpost.com/2014/07/23/teacher-turnover-rate_n_5614972.html (accessed 23 November 2015).

Pasteur, L. (1954) Inaugural lecture. University of Lille, Douai, France, December 7, 1854. In Houston Peterson (ed.) *A Treasury of the World's Great Speeches*. New York: Grolier.

Ritter, K. and Vanderslice, S. (eds) (2007) *Can It Really Be Taught?* Portsmouth, NH: Boynton/Cook.

Shenk, D. (2011) *The Genius in All of Us: New Insights into Genetics, Talent, and IQ*. New York: Anchor Books.

Shivani, A. (2012) Can writing be taught? Therapy for the disaffected masses. *The Huffington Post* 11 January 2012.

Shulman, L. (2005) Signature pedagogies in the professions. *Daedalus* 134 (3), 52-59.

Solomon, S.D. (2013) Debating, yet again, the worth of law school. *New York Times* 18 July. See http://dealbook.nytimes.com/2013/07/18/debating-yet-again-the-worth-of-law-school/ (accessed 9 October 2015).

Stevens, W. (1990) The idea of order at Key West. *The Palm at the End of the Mind*. New York: Vintage.

UCA See www.uca.edu.

Vandermeulen, C. (2011) *Negotiating the Personal in Creative Writing*. Bristol: Multilingual Matters.

Vanderslice, S. (2012) *Rethinking Creative Writing in Higher Education*. Cambs: Creative Writing Studies.

Wallace, D.F. (2014) The fictional future. In C. Harbach (ed.) *MFA vs. NYC: The Two Cultures of American Fiction*. New York: n + 1, 2014. 73–82.

Yocom, G. (2015) My shot: Gary Player. *Golf Digest*. Accessed 21 November 2015. See http://www.golfdigest.com/story/myshot_gd0210 (accessed 21 November 2015).

10 Terms & Trends: Creative Writing and the Academy

Rachel Haley Himmelheber, Anna Leahy, Julie Platt and James Ryan

'Terms & Trends' is important in the discussion of where our discipline stands both because of the individual authors' perspectives and the issues they address. This chapter brings three new voices to bear, including a graduate student and someone defining a hybrid-discipline career. In taking on some big questions, such as the position of creative writing studies, Rachel Haley Himmelheber, Anna Leahy, Julie Platt and James Ryan disagree on certain points and in fruitful ways that show consensus need not be the driving force of any academic field. As the authors tease apart trends and possibilities for the future of creative writing and their own careers, they demonstrate that variety, inclusiveness and innovation are goals for the field of creative writing.

Anna Leahy: Wendy Bishop was one of the few publishing about creative writing pedagogy when I started teaching. She fit neither in creative writing nor in composition studies, even as she looked across the divide from both sides for ideas that each field could adapt from each other. In a *College English* article, she argues that creative nonfiction has a lot to teach composition, 'yet viewing these areas of reading and writing productively *together* has been a hard sell in composition circles. The reverse is also true' (2003: 259). Bishop found that, when presented with a student's PhD reading list in nonfiction, composition colleagues feared incursion by the creative and creative writing colleagues feared incursion by the theoretical. Creative nonfiction and the essay are emblematic of larger tensions between camps – to whom does X belong?

James Ryan: The methodological distinction between composition studies and creative writing exists. Creative writing *studies* offers opportunity to blend the methods of these fields.

Anna Leahy: Attitudes have shifted. *Power and Identity in the Creative Writing Classroom* came out of that AWP panel, and AWP had more pedagogy panels in the last two years than in any other proposal category. So, traditional creative writing has made room for pedagogy scholarship. Still, there's work to be done in talking across the divides – across the sub-specialties within English and across other disciplinary boundaries, too.

Rachel Haley Himmelheber: My teaching position allows for intersection among my writing, teaching and scholarly and service work. That said, my scholarly work is often unsupported by those within creative writing and undervalued by those in composition and literary studies. Interdisciplinarity matters, as does kinship with other areas of English studies, as well as with various disciplines within fine arts. But there exists a need for tribalism within creative writing.

Who's in one's tribe is complicated, though. It's tough to figure out the boundaries since, for example, many teachers trained in creative writing end up teaching in other areas of English studies, particularly in composition. Many messy boundaries define and fail to define the field.

Julie Platt: It took me some time to explain that my choice to pursue a PhD in rhetoric and composition with a concentration in digital rhetoric was not a turning away from poetry, but a turning toward. I had assumed that rhetoric and composition would immediately understand what I was trying to do, but I needed to do a lot of work to clear and claim a space for my scholarship and to make it legible to both fields. Despite calls for collaboration and interdisciplinarity, academia should be more responsive to the challenges faced by hybrid scholars.

Anna Leahy: Interdisciplinarity is a buzzword on many campuses, but university structures make it difficult to accomplish in meaningful ways. Team-teaching can be costly, and tenure review committees may be primed to value traditional disciplinary work, so it's especially difficult for junior faculty to risk interdisciplinary work. Of course, once an individual has a record in a field, it can also be difficult for tenured faculty to adjust their standing habits and goals.

In *Academic Instincts*, Marjorie Garber states, 'The inevitable consequence of interdisciplinarity may not be the end of the scholarly world as we know it but the acknowledgment that our knowledge is always partial, rather than total' (2003: 79–80). Garber also points out that interdisciplinarity depends on the disciplines and vice versa. We cannot have interdisciplinarity without disciplines, and vice versa. An interdiscipline like writing studies cannot emerge, according to Garber, without the disciplines – and their boundaries – from which it draws and with which it plays. A university's physical structures and intellectual territories have a lot to do with those dynamics. Interdisciplinarity results from intellectual and creative collisions, and those collisions can sometimes be uncomfortable as well as fruitful.

Rachel Haley Himmelheber: I don't really face these tensions in my current position. I hold an MFA and a PhD in fiction, not composition-rhetoric, and I teach in an undergraduate course sequence at a small college, so I have the same students in the multi-genre introductory course as I do in introductory and advanced fiction courses. Research projects are an integral part of each course. My study of theory and history in creative writing informs my practice in the classroom, and I use that practice to obtain data for my scholarship, and, if I'm lucky, for my creative work, too. But my situation probably isn't the norm in creative writing.

Anna Leahy: I, too, hold an MFA and PhD in poetry. In my current position teaching in the BFA and MFA programs, I feel well supported and respected in my various creative and scholarly pursuits and see the various parts of my job as a cohesive whole (even when others don't). In all my academic positions (this is my fifth full-time position), both my creative and scholarly publications have been recognized. Most of these jobs have been at institutions that overtly value teaching over scholarship. Chapman University's goals emerge from its liberal arts tradition and the centrality of teaching, but it's also an entrepreneurial place with rankings ambitions that encourage innovation and even risk taking.

In other words, institutions vary. Individuals mature. And times change.

Julie Platt: Both creative writing and composition-rhetoric have changed over the last decade. The rise of digital technology is another touchstone, in addition to creative nonfiction, for both disciplines and as a way to build a career. My dissertation research looked at how poets use digital technology. Now, I am an assistant professor of professional writing and composition and teach courses face-to-face, hybrid and online. My pedagogical approach is informed by tracing how creative writing is defined and redefined by the shift from print to digital media in terms of composition, publication and distribution. These issues are shaping creative writing in ways about which we need to talk with students if we're going to be responsible teachers.

Rachel Haley Himmelheber: Likewise, my department and administration encourage innovative pedagogical inquiry and practice. As Tim Mayers points out in his article advocating for creative writing studies, 'creative writing has [...] operated under a dynamic according to which the role of creative publication [...] serves the same institutional function as does the production of scholarship in most other academic disciplines. Under this dynamic, university teachers of creative writing have most often lacked both the time and the institutional reward structure to pursue creative writing studies' (2009: 220).

Anna Leahy: Time is a huge issue for academics publishing in more than one area. Doing scholarship has undoubtedly slowed down my productivity as a poet and essayist, though each aspect of my work informs the whole. My job is designated for a poet, but I've made – or taken – time for writing about pedagogy and the profession because it makes sense of the parts that are the whole of my career and the field of creative writing. Reimagining what scholarship for a creative writer – and for other academics, too – might be and whom it might reach may be an important opportunity (and obligation) of an expansive vision for creative writing studies.

Rachel Haley Himmelheber: Teaching is a creative act, and I always had a lot of pedagogical ideas that I wasn't allowed to enact in restrictive, temporary positions. In 'Professional Writers/Writing Professionals: Revamping Teacher Training in Creative Writing PhD Programs' (2001) Kelly Ritter considers the PhD's 'marker of difference [...] the commitment to a life of teaching and scholarship symbolized by the PhD' while in 'Revisions from Within: the Potential of PhDs in Creative Writing' Kate Kostelnik poses this rhetorical question: 'who would pursue a PhD. without teaching aspirations and an understanding of the necessary research into pedagogy?' (2010: 3). Creative writing pedagogy was an area of focus in my doctoral exams, and, through increased understanding of the history of creative writing in the academy, I became interested in creative writing – the field, the discipline – in addition to the practice.

James Ryan: I first got involved in this field through an independent study with Steve Westbrook during my Master's degree, which introduced me to the work of scholars like Wendy Bishop, Patrick Bizarro, Katherine Haake, Anna Leahy, Tim Mayers, D.G. Myers, Hans Ostrom, Stephanie Vanderslice and many others.

Later, I discovered the Facebook group Creative Writing Pedagogy, or CWP. I asked that group whether the United States needed an academic journal of creative writing studies like *Text* from Australia or *New Writing* and *Writing in Practice* from the United Kingdom. The response was overwhelmingly positive, so now I'm editing a journal. It's an exciting opportunity, but also an overwhelming project for a first-year PhD student. Fortunately, many talented people asked me how they could help. Julie started working with me from the beginning.

Anna Leahy: The CWP page is space for vibrant conversation in which mentorship and innovation abound and scholarly opportunities and collaborations emerge. Development of a scholarly journal is exciting and much needed. *Pedagogy,* one of the few journals in the United States that considers the kind of scholarship we do, has a three-year backlog, last I checked. That said, my piece for this new journal argues against its title *Journal of Creative Writing Studies.*

Rachel Haley Himmelheber: Aversion to the term is worthy of further discussion, and the new journal is a good place for that exploration. Criticism from within creative writing seems to stem from two lines of thought: one, creative writing studies implies similarity to composition studies, and many don't want more alignment; and, two, some in creative writing find resonance in David Fenza's question: 'Will continued theorizing on pedagogy only lead to the lamentable time when creative writing will be taught not by accomplished poets, novelists, and dramatists, but by professors with graduate specialties in the theory of creative writing?' (1990: 240). Fenza's question is rhetorical here, but that *lamentable* is telling. These two positions have a singular origin in a kind of self-protection and defensiveness born of the hierarchies in English studies.

Anna Leahy: Aligning with composition studies, a field seen narrowly by many colleges and universities – especially institutions without graduate programs in the field – implies providing service courses toward general education. More importantly, though, differences between fields are strengths that we can use to create meaningful intersections. In his preface to *(Re)Writing Craft,* Tim Mayers uses scare quotes when he discusses such differences and attributes the difference mindset, in large part, to the fact that 'composition is almost always a required course while creative writing is almost always an elective' (2005: xii). But the separation between the two fields of writing cannot be racked up only to 'historical accident' (2005: xii); curricular patterns embody philosophy and methodology. Because the use of *studies* makes many creative writers who are steeped in philosophical and methodological approaches different from composition studies defensive, I'd rather not use it.

Why encourage connection with composition studies, as Mayers advocates, by dividing creative writing? Why limit participants in this conversation?

Another concern, which is what Fenza gets at, is that creative writing studies invites that age-old criticism that those who cannot do teach. Not all writers are good teachers. AWP makes it clear in its guidelines that publications aren't enough: 'it is recommended that a prospective teacher's individual competencies be examined closely.' That said, if creative writing is a discipline of practice, of doing, shouldn't the teachers of this practice also be practitioners themselves? This question is deeply philosophical and also utterly practical. Other practice-based disciplines like the visual arts, the performance arts, even law and medicine require such practice of their professoriate. As the chapter 'Text(ure), Modeling, Collage' asserts, creative writing is at least as akin to those arts disciplines as to composition studies.

Rachel Haley Himmelheber: A reductive and problematic – but common – way to conceive of the split between creative writing and creative writing studies is through the lens of degree: MFAs are artists unable to undertake scholarship; PhDs are scholars who failed as artists. This schism is further complicated by AWP's degree recommendations for teaching and by the demands of the job market in creative writing. While AWP, in its hallmarks for programs, still recommends the MFA as the necessary terminal degree for a teacher of writers, Kelly Ritter noted a trend towards the PhD back in 2001. In her article 'Professional Writers/Writing Professionals: Revamping Teacher Training in Creative Writing,' Ritter posits that 'a survey of the available positions in creative writing each year offers proof of this shift [away from the MFA], as many job advertisements now list a preference for the PhD, or list the PhD as a minimal requirement for employment, especially at liberal arts colleges that do not offer Master's degree programs' (2001: 206). This trend holds true today: out of the 100 full-time tenure-track positions in fiction, poetry and creative nonfiction that specify degree requirements listed on the 2014 and 2015 Academic Jobs Creative Writing Wiki site, only nine specify the MFA as the sole required degree while 20 require or prefer the PhD.

James Ryan: The term *creative writing studies* is discussed in Tim Mayers's 'One Simple Word' in *College English* (2009); Adam Koehler's 'Digitizing Craft' (2013) which reimagined Mayers's framework to include the digital; and, of course, Dianne Donnelly's book, *Establishing Creative Writing Studies as an Academic Discipline* (2012).

The term does important work. It names a field of inquiry distinct from, but related to, creative writing. While creative writing is a practice-led discipline, creative writing studies is a discipline of scholarship, so the 'simple word' *studies* marks an important distinction between these two fields.

Julie Platt: This term implies that one can, indeed, *study* creative writing. When I was pursuing my first master's degree, I was surprised that there was very little that made up the poetry-writing concentration aside from the creative thesis and a few workshops substituted for literature seminars. My MFA was more comprehensive, with courses on creative writing pedagogy and internships in literary publishing, but these were electives. Shifting to the term *creative writing studies* calls for a curriculum that is reflexive and entirely new.

Anna Leahy: Cathy Day, in another chapter, points out that some creative writers avoid more fully engaging with pedagogy because '[o]ne side thinks we aren't theoretical enough, and the other side thinks we're too theoretical' (p. 22). There exists a newly defined, academic Goldilocks space. 'We need to bring more writers from both sides into this space,' Day writes. The term *creative writing studies* attempts to fill this space but, in doing so – in whispering, *be more scholarly* – draws boundaries between varied roles a creative writer may embrace.

   Donnelly, who is also a co-author of another chapter, writes the following in her book: 'The academic goal of *creative writing studies* is to stand alongside composition studies and literary studies and any other university field of study as a separate-but-equal discipline' (2012: 2). Since creative writing already stands alongside these other areas of English studies, does this suggest that creative writing studies supplant creative writing and take its place in English departments alongside literature and composition-rhetoric? Can and will creative writing studies allow for theory, research and craft criticism to commingle as scholarship and for scholarship and creative work to commingle? Is this not what creative writing does already?

James Ryan: I can understand your concern about the sort of saber rattling that sometimes takes place among creative writing studies scholars. Many express their frustration with creative writing as it currently stands. This frustration has arisen due to the lack of academic spaces in which the scholarly study of creative writing can thrive. Maybe the tone of the rhetoric will change once creative writing studies gets its legs. In any case, I think *Studies* will find its place alongside creative writing rather than supplanting it.

Anna Leahy: Especially because creative writing has become important for enrollment in many English departments and because MFA programs are more numerous than they were a few decades ago, creative writing is unlikely to be supplanted any time soon. Keeping *creative writing* as the name for the field is not to say that theory and research shouldn't be done nor that a curriculum to support such projects shouldn't be cultivated. Indeed, the broadest, least divisive term, one that recognizes creative writing in the academy is connected to creative writing outside the academy, seems most prudent and fruitful.

Julie Platt: The problem is legitimizing a creative writing studies curriculum in the eyes of the academy, especially in the United States, for the term seems to be accepted in the United Kingdom. The scholarly identity of creative writing studies people is still not quite coherent in the way that being a compositionist or a poet is coherent. However, as more and more scholars identify as creative writing studies people, they will be producing scholarship and going on the job market. This contingent will reach critical mass.

Rachel Haley Himmelheber: The fight seems to be over: the term is more and more popular in usage, as James's references suggest. Julie's right about the critical mass – we're probably on the verge of that, and the resistance may be merely evidence of that. Our new initiatives in creative writing studies, including this book series, indicate we're probably there.

  The real goal should be to provide space for and open access to difficult discussions. To that end, scholars are advocating for the discipline's visibility and viability through the establishment of a professional organization, a conference and the peer-reviewed journal. I'm part of the leadership for the inaugural creative writing studies conference, slated for Fall 2016, which is an important step in legitimizing the field and bringing experts together.

Julie Platt: A few specific conversations must be a part of these efforts. One is how digital technology is shaping all aspects of writing creatively. Poetry has long been approached as a relatively transparent text; that is, we are familiar with looking *through* poetry to interpret it but have tended not to look *at* poetry – as circulated text, as mediated material, as rhetorical artifact.

Anna Leahy: N. Katherine Hayles, in her book *Writing Machines*, asserts, 'As the vibrant new field of electronic textuality flexes its muscle, it is becoming overwhelmingly clear that we can no longer afford to ignore the material basis of literary production. Materiality of the artifact can no longer be positioned as a subspecialty within literary studies [...]' (2002: 19). The rise of the digital heightens this need, which has existed all along, to consider all texts as mediated.

  In *Poetry's Afterlife: Verse in the Digital Age*, Kevin Stein writes, 'The advent of digital technology has given birth to video and new media poetries both created on and received via the computer. Each bristles with revolutionary fervor' (2010: 114). While not every creative writer or professor need go digital, Hayles and Stein indicate that recent changes in technology, media and textuality cannot be ignored by the field of creative writing.

Julie Platt: In the last 40 or so years, we've experienced a major shift in the way human beings create and consume media, and a handful of poets eagerly embraced and explored this shift even earlier than that. Christopher Funkhouser in his comprehensive 2007 study, *Prehistoric Digital Poetry*, writes that these poets first began working with digital technologies decades before personal computers were even accessible to the average person, let alone commonplace (2007: 1). That which we might call the mainstream of academic poetry writing in the United States has been slow to confront the reality of networked spaces. Very recently, however, there's been an explosion of interest in how creative writing and digital technology are interacting. Adam Koehler's 2013 piece for *College English* and the collection *Creative Writing in the Digital Age* (Clark *et al.*, 2015) are two high-profile works taking up incredibly important questions.

Anna Leahy: The possibilities of the digital seem especially relevant to poetry, which is overtly attentive to form and sound. I've started using blog software and Prezi in some of my classes, which I discuss in a chapter of *Creative Writing in the Digital Age*. I'm also collaborating with a graphic designer on *TAB: The Journal of Poetry & Poetics*. We're very consciously exploring both print and digital formats in relation to each other. These experiences convince me of the need for creative writing programs to account for the rise of the digital, and Chapman University is doing that through a set of new courses that include digital humanities, humanities computing and writing for video games.

Julie Platt: The other conversation that must be advanced is about identity and difference. In my experience as a graduate student, when we read poetry by a person of difference – Natasha Trethewey, for instance – we focused exclusively on the poems themselves or had brief, simplistic conversations about identity. What might it mean to be a multi-racial poet? What are one's responsibilities as a white reader and teacher of poetry? The voices that ask these questions are finally receiving recognition, such as David Mura's April 2015 essay in *Gulf Coast* in which he asserted that:

> the divide between the way whites and people of color see the social reality around them is always there in our society. But this divide often

remains invisible or obscured, especially in our current climate where the issues of race are avoided rather than discussed. But creative writing involves the very description of that reality, and so the gulf between the vision of whites and people of color is very present right there on the page.

If creative writing as a discipline has historically avoided these questions of privilege and difference, whether race, class, gender, sexual orientation, ability and so on, that must change.

When Junot Díaz's 'MFA vs. POC' article appeared in the *New Yorker*, I shared it with everyone I knew, all the while thinking, *This is a problem for all of us*. The whole field must be made to feel restless and unsatisfied – or downright angry – with the status quo. Ideally, creative writing studies is a space where that status quo can be named, confronted and taken apart.

Rachel Haley Himmelheber: Discussions must address whiteness within MFA program culture. The challenges about exclusivity and access currently being posed by writers like Diaz and Mura and through scholarly spaces like the excellent Thinking Its Presence: Race and Creative Writing Conference and VONA must not be skirted. Patriarchal norms within academic creative writing and within publishing are being questioned by organizations like VIDA, and that's a very exciting part of our field now.

Anna Leahy: This issue of difference – and the lack thereof – is rightly getting more attention at AWP, and many institutions are developing diversity and inclusion projects, in part because of pressure from accrediting bodies. But I don't see evidence that programs – that the faculty of each creative writing program – are addressing this issue day to day. These new initiatives, like a conference and a journal, could be incredibly important in making us all responsible for our part in constituting the larger field of creative writing.

James Ryan: Scholarship about these issues will emerge under Tonya Hegamin's editorship of the 'Diversity and Inclusion' section of the *Journal of Creative Writing Studies*. To my mind, the most important work in this field is currently being done by marginalized and underrepresented writers for whom the connections between craft and culture are self-evident. We will run a piece by David Mura whose essay 'The Student of Color in the Typical MFA Program' offered an insightful and devastating examination of the institutional racism enacted by creative writing programs. In that piece, Mura critiques the pedagogy of David Foster Wallace, finding

Wallace's lack of insight into his own cultural position as a white male both ethically problematic and representative of current tensions in creative writing.

Anna Leahy: Our classes often focus on practice, process and craft. In making poems, essays, stories, though, we are enmeshed in culture generally and in particular influences and identities.

James Ryan: Exactly. Creative writing would benefit from a close examination of our cultural enmeshment. The journal will offer the opportunity to explore such issues. Regional scholarly conferences are emerging for creative writing studies, too, that connect us with our closest geographical neighbors. The University of Montana, for example, hosts an annual conference called *Thinking Its Presence: Race, Creative Writing, and Literary Study* that featured Claudia Rankine as its keynote in 2015. The *Creative Writing and Innovative Pedagogies* conference (which will occur while this book is in production) looks promising as well.

Anna Leahy: When I think back 10 years, I can see that the body of work in creative writing pedagogy and the profession has grown quickly. Even over the last 18 months, the Creative Writing Pedagogy group on Facebook grew much faster than we'd seen before; as of this writing, has more than 4000 members, even though we screen membership. Ideas started exploding there. Social media allowed for connections to be made quickly and support to be gauged, and individuals like the three of you and others we've mentioned (and undoubtedly not mentioned) are making things happen.

James Ryan: We might be at the beginning of something big.

Anna Leahy: Like the novelist who's an overnight success after years of writing and revising.

These projects may become all-consuming for the individuals starting them, at least for a few years but perhaps for the length of a career. Perhaps, that's the point of creative writing studies as a discipline. Perhaps, creative writing studies is a way to fit creative work into a scholarly career, instead of the way I've fit scholarly work into my career in creative writing.

James Ryan: I don't draw a hard line between creative writing *practice* and *scholarship* or *service*. The kinds of writing that produce something other than text – like a play or a film or a conference or an organization – are also acts of creative writing. They are all *writing*, and they are all *creative*.

Anna Leahy: I understand that rhetorical point, but tenure review committees may not play by your book yet. In addition, especially after earning tenure, I've become less overtly scholarly and more creative in my pedagogy writing, as this book suggests. The piano and the guitar are both string instruments; though a person can learn to play both, it's unlikely that a person will excel to one's maximum potential in either if doing both. The choice of what to write matters.

James Ryan: While creative writing has defined itself by limiting its subject matter to craft practices in a handful of literary genres, creative writing studies explores the many intersections among creativity, writing, culture and technology. Scholarship becomes another genre in which to be creative.

Anna Leahy: Many of our creative writing colleagues don't do scholarship, of course, though some write book reviews and craft essays, which are a form of scholarly work in an artistic field.

Still, I think the commonalities among the kinds of things we write are clearer and more meaningful for there being a difference. As much as the modes are all writing and all creative, the distinctions remain and allow each to inform the other. Maybe the issue, then, is finding the right fit, a good mix, individual by individual and institution by institution.

Rachel Haley Himmelheber: The right mix and the right fit is quite idiosyncratic in this field. I've always felt a little separate from the artist-only types because I like scholarship and am compelled by it, and I feel the same way with scholar-only folks. But not everyone in creative writing is equally compelled by scholarly and creative pursuits, nor should they be. Moreover, not everyone's jobs support both artistic and scholarly production.

Julie Platt: I'm a junior faculty member, so I'm still learning how to do all of this. I was hired as a composition specialist, so the majority of my teaching and service reflects that focus. This places my own poetry and creative nonfiction writing lower on my priority list, but it means that I am free to pursue those creative projects without the intense pressure to publish them.

I also look for opportunities to integrate the questions of creative writing studies into my composition, professional writing and writing center research. As long as I remain first and foremost a compositionist, I'm free to pursue secondary interests as I like. However, I wait for the day when being a hybrid scholar – a creative writing studies person – can be accepted and valued as a primary identity. James and I are enacting that model already.

Rachel Haley Himmelheber: One pedagogical project I've been working on that enacts this new model and corresponds to my creative work is a research assignment called 'The Empathy Project,' which I teach in my beginning (200-level) fiction course. The purpose of the assignment is to try to consciously further one's own empathic development through research into a person or identity who feels *other.* This project's origins come from reflection on my own writing practice, which involves copious amounts of what I call *fiction writer research,* a style of inquiry that has rules and norms but was never taught to me explicitly.

Anna Leahy: A poet who writes about a bullet train without knowing much about bullets or trains, as one of my students did, limits himself without realizing it. Students don't always like to be sent to the library for in-depth research to work on a metaphor or a couple of lines, but it helps make for surprises and depth of thinking.

For many creative writers, research is part of the writing process. However, the sort of research we do probably doesn't make easy sense to our academic colleagues. Phillip Gerard, in 'The Art of Creative Research' (2006) states, 'For the writer, researching is about being resourceful in every sense of the word: finding research resources and exploiting them in your creative work, using all your ingenuity and inventiveness to develop an archive for your particular project and learning how to manage the precious and finite resources of time, energy, and money to accomplish it. It is based on our fascination with mystery, in the broadest possible sense: that which is hidden from us, the answer we crave to know in order to make sense out of our world.'

Rachel Haley Himmelheber: In the project I assign, I'm drawing upon arts-based research practice and methodology from social science disciplines. For example, aspects of grounded theory methodology organize my research. Patricia Leavy's *Method Meets Art* influences my approach, although the work I'm doing is the inverse of what Leavy discusses: instead of using fiction and narrative methods to understand things in the social science world, I'm drawing upon social science to understand narrative better.

I also use my own writing and its accompanying research to teach the project. I work alongside my students; that enriches both my creative work and my scholarship.

Julie Platt: When I was in a research methods class as a doctoral student, I reviewed *Method Meets Art* by Patricia Leavy and saw rich possibilities for its application in composition. Increasingly, rhetoric and composition is finding new, somewhat unconventional ways to perform research and interpret and present results.

Anna Leahy: Blurring boundaries between art and scholarship can make academics uncomfortable, of course. Can an essay that is orchestrated via email and edited into a conversation that draws, in part, from individual experiences be called scholarship? This book argues that it is. Or, rather, this book argues that these conversations are useful, perhaps necessary, to better understand what we're doing and what the possibilities might be. Leavy argues that usefulness is an important standard for judging the quality of arts-based research.

Julie Platt: The collection *ALT DIS: Alternative Discourses and the Academy*, edited by Christopher Schroeder, Helen Fox and Patricia Bizzell, sketches out some new possibilities. This book discusses the emergence of 'alternative' scholarship, in which 'traditional academic traits blend with traits from discourses not traditionally accepted in the academy to produce new forms with their own organic integrity' (2002: ix). While this book was published over a decade ago, we haven't yet reached a place where this kind of work is acceptable, say, in a tenure case. However, complex, hybrid and even multimodal writing that blends scholarly and creative work in critically important ways is emerging all the time, and older work, such as Theresa Hak Kyung Cha's 1982 autoethnography-as-novel *Dictée*, is now seen not just as art but as accomplished scholarship. Connecting artistic methods to scholarly products – and vice versa – might be a space where cooperative, meaningful, truly hybrid work can begin.

Anna Leahy: Indeed, when Leavy describes why she's embraced arts-based research, she talks about it as a way to include the range of her experience and knowledge as a researcher, teacher and mentor. She goes on to say, 'I also wanted to share it in a way where I didn't have to censor myself, which is another problematic aspect of traditional academic reporting' (2015: 2). Creative writers may struggle with traditional academic writing because it excludes much of how we think of ourselves and our roles as experts, and arts-based research provides a way through that struggle. On the flip side, academics might learn from creative writing, from the inclusion and self-consciousness we bring to our work and from the 'holistic and engaged,' to use Leavy's words, ways that artists combine theory and practice (2015: 4).

That Claudia Rankine's *Citizen* was a finalist for the National Book Critics Circle Award in both poetry and criticism points to the expansive nature of what creative writing is and can be. That a poet can do something recognized as poetry that is also accepted as cultural commentary matters to how we imagine our discipline. In that book, Rankine writes: '"The purpose of art," James Baldwin wrote, "is to lay bare the questions hidden by the answers." He might have been channeling Dostoyevsky's statement that we have all the answers. It is the questions we do not know' (2014: 115). Art has the ability to turn the tables on scholarship. Exactly how creative writing thrives and morphs as emerging scholars re-envision it remains to be seen. That responsibility falls to the three of you – and others like you.

References

AWP (Association of Writers and Writing Programs) *AWP Guidelines for Creative Writing Programs & Teachers of Creative Writing*. AWP. See https://www.awpwriter.org/guide/directors_handbook_guidelines_for_creative_writing_programs_and_teachers_of_creative_writing (accessed 13 May 2016).
AWP *AWP Hallmarks of an Effective BFA Program or BA Major in Creative Writing*. AWP. https://www.awpwriter.org/guide/directors_handbook_hallmarks_of_an_effective_bfa_program_or_ba_major_in_creative_writing.
Bishop, W. (2003) Suddenly sexy: Creative nonfiction rear-ends composition. *College English* 65 (3), 257–275.
Cha, T.H.K. (1982) *Dictée*. Berkeley: University of California.
Clark, M.D., Hergenrader, T. and Rein, J. (2015) *Creative Writing in the Digital Age: Theory, Practice, and Pedagogy*. New York: Bloomsbury.
Creative Writing Pedagogy. Facebook. See https://www.facebook.com/groups/395092 28012/ [Must be logged in to view or join].
Creative Writing (2014) *Academic Jobs Wiki*. See http://academicjobs.wikia.com/wiki/CreativeWriting_2014.
Creative Writing (2015) *Academic Jobs Wiki*. See http://academicjobs.wikia.com/wiki/CreativeWriting_2015.
Díaz, J. (2014/2015) MFA vs. POC. *The New Yorker*. Condé Nast, 30 April 2014. 15 June 2015.
Donnelly, D. (2012) *Establishing Creative Writing Studies as an Academic Discipline*. Bristol: Multilingual Matters.
Fenza, D.W. (1990) Review of creative writing in America: Theory and pedagogy. In J.M. Moxley (ed.) *College Composition and Communication* 41 (2), 239–240.
Funkhouser, C. (2007) *Prehistoric Digital Poetry: An Archaeology of Forms, 1959–1995*. Tuscaloosa: University of Alabama.
Garber, M. (2003) *Academic Instincts*. Princeton, NJ: Princeton University Press.
Gerard, P. (2006) The art of creative research. *The Writer's Chronicle* Oct/Nov 2006. See https://www.awpwriter.org/magazine_media/writers_chronicle_view/2258/the_art_of_creative_research.
Hayles, N.K. (2002) *Writing Machines*. Cambridge, MA: The MIT Press.
Koehler, A. (2013) Digitizing craft: Creative writing studies and new media: A proposal. *College English* 75, 379–397.
Kostelnik, K. (2010) Revisions from within: The potential of PhDs in creative writing. *Creative Writing: Teaching Theory and Practice* 2 (1), 1–32.
Leahy, A. (ed.) (2005) *Power and Identity in the Creative Writing Classroom: The Authority Project*. Clevedon: Multilingual Matters.

Leavy, P. (2015) *Method Meets Art: Arts-Based Research Practice*. New York: The Guilford Press.

Mayers, T. (2009) One simple word: From creative writing to creative writing studies. *College English* 71, 217–228.

Mayers, T. (2005) *(Re)Writing Craft: Composition, Creative Writing, and the Future of English*. Pittsburgh: University of Pittsburgh Press.

Mura, D. (2015) The student of color in the typical MFA program. *Gulf Coast*. 21 Apr. 2015, 26 Oct. 2015.

New Writing: The International Journal for the Practice and Theory of Creative Writing. See http://www.tandfonline.com/loi/rmnw20#.VXDllEuVM3g.

Rankine, C. (2014) *Citizen: An American Lyric*. Minneapolis, MN: Graywolf.

Ritter, K. (2001) Professional writers/writing professionals: Revamping teacher training in creative writing PhD programs. *College English* 64 (2), 205-227. Print.

Schroeder, C.L., Fox, H. and Bizzell, P. (eds) (2002) *ALT DIS: Alternative Discourses and the Academy*. Portsmouth, NH: Boynton/Cook—Heinemann.

Stein, K. (2010) *Poetry's Afterlife*. Ann Arbor: University of Michigan Press.

Text: Journal of Writing and Writing Courses. See http://www.textjournal.com.au.

Thinking Its Presence: Race, Creative Writing, and Literary Study. Conference 2014 and 2015. Missoula, Montana. See http://cas.umt.edu/tip/raceandcreativewriting/.

Voices of Our Nation Arts Foundation (VONA) Voices: Writing Workshops for Writers of Color. Workshops. See http://www.voicesatvona.org/ (accessed 15 November 2015).

Part 5
Careers

11 Peas in a Pod: Trajectories of Educations and Careers

Mary Cantrell, Rachel Hall, Anna Leahy and Audrey Petty

'Peas in a Pod' functions as a set of career case studies, with each of the four authors starting from roughly the same point as an undergraduate student at Knox College in the mid-1980s. This discussion captures the opportunities and choices they had over the last 30 years, the ways they negotiated resistance and accommodation, and where they stand in their careers as writers and teachers now – at a community college, at a state university, at a private university and in community-based educational organizations. Their careers remain dynamic and changing, and they learn by reflecting on how they got where they are and what may lie ahead. This chapter conveys that a degree in creative writing creates many opportunities and that, while a professor's experiences may help guide students, there exist a variety of trajectories and issues within and beyond the academy.

Anna Leahy: Fareed Zacharia, who is of our generation as well, writes in his defense of the liberal arts education, 'Loving to learn is a greater challenge today than it used to be' (2015: 61). My parents embraced the concept of a liberal arts education and seemed unconcerned about what exactly I'd pursue as a career. When I headed to college, I wanted to be a surgeon. I wanted to write, too, and planned to take creative writing classes, but I had no idea that such an urge or talent could build a life around such an endeavor.

Rachel Hall: Like any daughter, I didn't always listen to my mother, but I did when picking a college. She knew somehow that I would flourish at a small school. I went to Knox College thinking I'd be a psychology major, but those classes felt abstract and distant from my interest in people and why they did what they did. Without knowing it, I was really interested in fiction writing, with its focus on character and motivation.

Anna Leahy: The first undergraduate for whom I wrote a recommendation letter for an MFA program was a psychology major who took my creative writing class at the beginning of her senior year. She was the sort of student who always carried around a novel that hadn't been assigned and couldn't remember why she'd checked that psychology major box. While English major numbers have held relatively steady since the 1970s, according to the National Center for Educational Statistics, the number of undergraduates at large has almost doubled and the number of psychology majors (and also business majors) has almost tripled. Might a few of those students be more interested in character than personality?

Rachel Hall: When my roommate, Mary Cantrell, enrolled in an introductory fiction-writing class, I wanted to be in the class too. Friends influence each other's choices. This class was exciting in ways I hadn't experienced before. At that point, I hadn't been the most engaged college student, but I didn't miss a single class, and I read all the assignments and worked hard on them. The work was fun for me, engrossing. Through a series of decisions that I was sometimes only half-making myself, I found that I wanted to write – that I had something to say – and, after that, I knew what to do with my life.

Anna Leahy: Seemingly small decisions can matter to our students' trajectories. When we hand out a syllabus or have students complete an assignment, we affect a life or two. Of course, it depends on their openness, their interests, their willingness to become as engrossed as we were.

Mary Cantrell: In my case, those small – and big – decisions that my many excellent high school English teachers made sent me to Knox College, where I planned to study English or philosophy. During that first year of college, my composition professor, Ed Niehus, encouraged me to take Robin Metz's fiction-writing class, and Robin Metz encouraged me to write a novel. It's a cliché, but it's true: teachers created the inciting incidents in my life story. Or to use John Barth's jargon, they were the 'incremental perturbation' of the 'unstable homeostatic system' that was my youth (1999: 131). If I were an award-winning writer with many publications, perhaps it would be easier to attest to the profound ways English teachers shaped my future; instead, their influence is subtle and complex. I think about the world differently because I studied creative writing – my own writing and that of others – with really smart people.

Audrey Petty: I actually didn't major in creative writing at Knox. I graduated as a French major with a concentration in American History, but creative writing drew me in over time. I'd written poetry in grammar and middle school, and some of my college friends told me that workshops were really different from other classes. I enrolled in a poetry workshop with Robin Behn, and she created an inciting incident for me. It was fun learning how to read as a writer. That class introduced me to such an eclectic range of published work, collections by Rita Dove and Czleslaw Milosz, and the world became much bigger. Fareed Zacharia, in his book about a liberal education, had a similar experience: he took one class his first year 'simply out of sheer interest' (2015: 38). He says, that course 'made me realize that I should take my passion seriously, even without being sure what it might lead to in terms of a profession' (2015: 39).

Life at Knox outside of the classroom was sometimes difficult for me, though. As a black person, as someone who'd grown up in a racially inte-grated neighborhood, as someone who'd attended schools that were majority African American, I had some deeply painful experiences in college. I encoun-tered white privilege and racism more squarely. I eventually found some perspective about the culture shock I was experiencing through my course-work – especially United States history. Reading and writing provided me sanc-tuary, but these were also practices that helped me to struggle and connect.

Anna Leahy: I make a conscious effort, usually in one-on-one conferences, to find out what other classes my students are taking. Students reveal their interests so that I can help them make connections between those interests and their writing. Students sometimes also reveal their struggles, some of which have to do with identity, and I talk with them about those issues and recommend other reference points on campus.

Because creative writing is a field that values originality, intructors may be more likely to see students as individuals and, therefore, have an ethical responsibility to consider gender, race and class – identity – when guiding students as writers. In 2014 in *The New Yorker*, Junot Diaz called out the field for being 'too white.' By that, he meant the lack of people of color among both faculty and MFA students and, importantly, that the 'workshop repro-duced exactly the dominant culture's blind spots and assumptions about race and racism (and sexism and heteronormativity, etc.).' Creative writing has set aside these issues for too long. That's hypocritical, when we are – or should be – much more aware of *the writer* as part of the educational environ-ment and the practice of writing.

Mary Cantrell: Many community colleges are not 'too white.' Community college faculty cannot ignore issues of race, class and gender if we want to help these diverse groups of students navigate the challenges of the writing life and of the academic world in general.

Anna Leahy: I also help students negotiate what might be very different types of academic demands. We talk about how to allocate time during the last two weeks of the semester, for instance, to study for exams, write research papers, prepare presentations, pull together a final creative writing portfolio. Even as I try to get a sense of the individual writer, everything including identity, tends to lead back to craft.

Audrey Petty: Diaz's essay resonates with me, especially when I reflect on my college years. I think about his friend (and fellow 'Caliban') Athena, who dropped out of the MFA program at Cornell while he was there. I left Knox after my first year – not expecting to return – because of the alienation I experienced as a black woman. I came back one year later with a clearer agenda about what I would seek. Knox was in dramatic transition when I returned. Black students were mobilizing to demand changes to the curriculum. It was an exciting and turbulent time, and I was inside of it. I enrolled in Knox's first ever African-American Literature course, and I was gobsmacked by *Song of Solomon*. I took my first creative writing class around that same time. Fortunately, the guidance of the professors in those classes allowed us to meaningfully talk about race and racism and sexism and, to a lesser degree, heteronormativity. Workshop was a space for talking shop, and I loved learning how to do that. Those classes felt worldly. Without a doubt, my French studies, which were rooted in literature and capped by a year in Besançon, led me to love many Francophone works, too. All of this forced me to pay a new kind of attention to my mother tongue; I grew to understand the English language more deeply.

Anna Leahy: That Knox College had a language requirement seems important to me as well. Do undergraduate English degrees generally still require that? I encourage my students to study a foreign language because there exists no other way to understand syntax as well. Most people can go through life without understanding the subjunctive, but I'm not sure writers should. Studying Latin, even as a beginner, made me take less for granted about English and also consider how language, culture and cultural norms are varied and in flux. I was hardly a world citizen after a year of Latin and a three-week study abroad course in the Soviet Union, but these types of experiences help us – as writers and as human beings – question our assumptions about ourselves and about others and also develop empathy.

Audrey Petty: By the time I finished my studies at Knox, I was determined to become a writer for life. Coming from a long line of teachers, I had always held that in my imagination as an almost inevitable career path.

Mary Cantrell: Because of the profound impact my high school English teachers had on me, I also thought of teaching as an inevitable career path. Much to my surprise, though, graduating cum laude from Knox College with a degree in English did not qualify me to teach high school. I needed 36 more hours of education classes to earn my Oklahoma teacher certification. I'd taken two education classes at Knox: 'School and Society' and 'Feminist Theory,' classes that focused on what we now call the achievement gap and that did not count toward becoming a teacher.

Anna Leahy: I wonder how many students who pursue that education degree or teaching certificate might have taken, as you have, a different path to happier lives. The five-year dropout rate for new teachers, according to the US Department of Education, is 50% (Alliance for Excellent Education). For inner-city schools, half of new teachers leave within three years. High-school teachers are more likely to drop out than their students. Either education students are choosing the wrong major for their goals, or programs are not preparing students for the realities of teaching.

Rachel Hall: I've encouraged a number of students to pursue MFAs, but only once did I recommend that someone do so instead of getting teaching certification. I've always felt that students should pursue an MFA only if they are really passionate about writing and also talented. And I always tell them that an MFA isn't, as teaching certification is, job training. I know that teaching is a difficult job, and it isn't really treated as a profession, perhaps because it's a female-dominated profession. My mother was a junior high school teacher, and, given her experience, I did not want to be a teacher.

Mary Cantrell: The way we treat public school teachers shows a disregard for the real work teaching is and discourages some smart, ambitious people from pursuing that career. So does teacher training. After Knox, I figured I could be a good teacher, but I didn't want or think I needed to take (and pay for!) classes like Classroom Management. So, instead, I took a job as a secretary at a classic rock radio station and volunteered for *Nimrod International Journal*.

Anna Leahy: I took the classes I wanted to take, nothing beyond general chemistry to get into medical school. My interests led me to become something other than a surgeon.

Students often decide on a major early, especially at some institutions and in some fields. Some students don't want or need to explore, but others think twice when they become interested in classes outside their original major, as Fareed Zacharia did. I've spoken with several business students who won't change their major, often because of parental expectations, but want to know how to complete at least a creative writing minor. Will they be happy in accounting and marketing jobs? What might their lives and our culture be like if they majored in the arts and minored in business?

I wanted to hang out with the creative writing and humanities students. So, I took courses with them, and then I worked on the student literary journal. One thing leads to another.

Mary Cantrell: Yes, and often unpredictably. My volunteer work turned into a paying job with *Nimrod*, where I might have stayed if Rachel hadn't encouraged me to apply for a fellowship at Iowa State University. I earned a master's degree in the same amount of time that it would have taken me to earn my teaching certification.

Rachel Hall: I applied to a number of programs for graduate study. Some were MFA programs; others were MA programs. I knew the difference, but the line was blurrier then, as there were fewer MFA programs and more MA programs. Also at that time, an MA could land you a full-time college teaching job. Clearly, times have changed, so, while our experiences are important reference points, we need to keep in mind that the landscape of creative writing programs has changed and the options for our students are different than they were for us.

Three of us, in different years, applied to Iowa State University because Robin Behn, our poetry-writing professor at Knox College had recommended it. Her friend Mary Swander taught poetry writing there, and she knew that they had a good program and offered financial support. At the time, Jane Smiley taught there, too, and I liked her work. Creative writing is a small world, and our connections – our tribe – can help us create paths for ourselves and our students.

Anna Leahy: The connections are part of the strength of the discipline but also reinforce the status quo. I can think of only one black student in that MA program at the time the three of us attended and one differently abled student. Some of my first-year composition students had met a black person for the first time when they came to campus.

I wanted more time to figure out how to become a writer, and a teaching assistantship was the way I could do that. As the three of you can attest, when I was an undergraduate, the idea that I would stand in front of a class-room and speak was preposterous. In fact, despite taking courses on teaching, it took years for me to think of myself as a teacher. But there I was with Mary and Rachel at Iowa State University, writing, reading and going through the motions of teaching first-year composition so that I could earn an MA.

Audrey Petty: Truth be told: I couldn't have gone to graduate school without financial support. A fellowship and teaching assistantships (and a part-time job) made the MFA possible. I was curious about teaching, but at that point, I didn't really imagine myself going on to teach college. My criteria in applying to schools was shaped by my desire to take lots more Anglophone literature, and I wanted to be in a program that included people of color on faculty. I was looking for the most open space to risk more in my work, trying to find the greatest range of motion for myself as a writer. I didn't want to always be the only black person in the room. UMass was appealing, in great part, because of the opportunity to work with John Wideman, who became my mentor. I also studied Contemporary Latino/a Poetry with Martin Espada. Agha Shahid Ali joined the faculty after I got to there; it was mind-bending to be in his poetry workshop.

Anna Leahy: As an undergraduate and in the MA, I, too, worked in both fiction and poetry, and I found that mix of interests an important part of how I defined an intellectual community. But my MFA program didn't allow for that, as Audrey did. Quickly, though, I felt as if focusing on poetry would be important to my growth as a writer, and I couldn't have found better mentors than Stanley Plumly, Michael Collier and Phillis Levin.

While those workshops were crucial to the poet I am now, Neil Fraistat's literature course on Romanticism had as much impact on my thinking as a poet and future professor. Reading the work of Felicia Hemans and Dorothy Wordsworth in addition to the big five Romantics made me more interested in scholarship and helped me make sense as a woman poet. I was able to see how my reading and writing selves might be connected. I still didn't think of myself as a teacher, but I wanted to keep doing what I was doing – writing poems, writing about poets and poetry, connecting these two modes – with people who were also doing these things.

Audrey Petty: UMass required a significant amount of coursework in literature, and I dove into studying writers I hadn't encountered as a French major in college. I was thrilled to finally sink my teeth into some Edith Wharton novels and to take a seminar on Richard Wright, Ralph Ellison and

James Baldwin. The reading and writing self as connected – that clicked for me in grad school. I was consciously, actively an apprentice, and every class I took – the shape of my life – was devoted to that.

Anna Leahy: It's important for us to remember that our creative writing students are in someone else's literature class. We can encourage students to make connections across courses and figure out how all their work – reading, writing, thinking – might fit together. Connections, engagement, ambition, and even morale are interwoven for all our students.

Rachel Hall: I earned my MFA at Indiana University, and, at the time, the program was not really a happy place, in part because there wasn't adequate funding for all entering students, which led to competition, bitterness and low morale. I was accustomed to a more nurturing environment – and more praise – and had to learn to push on without that and to develop a thick skin. I really didn't do good writing there until my last year, after I'd learned to focus on my work rather than on the critics. Those lessons, alas, are some of the most important a writer can learn. It's not fun, but rejection and stiff competition are part of this writerly life.

Mary Cantrell: Resiliency and grit seem to be new buzzwords in education, and many articles have been written about the frailty of the millennial generation, so perhaps our training needs to include more about helping students deal with rejection and criticism. In her book *Mindset: The New Psychology of Success*, Carol S. Dweck provides a wealth of research that shows attitude matters when it comes to learning. People with a 'fixed mindset' attitude believe individuals are born with 'a certain amount of intelligence, a certain personality, and a certain moral character' whereas those who have a 'growth mindset' believe that individuals can improve upon their qualities through effort (2008: 6–7). Dweck explains that a key characteristic of the growth mindset is the belief that 'you can develop yourself,' which in turn makes you 'open to accurate information about your current abilities, even if it's unflattering' (11). Good teachers, therefore, 'tell students the truth [about their abilities] and then give them the tools to close the gap' (2008: 199). Learning to learn from criticism as well as from praise is something my best writing professors taught me. Offering constructive criticism and instilling well-placed confidence in our students might be as important as teaching the craft of writing.

Anna Leahy: In her recent book about persistence and writing practice, Jordan Rosenfeld distinguishes criticism, which she defines as 'personal opinion that has little or nothing to do with you,' from critique, which she defines as 'a well-reasoned, astute approach designed to help you improve your work' (2015: 138). The highest compliment I've ever received from a colleague about my teaching is when the then-chair, a literature professor, who observed my class expressed surprise that students were comfortable telling each other what was wrong with their stories; he didn't understand why or how students openly welcomed critique.

Researcher Angela Duckworth says in her TED Talk (2009), 'Having perseverance in the face of adversity [...] setbacks, failures, that's important.' Poet Jane Hirshfield writes, 'Difficulty itself may be a path toward concentration – expended effort weaves us into a task, and successful engagement, however laborious, becomes also a labor of love. [...] Difficulty, then, whether of life or of craft, is not a hindrance to an artist' (1997: 5). Steven Johnson, in *Where Good Ideas Come From*, asserts, 'Being right keeps you in place. Being wrong forces you to explore' (2010: 137). It takes a lot of orchestration, but guiding students to embrace critique and revision may be my most important task, no matter what their futures hold. Learning failure is a life skill.

Mary Cantrell: Most of our students, even at the MFA level, won't go on to publish, so we need to think about how to serve the variety of students who take our classes and can learn from studying and practicing creative writing. I'd like to say that I was incredibly noble and *chose* not to pursue an MFA because I wholeheartedly believed in the community college mission and wanted to apply my talents to teaching the first-generation, underserved students that make up Tulsa Community College.

But, when I applied for and (I realize now but not then) lucked into a full-time teaching job, I had no idea what I was getting into. Naively, I didn't for a moment imagine that teaching five classes a semester would interfere with becoming a writer. For a while, it didn't.

Perhaps I would have been more successful as a writer had I earned an MFA. Surely, I would have had more time to write. But would I have found a better job? For me, no. My interest in writing has always been connected to my belief in social justice, and I've come to see how the community college mission squares with my personal ethos.

Anna Leahy: I taught at a community college and at a correctional facility between my MA and MFA, and that was very rewarding work, though part time. It's not always easy to do good – work toward individual and public good – in one's career, and the hierarchy in higher education is often starkly delineated.

When I finished my MFA, I mistakenly thought the PhD was merely a longer MFA instead of the more academic degree that it is. Even as I started my PhD, I wasn't sure that I wanted to teach for the rest of my life.

Rachel Hall: At Indiana University, we were told repeatedly that we wouldn't get a college teaching job if we didn't have a book published. I decided to apply for teaching jobs anyway. I must have applied to a hundred jobs – some adjunct, some temporary, some tenure track. I had three interviews, was offered one temporary position and one tenure-track position, and took the tenure-track position at SUNY Geneseo. I've been there ever since.

Anna Leahy: All four of us landed full-time academic positions before we had published books, which is surprising. The MFA alone is not usually enough to land a full-time academic position at a four-year institution. That seemed obvious to me 25 years ago. The proliferation of MFA programs since then makes it more so. I've changed my pedagogy to push them toward publishing poems and book reviews and toward building chapbook-length projects.

Mary Cantrell: Maybe we should also be pushing students toward careers that don't depend on publishing. At the 2015 Association of Writers and Writing Programs annual conference, Simone Zelitch chaired a panel called 'Creative Writing as Job Training,' which argued that we who teach creative writing need to promote it as recession-proof job training: a course of study that imparts the so-called soft skills employers say they most want from college graduates. Neal Bowers, who taught both Anna and me poetry at Iowa State University, used to say the world needs more creative writers as opposed to, say, more lawyers. A recent editorial in the *New York Times* makes his point even more relevant today: 'Forty-three percent of all 2013 law school graduates did not have long-term full-time legal jobs nine months after graduation, and the numbers are only getting worse. In 2012, the average law graduate's debt was $140,000, 59% higher than eight years earlier' ('The Law School Debt Crisis'). A degree in creative writing can result in debt and lack of employment as well, but the skills one develops through an intensive study of reading and writing translate to many possible career pathways.

Anna Leahy: We've seen articles recently that claim CEOs are looking for skills liberal arts students have or that creative thinking, strong communication and problem-solving are what employers want, and that's important to cultivate, even though the middle managers who do the hiring may not judge applicants the same way. We can and should make that case – heighten the buzz – and help our students make that case by clearly articulating their skills and experiences.

Meanwhile, because of the academic market, the PhD may now be the terminal academic degree, while the MFA is the terminal artistic degree. The value placed on each varies by hiring institution and by individual degree holder, and there exist mixed feelings about how the PhD has changed the field.

Mary Cantrell: When I served on hiring committee for a full-time position years ago, my associate dean didn't want to interview applicants with an MFA; she thought they just wanted the full-time gig so they could spend all their time writing a novel. What, I asked her, could be *less* conducive to writing a novel than teaching five sections of composition?

Rachel Hall: I never considered a PhD. In fact, I was surprised when one of my professors suggested that I'd be a good candidate for one. Now, it seems a PhD is pretty much required. We recently did a search at SUNY-Geneseo, and the number of candidates with both MFAs and PhDs was stunning.

Anna Leahy: Having the PhD helped me land a job and carries weight with colleagues. The PhD may matter especially at smaller schools and institutions without large arts programs and also with some hiring committees. When I applied to PhD programs, I didn't know this and just wanted more time to read, write and hang out with writers. Two programs accepted me, but neither offered me funding, so I deferred for a year, then was offered an assistantship. It did not occur to me to attend graduate school without full funding.

Audrey Petty: I took advantage of my three years in graduate school, with funding, to experiment. I wasn't really thinking much about being published back then, and I didn't envision myself going on to teach college. I found a tribe of fellow graduate students who'd become my close friends. Whether they were candidates in political science or architecture or fellow creative writers, being in the company of others steeped in their own disciplines and committed to their own intellectual interests – all of this was thrilling. Even as we were kicking back at a local bar, we were sharing our passions, and it was energizing. What I wanted was studio time and to be part of a vital intellectual community, and that's what I got as an MFA student.

Mary Cantrell: Years ago, I had a student in my class who had quit his full-time job managing a Quick Trip to write a bestseller, and I still worry that I didn't temper my encouragement enough.

For myriad reasons, students believe a degree in creative writing leads to tenured professor and/or published author. We know that both scenarios are unlikely. The number of part-time faculty positions increased by more than 300% between 1975 and 2011 (Curtis & Thornton, 2013: 4), as the number of tenure-track faculty declined. The publishing industry has changed dramatically, too, with everyone scrambling to adapt to the digital age, the rise of Amazon and fall of Borders and large job losses during the recent economic downturn. Isn't it incumbent upon us to help students understand the marketplace and to appreciate the other ways learning the craft of writing can benefit them?

Anna Leahy: I could have done something else; another path would have been fine. Between my MFA and PhD programs, I worked full time as a production editor for science journals. I did copyediting and layout; I even wrote a children's coloring book. I was a good editor and could still do that if I needed to. Had I not found full-time teaching (a one-year contract) just as I was finishing my PhD, I would have gone full time at The Gap, where I already was working, and probably would have written a lot more in those early years.

Most undergraduate creative writing majors will not go on to pursue an MFA. Most MFA students will not land tenure-track academic jobs. The chances of one of my students becoming a version of me are slim. AWP's annual job reports indicate that roughly 4000 individuals earn graduate degrees in creative writing each year for the roughly 100 tenure-track creative writing positions that are advertised (Flood, 2012–2013). Plus, there are last year's graduates and the year before that. Students should build a variety of skills and, even more importantly, be aware that they have marketable skills so that they can convince prospective employers of their value.

The four of us are testament that even the same starting point leads to different places. It's difficult to predict an academic career or a career as a publishing writer.

Rachel Hall: If I hadn't found a teaching job after my MFA, I planned to go into publishing. I wanted to become a professor, but I had good alternatives in mind.

Audrey Petty: Since finishing my MFA, I've been focused on teaching almost exclusively. My first position was as a Visiting Writer at Knox

College – Rachel, Anna, and I all caught that great break from our alma mater, so we share two career starting points. Later, I was tenured at the University of Illinois. When my mom became gravely ill – when she was at the end of her life – my husband and daughter and I uprooted from Urbana to be back home in Chicago, and we resettled there. I commuted to work in Urbana for a while before I eventually understood that, day-to-day, my life needed to happen in one place. I walked away from a tenured position at a major university – what some consider a dream job – because I wanted a different life for myself.

Now I'm teaching in a humanities program for high-school students on the far South Side of Chicago, collaborating with a veteran high-school teacher and several faculty from colleges and universities in Chicago to offer interdisciplinary courses about coming-of-age and migration. I was also a visiting professor at Northwestern last spring. In the summer, I taught a memoir workshop through the Prison and Neighborhood Arts Project at Stateville Prison. I'm in a good place for now, but it's not one I could have set my sights on at the beginning.

Mary Cantrell: For the last three years, I've been teaching high school seniors, too, as part of Tulsa Community College's dual enrollment program, which offers students (many of whom are first-generation, low-income students) the opportunity to earn college credits at a reduced cost at their high schools.

It's interesting that both Audrey and I found circuitous routes into a public school setting. While I have mixed feelings about the nationwide trend of offering college classes in a high-school setting, I saw an opportunity to be the kind of high-school English teacher that set me on my trajectory toward creative writing, so I signed up to teach the classes. I enjoy working with 17- and 18-year-olds without other work that burdens high-school faculty – work that no doubt contributes that high attrition rate that Anna mentions. It's difficult to encourage someone to go into public-school teaching in Oklahoma, but a teaching certification is a practical way to supplement an MFA.

Anna Leahy: I taught at a correctional facility between my MA and MFA programs, and I know other creative writers who've taught in nursing homes or libraries. Many possibilities exist for lives that combine writing and teaching, as our different paths show. Looking at me now, people probably don't see that I might have done other jobs and been happy, nor that I had several academic jobs before this one. I would have kept writing no matter what.

Mary Cantrell: People can and do balance writing, whatever their careers. The career doesn't matter as much as passion and discipline – grit – and having long-term connections with other writers. Although writing has been an awkward and sporadic fit for my adult life, I keep writing in part because of what I learned in college and graduate school, but also because I maintain friendships with talented and productive writers like the three of you. Earning a college degree, whether in business or creative writing, offers opportunities to connect with others. Maintaining those connections is as essential for writing as for any other career, maybe even more important for those of us who didn't pursue a tenure-track position at a four-year college or university.

Anna Leahy: As a student, even though I was also a teaching assistant and sometimes working part-time in retail, I didn't realize how difficult it would be to maintain regular writing and reading habits over a career. I especially have trouble writing regularly in the second half of a semester, unless I have an external deadline. That seems unsustainable now. Summers (though my new administrative position runs all year) and university breaks have become increasingly important, as have writing residencies that remove me from my usual day-to-day obligations.

Mary Cantrell: Other than writing, teaching is the only thing I do well, and the truth is, it's much easier to draft a syllabus than a story, more rewarding to read a good paper from a struggling student than a rejection letter from a great journal and, in some ways, more gratifying to hear a student's thank-you than to see my name in print. I passionately want to help the single mother of three who stays up all night revising her essay or the high school drop-out who can't comprehend the three-page editorial I've assigned or the first-generation English-language learner who sends me an incomprehensible email about her failing grade. Some days, I think about my struggling students, and writing doesn't matter at all.

Audrey Petty: When I was in graduate school and during my first years out, I worked on stories and poetry – mostly stories – at a pretty steady pace. The routine was deep. I kept a notebook, and summers made for a stretch of time to kick into a higher gear.

Since becoming a parent, my own writing projects – essays – have arisen thanks to assignments and deadlines. My most recent extended project was a book-length oral history project called *High Rise Stories.* I spent nearly three years in conversations with people who lived in high-rise public housing communities in Chicago – places that no longer exist, at least not in physical form. I was able to devote lots of time to this work because of a fellowship from University of Illinois and an extra semester on unpaid leave. The shaping of lengthy transcripts into stand-alone stories was a consuming task, one that I now recognize as a creative act.

Anna Leahy: We are more willing to expand our definitions of writing and creativity as our lives become more complex. Working on this book of conversation essays, I put aside other writing to make sure this project happens because I believe in the difference our conversations might make in the lives of others like – and maybe not so like – us.

Still, I'm anxious for that writing residency that looms in the not-too-distant future, when I can refocus on the more officially creative projects. That engagement with my own creative writing, is, more and more, what makes me the person I want to be, even as I enjoy and find reward in the other roles I play.

Rachel Hall: Fiction writing is the part of my career that is the most important to me, too. I'm a good teacher and I enjoy it, but writing is my true love. During the school year, I don't get to write as much as I'd like. Instead of finding more time after earning tenure, I've found that I have more responsibilities and obligations. I'm learning to find a balance as well as delegate. I'm still learning to say *NO*, too.

Anna Leahy: I've had a similar experience post-tenure. I've never worked harder, nor on as many disparate tasks. As I wrote in an essay for *Minerva Rising*'s blog, I like leading a life of *yes and*. It's full of experimentation, adrenaline, reward. But the curse of competence and the cult of busyness, as Barbara Erhenreich and others have termed it, are real.

In addition, a study by Misra *et al.* in 2011 defines 'The Ivory Ceiling of Service Work': '[W]omen associate professors taught an hour more each week than men, mentored an additional two hours a week, and spent nearly five hours more a week on service.' They estimate that male associate professors spend 200 more hours per year on their research. What if the four of us were writing an additional 7.5 hours every week?

Recently, I was tapped to join an institutional advisory committee on diversity that focused on women. I sent three pages of links to recent articles about gender in the academy – in relation to both faculty and student issues – but wrote, 'I can't take on any more service while my male creative writing colleagues are focusing their time on writing books. I'm terrible at saying *no*, but it's an important skill for any writer and especially for the woman writer.

Mary Cantrell: I don't say *no* often enough, either, but maybe that's because I enjoy, am challenged by, and find reward in the other roles I play. A recent article by Rivard, 'Grating Expectations' (2014) noted that our male colleagues may focus more on writing their books than we do, but males also outnumber women in leadership positions, which are often time consuming. I'm thrilled that TCC has recently hired our first female president and our first female Chief Academic Officer, a former English teacher. In every business and at every level, we need women, just as we need books published by women. The world also needs people who love and appreciate the power of language and storytelling, whatever their profession.

Audrey Petty: I'm now getting to work on a novel and will need to make new habits to advance it. Key is adhering to some sturdy system of accountability. I also must make some time for daydreaming, experimentation, exercises, play. I recently reread Lynda Barry's *What It Is* (2008), and she reminded me that play is serious business! For a short spell, the business of publishing as an academic – especially pre-tenure – gummed up the works for me. Barry's book challenges us to calm down and pay attention and to make time for writing as play.

Anna Leahy: Barry's book is incredibly playful, with drawings, surprising juxtapositions and important questions. Near the beginning, she asserts that an idea is made of 'future, present and also meanwhile.' My mindset as a writer needs to be playful, more attentive to the meanwhile.

A quick, quirky book I used in a graduate poetry workshop for this purpose is *Steal Like Artist* (2012); in it, Austin Kleon says, among other straightforward wisdom, that we should lead boring lives because that's how the work gets done. Another book whose advice is terrific to keep in mind but difficult to fully practice is *The ONE Thing* (2013); there, Gary Keller reminds readers that *priority* means *first*, which doesn't really work as a plural, and that success is built sequentially, one thing at a time. These are not writing guides, but they can be applied to the writing life. I also talk with my students about how they might put and do writing first.

Rachel Hall: I'm a better writing professor when I'm also writing. This way, I'm in touch with all the emotions that accompany writing – the struggle to find my way into a particular story or the triumph of finding the exact and exactly right phrase, the pleasures and the intense frustrations involved in writing. My writing practice benefits my students as well as me. When I'm not writing, I get crabby and become a harsher critic.

Audrey Petty: I feel the same way. And it often seems impossible for me to pull off this two-step, but when I have a deadline nipping at my heels, I deliver. Still, making space to let my mind wander and play? I easily forget that this is what I once did as habit.

Mary Cantrell: Eventually, I block time to make myself work, and, somewhere in the process, I remember that writing is, as Carolyn See insists, *fun* 'in the very highest and most profound sense' (2002: 254).

An essay about writing that was handed out in the pedagogy class that Anna and I took has stuck with me all these years. In it, Sue Lorch writes about how she came to understand the role of revision and to appreciate the difficulty of writing well. 'I lurch,' she writes. 'I shudder. I come to screeching halts only to leap forward again. I bump; I scrape; I rattle' (1985: 170). Writing is a lurching, bumpy process in which we only occasionally arrive. At the end of the piece, Lorch writes, 'I do not like to write; it is an always slow, frequently difficult, sometimes painful process. Few things, however, offer the satisfaction of having written' (1985: 171).

My educational background taught me the difficulties of writing but also the unique joy of having written, and because of this, I'll always fit writing into my life.

Anna Leahy: Really, that's what any writer must learn or teach herself and what we must instill in our students. The way to become a writer is to write, which is often difficult and without guarantee of getting anywhere in particular. The way to sustain writing – to go back to it again and again over time – is to experience the joy of writing so that you want to experience it again.

I'd like to list that as our creative writing program's only student learning outcome: to experience the joy of having written. That would be immeasurable.

References

Alliance for Excellent Education (2014) On the path to equity: Improving the effectiveness of beginning teachers. July 2014. See http://all4ed.org/wp-content/uploads/2014/07/PathToEquity.pdf (accessed 13 May 2016).

Barry, L. (2008) *What It Is.* Montreal: Drawn and Quarterly.

Barth, J. (1999) Incremental perturbation: How to know whether you've got a plot or not. In J. Checkoway (ed.) *Creating Fiction.* Cincinnati: Story Press. Print.

Curtis, J.W. and Thornton, S. (2013) Here's the News: The Annual Report on The Economic Status of the Profession, 2012–13. *Academe.* Mar./Apr. 2013.

Diaz, J. (2014) MFA vs. POC. *The New Yorker* 30 April 2014. See http://www.newyorker. com/books/page-turner/mfa-vs-poc (accessed 17 October 2015).

Duckworth, A. (2009) True grit; can perseverance be taught? TEDTalk 18 October 2009. See http://tedxtalks.ted.com/video/TEDxBlue-Angela-Lee-Duckworth-P (accessed 17 October 2015).

Dweck, C.S. (2008) *Mindset: The New Psychology of Success.* New York: Ballantine Books.

Ehrenreich, B. (1985) HERS. *New York Times. 21 February* 1985. See http://www.nytimes. com/1985/02/21/garden/hers.html.

Flood, S. 2012–2013 Annual Report on the Academic Job Market. Association of Writers and Writing Programs. See https://www.awpwriter.org/careers/career_advice_view/2926/2012-13_annual_report_on_the_academic_job_market.

Hirshfield, J. (1997) *Nine Gates: Entering the Mind of Poetry.* New York: HarperCollins.

Johnson, S. (2010) *Where Good Ideas Come From.* New York: Riverhead.

Keller, G. (2013) *The ONE Thing.* Austin, TX: Relleck.

Kleon, A. (2012) *Steal Like an Artist.* New York: Workman.

The Law School Debt Crisis. Editorial. *New York Times.* 24 Oct 2015. See http://www. nytimes.com/2015/10/25/opinion/sunday/the-law-school-debt-crisis.html.

Leahy, A. (2013) Yes and no. *Minerva Rising* blog. 26 September 2013. See http://minerva-rising.com/contributors-blog-yes-and-no-by-anna-leahy/.

Lorch, S. (1985) Confessions of a former sailor. In T. Waldrep (ed.) *Writers on Writing* (pp. 165–171). New York: Random House.

Misra, J. *et al.* (2011) The ivory ceiling of service work. *Academe* Jan./Feb. 2011. See http://www.aaup.org/article/ivory-ceiling-service-work#.VXzfwkuVM3g.

Nimrod International Journal of Prose and Poetry. See http://utulsa.edu/nimrod/index.html.

Petty, A. (2013) *High Rise Stories: Voices from Chicago Public Housing.* San Francisco: McSweeney's.

Rivard, R. (2014) Grating expectations. *Inside Higher Ed.* 24 April 2014. See https://www. insidehighered.com/news/2014/04/24/female-leaders-colleges-report-discouragement-can-be-role-models.

Rosenfeld, J. (2015) *A Winter's Guide to Persistence.* Blue Ash, OH: F+W Media.

See, C. (2002) *Making A Literary Life.* New York: Ballantine.

'Table 322.10: Bachelor's degrees conferred by post-secondary institutions.' National Center for Educational Statistics. See https://nces.ed.gov/programs/digest/d14/tables/dt14_322.10.asp (accessed 13 October 2015).

Zacharia, F. (2015) *In Defense of a Liberal Education.* New York: W.W. Norton.

Zelitch, S. (2015) Creative writing as job training. Association of Writers and Writing Programs Conference.

12 The First Book

Nicole Cooley, Kate Greenstreet, Nancy Kuhl and Anna Leahy

What does it mean to be an emerging writer? How does the first book matter? When Nicole Cooley, Kate Greenstreet, Nancy Kuhl and Anna Leahy initially formed this conversation, they had each published their first poetry books in recent years. They discovered through conversation, however, that each had different experiences getting to and through that first book publication and that each began dealing in different ways with what was next. In this chapter, each author is at a somewhat different reflective distance beyond that first book, but all feel as if they are in the process of being an *emerging* writer.

Kate Greenstreet: I understand why some people resist that label: *emerging poet*. But I had stopped writing for quite a few years, and, when I started again, it felt like emerging. Beginning to get published was another kind of coming out. In my case, the term still feels accurate.

Nancy Kuhl: I have mixed feelings about the term – on the one hand, of course, it might be said that we are all always emerging, but at what point has one *emerged*? And after emerging, then what? Has Nicole, with her third and now fourth collection, slipped or propelled herself into that other dubious category: *mid-career*? I know other terms are no better or more accurate – many who might be called emerging poets are not *new* or *young* or *beginning* – but I do wish we had a reasonable alternative. Maybe simply *first-book poets*.

Nicole Cooley: I too have mixed feeling about the term *emerging* and about the term *mid-career*. What has surprised me is that with each book – my first and second and the one I was finishing when we first had this conversation – it always feels like I'm starting over as a writer. Re-emerging each time perhaps?

Anna Leahy: Certainly, we were emerging before our first books, but, yes, the first book is a distinct career accomplishment, a benchmark of sorts. Kate, that's surely part of why you conducted more than a hundred interviews with individual poets who'd published their first books – and why you asked each poet at this stage how that first book publication changed his or her life. That term – *first-book poet* – demarcates the move from manuscript in flux to book, which I understood only in hindsight. *Ordering the Storm* is a collection of essays about putting book manuscripts together that I've used in MFA courses I've taught. While that sort of reference is helpful, the transition from manuscript to book was complicated for me.

When I finished graduate school, I sent my manuscript to a slew of contests and was occasionally heartened when I was a finalist, perhaps because well-published writers assured me that, once finalist notes arrive, it's just a matter of time. Time wore me out, and I started writing new poems that weren't easily swapped into the existing manuscript. In 2003, I read Beth Ann Fennelly's article 'The Winnowing of Wildness: On First Book Contests and Style.' I stopped submitting my manuscript. That was really difficult because submitting felt like action, and, as I've heard Nancy echo the lottery slogan, *you can't win if you don't play.* But you can't win if you don't really have a book either.

It took me at least 18 months to overhaul my collection. This time, things moved quickly. What led to the Wick Poetry Prize, I'm convinced, was an overarching theme – science metaphors and terminology – to pull the poems together into the semblance of a coherence or cohesiveness instead a pile of poems. When I began imposing that theme to try it out, it felt contrived, but I was soon able to make sense of my writing in a way that delighted me.

Nancy Kuhl: My book was also in the contest market for a while – in the five years before it found a publisher, it was a finalist or semi-finalist more than 15 times. Having the manuscript acknowledged was great, but the bottom line, of course, is that being a finalist doesn't get you any closer to the winner's circle in the next contest. It just gives you the right mix of hope and confidence to keep you sending the manuscript to more contests, paying more reading fees. I continued to make minor revisions during that time, rearranging things, adding or subtracting a poem or two, but the book didn't really change substantially.

Finally, at my husband's suggestion, I sent the manuscript to Shearsman Books in the United Kingdom. I knew Shearsman because my work had appeared in the press's magazine, and I'd admired Shearsman's list of international poets for some time. I was thrilled when the editor, Tony Frazer, told me he wanted to publish the book. As luck would have it, the manuscript was a finalist in a contest with a fat cash prize at the time; Tony graciously agreed to let me ride that out before officially committing *The Wife of the Left Hand* to Shearsman. Since the four of us first had this conversation, I've placed two more books with this press.

Kate Greenstreet: I also sent my first manuscript out for a couple of years. Nothing happened. As time passed, I reordered and improved it with new work, but eventually I just wanted to write a different book. So, while I continued to submit the first, I began a second manuscript, which became my first book, *case sensitive.*

Anna Leahy: Now that you say that you started a new manuscript, I have to admit that I wasn't really tinkering or even revamping my defunct one. I was beginning something new. But I couldn't think of *Constituents of Matter* as a different manuscript at first.

Kate Greenstreet: For me, the two manuscripts were completely separate. I didn't use anything from the first in the second. When the new one was finished, I sent it to Ahsahta Press during their 2004 open submissions period. Janet Holmes wrote to say she'd love to publish it, but couldn't do it until 2006. I was thrilled to be published by Ahsahta, so I didn't mind waiting.

A few weeks after Janet wrote, Colleen Lookingbill of Etherdome Press contacted me to ask if I had a chapbook manuscript. She'd seen two poems of mine in an online journal. Since *case sensitive* is divided into five sections meant to be the chapbooks of the protagonist, I thought: great, take your pick. But Colleen didn't want to publish a group of poems that would be part of the forthcoming book. So I decided to take apart my first manuscript, *Leaving the Old Neighborhood*, and use those poems (sometimes cut up, reworked, retitled) to make *Learning the Language*, a chapbook that Etherdome published in September 2005. *case sensitive* came out a year later. There's a two-poem overlap because I ended up using two poems from the *case sensitive* manuscript in the chapbook (not the other way around).

I approached my first two manuscripts from opposite directions. *Leaving the Old Neighborhood* grew as new poems accumulated and was never intended as anything but a collection of poems. *case sensitive,* on the other hand, began as notes for a story – I thought it might be a novel. And it was built around a fictional character, whereas the first manuscript was more autobiographical.

Nicole Cooley: My experience is somewhat like your process for *case sensitive,* I see, because I earned my MFA in fiction, but all along I was secretly writing poems. Oddly – or maybe not – I constructed the manuscript of my first book *Resurrection* as if it were a novel, envisioning my poems like chapters. Then, after a few years of writing, I laid my poems out over the floor and walked around and around and in between them, putting them in order, considering them as a book. Because my background was in fiction, I felt a great deal of freedom within my poetry. I borrowed ideas of voice and persona from fiction and worked to link my poems together as a project.

Anna Leahy: It sounds as if you had a structure – a narrative arc of sorts – as the poems were written, whereas I had to find a structure and rework.
     Of course, after the manuscript is really formed, we have to submit it.

Nicole Cooley: I have always worked hard to separate the work of writing from the work of submitting, and I try to approach all submissions in a detached way – to be businesslike and non-emotional, in so far as that is possible. The year I won the Whitman Award, I was a graduate student with a job in the law library computer lab, which meant that one or two nights a week, I sat at a computer overseeing the lab, and, since I couldn't focus enough to read or write or study in that setting, I worked on submissions to magazines and contests. I am convinced that attending to the business end of writing for so many hours a week that year helped me to move forward.
     Winning the Walt Whitman Award was amazing luck, all the more meaningful to me because, as it turned out, my first book would be published by Louisiana State University Press. I'm from New Orleans and many of the poems focused on the landscape of the Gulf Coast. This was wonderful synchronicity. I was able to give a number of readings in Louisiana and the South and to have my family and friends from the area be part of bringing my book into the world.

Anna Leahy: I felt lucky, too, even though I'd worked hard for a long time. The odds are tremendous. On the morning I left for a research vacation in 2006, I saw the e-mail asking me to call the Wick Poetry Center and knew – or hoped, but really knew – what it was. I couldn't stop smiling for two days and had to check that message several times, even after the phone call.
     Nancy had won a Wick Chapbook Prize several years earlier and had wonderful things to say about the center and then-director Maggie Anderson, so I was excited to have my book in good hands. That matters more than I'd expected, though I'm sure most poetry presses care about their books a great deal. Kent State University Press allowed me (encouraged me even) to secure

the cover art (and Lylie Fisher was generous to provide it in exchange for copies of the book), and the marketing staff sent out review copies, book contest nominations and catalogs that include *Constituents of Matter.* Library acquisitions were good as well. A weeklong residency at Kent State University – to teach a workshop, give a reading with judge Alberto Ríos and give a lecture – was part of the prize as well and a wonderful experience.

Part of my work as a poet was to usher the book to readers. I had post-cards printed and contacted acquaintances at other institutions to set up readings. And I had someone develop a website, though I've since switched to Wordpress and do most of the website management myself. This work in the wake of book publication seems trial and error and demanded more time than I'd anticipated, with somewhat unknown results.

Nicole Cooley: Louisiana State University Press is also wonderful to work with, and I was very happy with the covers they did for my books and the way they designed the books. I really enjoyed the marketing of *Resurrection* – I loved giving readings at colleges and universities, traveling by train, car, bus and plane through the South in particular. I was a graduate student at the time, so my schedule was comparatively flexible, and I could do things like take a Greyhound bus through Louisiana to different colleges for readings. It was incredibly fun.

Kate Greenstreet: My job allows me to work from home or the road, so I've been able to read all over the country, in all sorts of venues. Before *case sensitive* was published, I was extremely reclusive. I really was the kind of person who rarely left the house except to take a walk or drive to the grocery store. I'm writing this from a motel room on the other side of the country from where I live, at the beginning of a three-week tour with dates in Washington, Idaho, Montana, Wyoming, Colorado, New Mexico, Arizona and Nevada. I've done a lot of readings with my publisher, Janet Holmes, whose fourth book came out soon after my first – that's been great.

Also, Janet allowed my husband and me to design the cover of *case sensitive* (and my next books). We're designers, but we'd never done a book cover, so working with Ahsahta has been an opportunity to expand in several ways.

Anna Leahy: In her book *Making a Literary Life*, Carolyn See asserts, 'After you write your book, *you* must sell it. The three months before and after publication are just as important as the years you spend writing. [...] Nobody else cares as much as you' (2002: 220). She's talking about her experience as a fiction writer with trade publishers, but all authors face pressure to market their work. Rob Eagar's *Sell Your Book Like Wildfire* is chock-full of practical ways to form your author brand and network. He's well aware, though, that social media can be a time suck and that some of the lore about what authors must do doesn't translate into book sales. While I've become much more active in making myself visible as an author, we're not experts at marketing tasks, and this work can be exhausting.

Nancy Kuhl: Tours and travels sound exciting, and part of me is deeply envious, but another part of me is exhausted at the thought of it. My own professional work, as a rare book and manuscript curator, is not at all reclusive, and I've found that adding traveling for readings to the demands of my day job has made it increasingly difficult to find time to write. Always it is a struggle for balance, managing a challenging and intellectually stimulating job with a writing life – but any new demand, even a pleasurable one like traveling to give a reading, can easily eat into writing time. So, though I've valued the opportunity to read and especially to use readings as an opportunity to connect with poets in other parts of the country, I haven't done nearly as many as Kate or Nicole.

Thinking of all this now, how complex time management can become in the wake of the new book, I am glad that I'd already written a second manuscript and most of a third before my first book actually arrived in print. The fact of the book itself, coupled with the demands of promoting it, might have made it difficult to move on to some *next thing*. Finishing my MFA thesis, for example, left me with a sort of post-partum grief; I didn't write anything of substance for a long time. But when my first book found a home, I was already writing beyond it.

Anna Leahy: Though I worked on other kinds of writing, like scholarly essays on Natasha Trethewey's poetry, it was almost a year after the book acceptance that I was able to think about a new manuscript and again start writing new poems with any regularity. And I have to admit that I went back to my defunct first manuscript to salvage at least a section as a foundation for some *next thing*.

I wonder whether we, at times, need ruminating or shoring up – more positive phrases than *writer's block* – in order to move on with creative work. In a *Scientific American Mind* article entitled 'Unleashing Creativity' (2005), which I read years ago but which stuck with me, Ulrich Kraft points out, 'the brain [continues] to work on a problem once it has been supplied with the raw materials.' He goes on to write, 'A little relaxation and distance changes the mind's perspective on a problem – without us being aware of it. This change of perspective allows for alternative insights and creates the preconditions for a fresh, and perhaps more creative, approach.'

I wonder, too, whether seeing individual poems as potentially part of a book even before I'd written them – since now one book exists, and I surely want another – created a sort of block. Neurologist Alice Flaherty, in the somewhat unsettling *The Midnight Disease: The Drive to Write, Writer's Block, and the Creative Brain*, claims that writer's block may 'stem less from emotional problems than from deficits in cognitive skills,' 'too-early editing' or 'hard projects' (2004: 88). It was difficult for me not to let the idea of *book* overwhelm the idea of *poem*.

Once I sat down with a bunch of old and new poems to see what's what, I felt better. Rearranging and revising a few existing poems created the drive to write new ones. I wrote a lousy set in fixed forms that prepared me to write a crown of sonnets about moving west, some sections of which have been published. Then I began a sequence in a historical persona that excited me and, only recently, several years later, was published as a chapbook.

Kate Greenstreet: I had the urge to write a book-length poem for a while before I finished *case sensitive*. It began to come to me in pieces as I was working on the final edits – I had five or six pages by the time I submitted *case sensitive* to Ahsahta Press. I worked on it for a couple more years before I felt it was finished. That manuscript, called *The Last 4 Things*, was published by Ahsahta in 2009.

Anna Leahy: For those of us who win first-book prizes, it's terrific. But my press publishes only books through that contest, so I can't place my next full-length collection there. Poetry publishers don't necessarily keep publishing a poet for the length of a career, though some presses do that to great effect. *Oh, there's Nancy Kuhl; she's a Shearsman poet. Ah, yes, Kate Greenstreet is an Ahsahta poet.* That's a mutually beneficial relationship built on aesthetics, trust and, yes, branding.

Kate Greenstreet: As we built this conversation initially, I was working on a new manuscript (which became *Young Tambling,* published by Ahsahta in 2013). I'd started it before *The Last 4 Things* was finished – that's just the way it seems to happen for me. But the time and energy I've given to promotion does interfere with the progress of new work. I'm not able to write much on the road. So when I'm on a reading tour, I look forward to being at home again and back to writing.

Nancy Kuhl: Writing my new manuscripts was really different from writing *The Wife of the Left Hand.* My writing process has changed and evolved from the period when I wrote the bulk of my first book – I was less settled in some ways, then, in terms of jobs, graduate school and those sorts of regular life pursuits. So while sometimes I had virtually no time to write (when I was full time in library school and working two jobs, for instance), and other times I had much more flexibility (in my first few years out of library school, when I rarely had any reason to take work home or even think about work after hours). Now that I have my current job, one which isn't strictly 9–5, everything is different. For the first couple years, I was working so intensely that I had little time for serious writing. Once I felt more comfortable in my professional position, I knew that I had to figure out a way to fit writing into my life in a more substantial way. So I started applying for grants and fellowships and ended up with a residency at the Vermont Studio Center and, later, the MacDowell Colony. That VSC residency was, I think, the first time I really devoted myself completely to writing – even as a graduate student I had the distractions of classes and grading student papers. During the writing residency, I was able to be really productive, but what was more significant was that I also developed some serious momentum and the motivation to restructure things in my life a bit to make more room for writing.

Anna Leahy: Writing residencies have become an integral part of my life. It'd be great if I maintained a daily writing habit, no matter the point in the semester or whether my administrative tasks increase. But I've come to terms with the reality that that's not the only way to be a writer. Vermont Studio Center was my first residency, too, followed by Ragdale a few years later, and I now sometimes spend time at Dorland Mountain Arts Colony, which, thankfully, has no wifi. These places alter reality; we are removed from our daily routines, and the space is designed to foster and validate our art making. Writing space and mindset can matter to what we allow ourselves to risk and accomplish.

Nicole Cooley: After I finished my first book, I wanted to do something completely and utterly different for my second project. But despite that impulse, I found it hard to execute. I recalled the ideas I talked about in class with my creative writing students. I always tell them you have to try to write the poem that you don't feel capable of writing, the project you feel will be too difficult, too hard to take on. And at the same time, you have to shake up all your ideas about poetry whenever you write a new poem.

At the time, my husband and I had put huge pieces of paper up all over the walls of our apartment. This was my way of radically altering my writing space and escaping the smallness of a poem on a single sheet of paper or a computer screen. And so I started writing on that paper, and returning to my childhood fascination with the Salem Witch Trials. This led to my second book – *The Afflicted Girls* – which focused on the trials and took me into many different worlds.

I was fortunate to spend a summer at The American Antiquarian Society in Worcester, Massachusetts, researching the book. The AAS offers fellowships for creative artists. There, I met historians, literary scholars, descendants of people involved in the trials and genealogists who knew and researched Salem. The sustained time to research was a joy, and the broadening of my circle of readers was also a true pleasure. Most of all, working on this new project challenged me as a writer because it raised new questions, about history and voice, that I had not considered fully before.

In fact, I continued to explore this line of questioning in my more recent book, *Breach*, which focuses on Hurricane Katrina and its aftermath. I believe that each project should be completely different from the last, but, at the same time, each one leads you to the next, provides a kind of stepping stone.

Anna Leahy: All of us are, then, continually *re-emerging*, for, as we approach anything akin to mastery, we move on to new challenges. While a first book may not demarcate mastery, it has, for each of us, signified a step or benchmark that allowed us both to understand what we had already written and to discover what's next. As Robert Frost wrote in 'The Figure a Poem Makes', 'For me the initial delight is in the surprise of remembering something I didn't know I knew.'

Before the first book is out, it seems a goal; in hindsight, it seems a motivation.

References

Eagar, R. (2012) *Sell Your Book Like Wildfire*. Blue Ash, OH: F + W Media.

Fennelly, B.A. (2003) The Winnowing of Wildness: On first book contests and style. *The Writer's Chronicle* October/November 2003 (accessed 7 October 2015 via AWP member website).

Flaherty, A. (2004) *The Midnight Disease: The Drive to Write, Writer's Block, and the Creative Brain*. New York: Houghton Mifflin.

Frost, R. (1972) The figure a poem makes. In E.C. Lathem and L. Thompson (eds) *Poetry & Prose* (pp. 393–396). New York: Holt, Rinehart and Wilson.

Greenstreet, K. (2015) First Book Interviews. See http://www.kickingwind.com/interviews.html (accessed 15 November 2015).

Grimm, S. (ed.) (2006) *Ordering the Storm: How to Put Together a Book of Poems*. Cleveland, OH: Cleveland State University Poetry Center.

Kraft, U. (2005) Unleashing creativity. *Scientific American Mind* 16 (1), 16–23 (accessed 7 October 2015 via EBSCO).

See, C. (2002) *Making a Literary Life: Advice for Writers and Other Dreamers*. New York: Random House.

13 Taking the Stage, Stage Fright, Center Stage: Careers Over Time

Karen Craigo and Anna Leahy

The process of aging as a writer and as a teacher is rarely discussed. The paths and paces of our careers, including the ways in which success does and does not change our lives, vary from individual to individual. 'I often find myself downplaying the difficulties of my career path,' novelist Christine Sneed writes in an article at *The Billfold*. She goes on, 'Students want to hear success stories, overnight success stories, if possible, ones where young writers are showered, in short order, with awards and piles of money.' Karen Craigo and Anna Leahy are both poets in the middle of their careers – or at least situated somewhere between youth and old age – not fresh out of an MFA program and with, they hope, more opportunities ahead. The word *career* comes from the Latin for road, which were carriageways with tracks. A set path. Later, the word came to suggest running at full speed, perhaps on a set path but with risk of careening off course. Most creative writing careers, however, develop somewhat circuitously and seldom at full speed from the writer's perspective, as an overnight success might easily take a decade or more.

Karen Craigo: I'm only 46, but sometimes I feel like the oldest living poet. When I hit 40 and realized I was no longer eligible for a prestigious younger poets prize, it seemed as if I should either hang it up (after all, Jesus and John Keats had both done their best work years younger) or else wait a bit until I could fully embrace my identity as the Grandma Moses of the poetry world. The ageism in our field is discouraging. Since then, the prize in question relaxed its age requirement. Now, I'm just an older younger poet, it would appear!

Anna Leahy: As we write this, I'm turning 50, a traditional time to look back and reflect on how I ended up where I am, especially because I didn't have this planned.

By the time I graduated from college, I knew I wanted to be a writer, but I didn't yet understand how a person went about doing such a thing, except in the moment of writing, and I wasn't very good at planning long term. After a semester working retail, I headed off to Iowa State University to earn an MA. I thought of it as two more years of working with other writers and reading critically. As an undergraduate, I'd barely spoken in class, so, even with training in how to teach first-year composition, I didn't think of myself as a future professor. I wouldn't have gone to graduate school without full funding, and, through my MFA and most of my PhD, I didn't think of teaching as anything more than the efficient way to pay for school.

Karen Craigo: Like a lot of writers, I can't remember a time when I wasn't scribbling in my notebook, dotting my 'i's with smileys. I got very serious about writing, very quickly, when I was an undergraduate in a class taught by Michelle Boisseau, the lead author of the textbook *Writing Poems*. Michelle was (and still is) a natural teacher, someone who could point at your overwrought rainbow image and get you laughing at yourself. There was no looking back after she set me on a proper poetic path.

I majored in English and journalism, and I was a reporter for several years between my undergraduate and graduate training. I loved the work, and, while the pay was small as professional wages go, it was awfully hard to leave it for a graduate student's stipend. I taught composition as a graduate student, and I had a talent for it and an interest, so I kept going, accepting a full-time composition instructorship upon graduation. I've been doing the teaching thing ever since, and I really enjoy it – the students, the lifestyle, the workplace.

Anna Leahy: I was 28 years old when I finished my MFA at the University of Maryland. It never crossed my mind, with only a few publications to my name then, to apply for teaching positions. I applied to a few PhD programs because I thought, naively, that the PhD would be like another MFA – more writing time with guidance. Two programs accepted me, but neither offered me an assistantship, so I deferred enrollment at one to see whether money would come through the following year.

So, after my MFA, I became a journal production editor for the Entomological Society of America. I'm good at editorial and production work, probably more consistently so than at poetry writing or teaching; it's demanding but straightforward work for me. I could have done that sort of

204 Part 5: Careers

work forever. Very few of my peers then or my graduate students now articulate that kind of path, though I'm not sure why, for editorial work seems more closely related to writing than does teaching or being a professor.

Karen Craigo: Part of that may be age and one's lack of ability to plan ahead or consider alternatives to a presumed norm. I remember feeling really old in my MFA program. I turned 30 there, and I recall taking two big boxes of cupcakes to class with me on my birthday. The cupcakes got all shuffled and banged around, and they didn't look very appetizing by the time I schlepped them across campus, so I ended up eating most of them myself, happy-birthday-to-me.

Most of my peers were fresh out of their undergrad institutions, and the difference between 22 and 29 felt huge, perhaps because a truly important career as a reporter had happened in the interim for me. I could not eye-roll hard enough when my peers complained about how busy they were, teaching a composition class and taking a few graduate classes. Let's just say that reporters are somewhat busier than that.

Anna Leahy: Taking and teaching classes while working retail part time wasn't very demanding, at least not from my perspective now. That said, the MFA program is a heightened situation.

All writers must grapple with the balance between self-confidence and self-doubt, and the MFA brings together a bunch of people at roughly the same stage of doing that. In 'A Mini-Manifesto' fiction writer George Saunders calls the MFA program 'a pretty freaky but short-term immersion' (2014: 8). Each individual is 'doing it to get a little baptism by fire' (2014: 8). I found the MFA especially intense as an individual because I was hanging out with a bunch of other writers going through the same two-year fire, though *fire* may be the wrong metaphor, because I had a lot of fun and, as you point out, had a lot of control over my schedule. But I was working through some heady notions and challenging myself as a writer and as a person – and my professors pushed me, too. Maria Adelman describes the MFA this way: 'We were bound together, like a congregation or an AA group, by something more powerful than ourselves – not the degree or even the writing, but the craving to create our own terms' (2014: 45). In my experience, which is now pretty dated, that included commiserating over beer at a local watering hole – not an ideal AA group – about writing and especially about teaching. I started growing up as a writer and as a teacher, and the MFA environment shaped that growth a lot.

Karen Craigo: I rather miss the commiseration, even though it seemed like bullshit commiseration at the time. Life wasn't hard, teaching for 150 minutes per week and having a stack of papers every two weeks. But it was clear that we were in the trenches together, navigating identities as *writers-and* (since no poet I know has the luxury of being *only* a writer) and generally giving ourselves permission to move through the world as artists.

Anna Leahy: For many, the MFA program is mostly a comfortable place compared to the so-called real world of family who think writing is fun or easy. Editors don't critique like a workshop conversation. But I sensed what Saunders says: 'There is something gross about a culture telling a bunch of people who are never going to be artists that they maybe are, even if only by implication' (2014: 11). That raises the stakes, if you recognize that it's really on you, not the program or pedigree. The MFA was a way to give myself a chance to become a writer, but that immersion also helped me understand how slim the odds were. That was two years of figuring out how I might thrive as a writer, with a lot of guidance and camaraderie.

And then you graduate; you leave and are alone to write. I stuck with it, but some really terrific writers don't.

Karen Craigo: When you leave a writing program, you can feel conflicted, calling yourself a poet when you don't have a book or very many significant publication credits. After I graduated, I became a full-time, non-tenure-track faculty member at the place where I got my degree, and I was doing well – fully a member of the writing community, a founding member of the faculty union, one of the first non-tenure track faculty members to serve on the faculty senate. Since unionization, my old colleagues have become permanent lecturers, instead of contract-to-contract instructors, and that would have been my fate, too – a small step up.

Anna Leahy: There's probably the assumption that someone like me, who now has tenure and even a fancy administrative title, waltzed straight into this situation. The last year of my PhD, I was finishing my dissertation, teaching a couple of classes as an adjunct at branch campuses and working at The Gap. I didn't have a book, so I started interviewing for full-time editorial positions and talked with my store manager about going full time. By then, I was a much better teacher and invested in how pedagogy could work, but I'm glad it didn't occur to me to piece together part-time teaching after earning my degree. Luckily, a former professor at my undergraduate alma mater called very late that spring to offer me a one-year position because their poet was moving to a new job.

After that, I landed a three-year position at a private college outside Chicago, which I left after a year for a tenure-track position at a state university in Missouri. These early positions were a great transition for me, as I learned how to be a better teacher in different courses with different types of students and also learned how different institutions function. I returned to the suburban college in a tenure-track position and stayed for several years but, eventually, looked for an institution that better encouraged my professional ambitions and varied interests. I was willing to relocate and had won a poetry book prize; these things gave me options. I was almost 10 years out of graduate school then.

That first year back on the job market, I had seven MLA interviews and no on-campus follow-ups. I felt more seasoned but probably without that excitement or energy that I'd had eight years earlier, that other – perhaps younger or perhaps more well-published – candidates conveyed. The second year on the market, I had fewer MLA interviews but several on-campus interviews. My dream job, though, went to an inside candidate that year. I'd done well; one professor there hugged me good-bye. I landed a different job. The timeframe meant that the top candidates hadn't panned out, and you'd think I'd have been bummed that I was the backup, but that gave me a nego-tiating edge. And this current job has been amazing for my professional growth, seven years and counting.

Karen Craigo: Everything was going well for me at Bowling Green State University for several years, and unionization meant that my job was going to get even better. A few years ago, I moved, though, to Missouri, and I started working at a small liberal arts institution. It was one I'd never heard of, and I honestly don't expect it to be around in 10 years because it's in an administrative and budgetary tailspin.

It's worth noting that the institution where you work matters, especially in the current climate, with some institutions failing and others moving toward a more commercial model. Faculty can be worked pretty hard in an unhealthy institution, and that leaves little time for one's art. At the outset, though, at my little university, things were going well, and my chair and I had hopes that I would move over to the tenure track after a few successful years there. There was a lot of recent precedent for this kind of move, and we felt confident.

What ended up happening, though, is that my contract was non-renewed after three years to save some money. I'm now teaching as an adjunct at three other universities in the area as I try to get my freelance writing and editing career off the ground. Wish me luck – I'm trying to be optimistic, but this all feels a little like a step backward.

Poet Amy Woolard said something interesting in a recent interview in *Bull City Review* (reprinted in *The Atlantic*). When asked how her work affects her writing, she replied, '[W]henever you have to perform a couple of different identities within your life, each is affected by the other in some way. My job provides a nice counter-balance to the anything-goes world of poems – it's still a persuasion-based job, but definitely in a rational, intellectual, responsible, real-world sort of way' (qtd. in Bassett, 2013). Woolard is an attorney in a nonprofit, so there's a useful distance between her day job and writing. That distance shrinks when you're teaching nine classes and reading rough drafts, final drafts and revisions of 900 papers over the course of 16 weeks. Our work life matters. We need to choose and shape it carefully.

Anna Leahy: What a strange word: *non-renewed*. Like *untruth*, an attempt to not say the distasteful thing as you're saying it.

I look back at my career and think of numerous times when I expected to fall backwards, but then something clicked at the right time and I fell forward. I've worked hard, so I'm not going to brush off my success by saying that it was mere luck.

You've done everything as well as anybody; you've built a great career, and institutional circumstances kicked your butt anyway. I look at recent MFA alums who are thrilled to get a few courses here and there as adjuncts, who haven't established careers like yours as a writer, a teacher and an editor, and they probably have hopes that they'll be hired full time somewhere anyway. A career is incredibly unpredictable, and the odds in a poetry book contest or on the academic job market are terrible. Few who don't work really hard succeed in an academic career, but you can work hard as a writer and as a teacher and not catch the break at the right time.

Karen Craigo: The most significant danger is that we age out of teaching, of course. We don't often note this about academia, but it seems to me to be an incredibly ageist field. At the instructor level in particular, the workforce is young; people either find a tenure-track job or they leave for a more lucrative, less demanding position outside of academia. I remember being a very young instructor and witnessing how my older colleagues were received – they weren't always taken seriously, they weren't youthful, the bulk of their training was in the past – and I made an inward vow not to be seen that way, if I could help it. I would keep current on research, I would be energetic in committee work, I would mix and mingle with my younger colleagues. I knew it would be important to, say, cover the gray.

To put it plainly, I've sat on hiring committees and heard those dangerous phrases uttered: *He has a lot of energy. She brings lots of new ideas.* All of this is code for youth, of course.

Anna Leahy: The ageism is gendered, too. As a graduate student sitting on a search committee, I pointed out that it was inappropriate to ask the middle-aged female candidate in the final group what her husband did and whether he was willing to move. Some of the faculty didn't understand why that question wasn't fair, and I felt like the troublemaker my parents raised me to be. Too many members of search committees don't understand what it means to discuss a candidate's hairdo and fashion choices as well as where the candidate is in her reproductive years.

Being too old undercuts a person, but being young works against a woman, too. She can lack *gravitas,* a word I heard when I served on a search committee at a previous institution, code for masculine confidence – a body that takes up space, a deep voice, a speaking style that doesn't qualify itself. An article in *Inside Higher Ed* a few years ago reported research on job recommendation letters that suggests praise like *nurturing, communal, supportive,* which are more often used to describe women, work against female candidates. Agentive language like *ambitious* and *independent* work better for both genders in recommendation letters but are more common in letters written for men, regardless of the gender of the letter writer (Jaschik).

Even though she'd planned her schedule around my birth, my mother had to sit out for a semester of law school because she revealed to the dean that she was pregnant; he probably didn't think she'd come back and definitely made it clear that she'd taken the spot of a man who wouldn't be stepping out of his career to raise children. That attitude, that suspicion that women will be distracted from their work, lingers even 50 years later, perhaps in subtler ways.

Karen Craigo: Kids *can* be distracting, like any aspect of life that you care about. I had a son when I was 38 – mature enough to do the job with a clear and level head, but maybe without some of a younger woman's verve. Particularly until you send them to school, they're a full-time and relentless job. Academia is accommodating, though, because it offers flexibility, especially in terms of day-to-day schedule. You just have to save a little compassion for the people whose onesies you're not snapping into place 10 times a day, and that can be a challenge. I know how to do that; I have the experience and maturity to handle having it all, as they say.

Anna Leahy: I don't have children. That decision was the accumulation of other decisions and a vague attitude of *not yet.* I didn't earn tenure until I was 45. At that age, chance of getting pregnant with your own eggs is 1% and the risk of Down Syndrome is one in 30. *Not yet* was always the right decision for me. Surely, the way we, especially women, negotiate and pace our careers – as well as our daily and weekly schedules – depends on when and whether we have children and also on aging parents.

Karen Craigo: It's very dangerous at my age to find myself out of academic work, because the new-ideas crowd is hungry, is more physically attractive and gets higher evaluations from students. What would I need to get a tenure-track job now? Probably a couple of books and prestigious grants – maybe a doctorate, although the hell with that, at this stage of my life.

Anna Leahy: I wonder whether, even though my PhD suggests intellectual maturity, aging – my gray hair, my new wrinkles, my general lack of being hip to the latest music and gadgets – suggests that I'm over the hill, that my intellect might have reached its peak several years ago and it's all downhill now.

Karen Craigo: Maybe. A PhD is an appropriate terminal degree for someone with a deep interest in research, and an MFA is an appropriate terminal degree for a practicing artist. Obviously, of course, people with doctorates can make art, and people with MFAs can do research, too. Does my MFA suggest artistic maturity? It should. At one time it may have, before the PhD in creative writing became the degree to get. Let's face it – the economy tanked, and people took shelter in universities, since professional positions were hard to come by. It has started to change the landscape, and it's a dangerous world for people with MFAs when doctorates become the norm. I believe in the MFA as a terminal degree, and that's a position that the Association of Writers and Writing Programs supports as well. I can hear the clock ticking, though.

Anna Leahy: The doctorate drew me back into the academy after my MFA; otherwise, I would have kept doing editorial work. Also, the PhD carries weight with administrators. That suburban college was leery of the MFA as a terminal degree. In addition, the percentage of PhDs is sometimes one little factor in rankings, so smaller institutions tend to value it more.

When I was hired in my current position, I joined three male creative writing colleagues, two of whom were long tenured and held PhDs and one of whom was well published and had taught here for decades with an MA. The PhD was a credential that helped me carve out respect.

For a long time, my father said that he was glad to have served his requisite two years in the Army because it built his character but that he'd never do it again. I feel similarly about the PhD. Or, as Saunders says in his manifesto about the MFA, 'If someone wants to go to a CW program, then goes to a CW program and it sucks, she probably won't die from it' (2014: 8).

The PhD prepared me for the career I ended up with; I ended up with a career built on a PhD. I learned a lot, but I wouldn't put up with those four years at this stage of my life. The MFA, teaching experience, publication record – that's a good fit for most full-time positions in creative writing.

Karen Craigo: The PhD was, and is, out for me. I don't care to focus on research; I want to be an artist. I'll take my licks in the academy. I suppose I could dye my hair and lose some weight and smile like it's some kind of beauty pageant. On my very best day, however, I don't really rise above fetching or maybe cute.

I'm a serious academic who is dedicated to my students and who publishes frequently, but I don't have anything approaching gravitas. Honestly, I make the dimpled mom thing work for me. I make a comfortable and caring environment for my students, and I project a quirky artsy persona, too, but, aside from a streak of natural fierceness, I doubt *serious* is the first adjective that comes to mind when colleagues or students describe me. I'm dead serious about poetry and writing, but I approach it in a loose, artistic, collaborative, creative way and try to keep it fun. It works for me. Screw gravitas. We all have different styles.

Anna Leahy: That variety of styles is incredibly important to the vitality of the larger field and part of why I structured this book as conversation essays.

Recently, at her retirement party, a well-respected administrator and rhetoric-composition scholar joked that she had used swearing as a management style. Both she and my mother understood that, in some circumstances, the label *bitch* might be worn with pride by a woman of a certain level of accomplishment.

When I started my current job, I was 42 years old. I didn't feel old; I was ready for the next stage in my career, as if I were at the beginning. Recently, I heard a female colleague with a combination staff-faculty position say that she's been advised to find the job she wants by the time she's 45. Otherwise, especially for women, you're stuck. My book publication came at exactly the right time for my academic career – it allowed me to switch jobs and earn tenure in a job I like by the time I was 45. I don't think I was ready for this type of job 20 years ago when I finished my MFA. I certainly hadn't published much.

Karen Craigo: I was racking up a few publications – good ones – before I entered graduate school, and that was unusual, at the time. My first poem was published in a journal called *Farmer's Market* when I was 25 or so. I felt like I'd won the lottery.

Anna Leahy: *Farmer's Market* was my first publication, too, and I was just about that age. That journal was based in Galesburg, Illinois, so I knew the editor from when I'd been an undergraduate – connections matter and also don't matter one whit when it comes to getting published. Having a poem published in a legitimate national journal helped me validate my decision to move halfway across the country to study poetry for two years.

Suddenly, having run into you here and there in person and online over the years, we've discovered that our careers – at least as publishing poets – launched from exactly the same point.

Karen Craigo: I love knowing that about you! I was a very busy reporter in a small town when that publication happened, and I was feeling more and more removed from my writing self. Sure, I could write three or more front-page stories a day about the shenanigans of the county commissioners, but I knew that I had work in me that was more permanent than the news, which is irrelevant after a day. Getting published meant that someone outside of my town of five thousand believed I had something to say.

Around the same time as that first publication, I wrote a fan letter to the poet William Matthews, and I told him what his work meant to me. He actually replied with a postcard, and it included this most thrilling sentence: 'A reporter is to a small town what a poet is to the language.' That one beautiful throwaway sentence from Matthews made everything click – it made sense of my life and gave focus to my efforts.

Anna Leahy: That story gives me goose bumps. Careers are made of such moments.

When I was finishing my PhD, I'd started sending out a chapbook and a book manuscript to contests. A friend and I had started getting finalist nods, but we'd become discouraged. We were commiserating about our shared circumstance and ran into the writer Bill Roorbach, who told us that, once you were a finalist, it was only a matter of time. That one comment kept me going, even though it'd be another nine years before my book was published.

Karen Craigo: Hello, my name is Karen, and I'm an emerging writer. I also did the thing where you send off your crappy master's thesis and call it a book manuscript, but generally it's not, and that worked about as well as you would expect. Then I had a dry spell for a long time – to be honest, a few unkind words from people close to me made me doubt my authenticity and lose faith in myself for several years – but I came back swinging, writing a bunch and forming a new manuscript. I will be 47 when my first full-length poetry book is published – it was just accepted, and that brought me such joy. That finally hit this year, and it made me feel, well, *real*.

I've published a lot in journals; I've been in *Poetry* and other distinguished magazines. Maybe I'm emerging, maybe not. I do think the word *emerging* is usually reserved for a writer in her thirties (or younger) at the time that first full-length book is released. Publishers love discovering younger writers and propelling them onto the scene, especially if they can muster up an attractive photo and some sexy work. Robin Black's excellent essay in *The New York Times*, 'What's So Great About Young Writers?' suggests prizes that discriminate against writers over a particular (young) age, 35 or 40, link reward to existing privilege. Black writes, 'Not everyone can afford to write when young. Some are already working more than one job.' (That was me.) 'Others are raising children, as I was for many years. Still others may not feel safe expressing themselves, for any number of reasons.' Black was an emerging writer in her late forties, like me, and she shares my sense that such prizes should be based on stage, not age. She puts it succinctly: 'Emerging writers are emerging writers.'

Anna Leahy: I look back on that process of evolving thesis to book – nine years – and wonder what I was thinking. The manuscript that won the Wick Poetry Prize was certainly not the one I'd sent out years earlier, and I had taken some years away from submitting as I rethought it entirely. And after nine more years, I don't have a second full-length collection out, even though I've been getting finalist nods these last two years and have a chapbook just out. Am I still emerging, was that first book a false start or am I stuck?

Carolyn See, in her book *Making a Literary Life*, encourages readers to make rejection a process. Oh great, it's not an event; instead, it goes on and on. She calls this process 'cosmic badminton' (2002: 100). (Badminton was the one sport in which I held my own in high school gym class.) That sort of patience we have must look insane to non-writers.

Karen Craigo: We all hit milestones at a different point in life – I have a two-year-old, for Christ's sake. The poems come when they come – and when we have time to receive them.

Of course, getting that second book out? Well, now that's another thing altogether. I know many poets whose second-book manuscripts gather dust because there just aren't as many opportunities for them. Most prizes are first-book prizes. There are even some prizes for either first or second books. Got a third book? You're on your own, sister.

Anna Leahy: Young. New. First. What excitement!

In her book about persistence, Jordan Rosenfeld argues that there's a time to walk away: 'So don't waste your time lamenting the doors that haven't opened or never will' (2015: 66). She rightly points out that we can put more energy into our writing projects, but 'What you can't control is everything else: people's decisions, approval, or willingness to take a chance; timing; and who got there "first"' (2015: 66). Maybe I *should* walk away. I've definitely hedged my poetry bets with creative nonfiction, scholarship and even a little fiction.

Dani Shapiro, in her book about writing, writes, 'Unlike other artists – dancers, sculptors, or cellists, say – as long as we hold onto our faculties, writers can continue to grow creatively until we die. The middle of the writing life is much like being in the midst of a book itself. Here we often discover our weaknesses and strengths' (2013: 93). Many novelists talk about being stuck in the middle of a book, but maybe life is a story too. Maybe I'm stuck in the middle but tumbling toward old age. Chuck Wendig, though, offers '25 Ways to Fight Your Story's Mushy Middle,' starting with, 'Fuck the three-act structure [...].' Maybe a writer-professor's career doesn't work on the premise of a beginning, middle and end. Or as Mr. Rogers said, 'Often when you think you're at the end of something, you're at the beginning of something else.'

Does a long, hard, messy middle go on and on as long as we need it? Somehow, the process sustains us, whether or not the next book is published in a timely manner. I'm actually more excited about my career now than when my book came out.

Karen Craigo: A writer's perspective broadens with age (and with reading), but the writing itself only benefits for as long as our faculties are intact. Stanley Kunitz published his last book in 2005 when he was 100! I don't really buy into the complaints of some writers who say that the publishing game favors the young – not much, anyway. It's clear that some journals have graduate student staffs, and it can be hard for a certain quiet poem to hit the mark with them, but there are a lot of magazines, and good work will find a home.

There's no sense in the poetry world insisting, as does the broader world, on a culture of youth. As I mentioned, I don't like ageism on the lower end – younger poets prizes, residencies for emerging poets under age 40, that kind of thing – but I don't like it on the upper end, either, although it is arguably more necessary to have special opportunities for writers who are over 50. Let's focus on the work, shall we?

Anna Leahy: Malcolm Gladwell, in an article called 'Late Bloomers,' writes of Ben Fountain's rise to fame as a writer and asserts that it was an arduous

18-year route to the big break. Gladwell (2008) also summarizes economist David Galenson's research that argues, 'Some poets do their best work at the beginning of their careers. Others do their best work decades later. Forty-two percent of Frost's anthologized poems were written after the age of fifty. For [William Carlos] Williams, it's 44 percent. For [Wallace] Stevens, it's 49 percent.' I wish he'd included women poets, too.

Shapiro recalls – and this rings true in my own observations of friends from writing programs and my students – that the most talented and the most quickly successful are not necessarily the writers who stick with it. The writers who do sustain a writing life 'have learned that there is no brass ring. That we can never know how it's going to turn out. That the race is not to the swiftest' (2013: 191).

Karen Craigo: Being a writer is about a few things. It's about having something to say and an interest in saying it distinctly. It's about having time – time to learn and hone your craft, whether by reading or formal study, and time to write and revise. It's about developing the mind and spirit, and feeling wonder at the evolution of understanding. One could argue that being older is of tremendous benefit to a poet, although I'd be cautious about that kind of sweeping statement. I love many young poets, and I marvel at their creations.

When we arrive, poetically, varies from writer to writer. Sometimes I think I am continually arriving and departing – getting it and losing it, and getting the barest glimpse of it again. We emerge in poetry time, which is not the same as clock or calendar time. I'm going to enjoy being the new kid on the block next year, as my new book comes out somewhere between Mother-May-I and menopause. I've waited a long time to begin.

Anna Leahy: We haven't used the words *finish;* we haven't laid out our retirement plans here – that's telling.

References

Adelman, M. (2014) Basket weaving 101. In C. Harback (ed.) *MFA vs. NYC* (pp. 41–49). New York: Faber and Faber.

Association of Writers and Writing Programs. AWP Guidelines for Creative Writing Programs & Teachers of Creative Writing. AWP. See https://www.awpwriter.org/guide/directors_handbook_guidelines_for_creative_writing_programs_and_teachers_of_creative_writing (accessed 13 May 2016).

Bassett, W. (2013) What's the ideal day job for a poet? *The Atlantic* 4 November. Web. 30 Oct. 2015. See http://www.theatlantic.com/entertainment/archive/2013/11/whats-the-ideal-day-job-for-a-poet/281081/ (accessed 30 October 2015).

Black, R. (2015) What's so great about young writers?' *The New York Times* 24 April. See http://www.nytimes.com/2015/04/25/opinion/whats-so-great-about-young-writers.html.

Boisseau, M. (2011) *Writing Poems* (8th edn). New York: Longman.

Gladwell, M. (2008) Late bloomers: Why do we equate genius with precicity? *The New Yorker* 20 October. See http://www.newyorker.com/magazine/2008/10/20/late-bloomers-2.

Jaschik, S. (2010) Too nice to land a job. *Inside Higher Ed.* 10 November. See www.insidehighered.com/news/2010/11/10/letters (accessed 25 November 2015).

Rogers, F. (2003) *The World According to Mr. Rogers.* New York: Hachette.

Rosenfeld, J. (2015) *A Writer's Guide to Persistence.* Blue Ash, OH: F + W Media.

Saunders, G. (2014) A mini-manifesto.' *MFA vs. NYC.* Ed. Chad Harbach. New York: Faber and Faber, 2014: 31-38.

See, C. (2002) *Making a Literary Life: Advice for Writers and Other Dreamers.* New York: Random House.

Shapiro, D. (2013) *Still Writing: The Perils and Pleasures of a Creative Life.* New York: Grove.

Sneed, C. (2015) Publish a book and change your life, or, well, maybe not. *The Billfold* 24 June. See http://thebillfold.com/2015/06/publish-a-book-and-change-your-life-or-well-maybe-not/.

Southern California Center for Reproductive Medicine. Age & Fertility Infographic. Newport Beach, CA: Southern California Center for Reproductive Medicine. See http://www.socalfertility.com/age-and-fertility-infographic.

Wendig, C. (2012) 25 Ways to fight your story's mushy middle. TerribleMindsblog. See http://terribleminds.com/ramble/2012/06/05/25-ways-to-fight-your-storys-mushy-middle/.

Part 6
Conclusions

14 Political, Practical and Philosophical Considerations for the Future

Anna Leahy

What We Talk about When We Talk about Creative Writing covers a lot of ground, focusing on pedagogy, programs and the profession, including career trajectories of creative writers. Its approach, however, has not been comprehensive. Although the number of authors and perspectives in this volume represents a great deal of thoughtful consideration about what we do and why we do it (especially for those in the United States), there remain several areas that deserve further discussion and analysis. Among these, the most important for the long-term vibrancy of creative writing as an academic field are the role of identity and issues of inclusivity, the discipline's position of and connection with the academy and the unfolding changes in publishing and the larger culture.

Identity and Inclusivity

The year 2015 challenged the field of creative writing like no time before, though the current discussion of identity in the field is rooted in very long-standing issues inside higher education and in the larger culture. Junot Diaz's much-mentioned article 'MFA vs. POC' appeared in April 2014. The most comprehensive overview of the goings-on to date is 'The Program Era and the Mainly White Room' by Juliana Spahr and Stephanie Young. That article discusses, among other events, the rise of the Mongrel Coalition Against Gringpo, the Kenneth Goldsmith reading of the manipulated text of an autopsy report of Michael Brown's body and the use of a Chinese classmate's name as a pseudonym by Michael Derrick Hudson. As a board member of the Association of Writers and Writing Programs, I was part of the decision to remove Vanessa Place, a conceptual artist among whose projects is tweeting the copyrighted text of *Gone With the Wind* and a connected Facebook page featuring images of Mammy, from the conference subcommittee charged with evaluating panel proposals for the 2016 conference.

As Spahr and Young point out, a lot of frustration has been building around issues of identity, and a lot of factors have been working against inclusivity. Their article's scope is sweeping, looking at urban gentrification, shifts in student loan programs and the rise of contingent academic positions as all contributing to the perpetuation of the white room of creative writing. They also ran a lot of numbers, a striking example of which is that only 18% of MFA graduates identified as other than white in 2013, up from 12% in 1995, a relatively meager increase for two decades and far below the 36% of Master's degree students overall who identified as other than white in 2013. Why in the world should creative writing, of all disciplines, lag behind when it comes to inclusivity?

As Beverly Daniel Tatum rightly asserts in '*Why Are All the Black Kids Sitting Together in the Cafeteria?*,' unchallenged personal, cultural and institutional racism results in the loss of human potential, lowered productivity and a rising tide of fear and violence in our society' (1997: 200). Although creative writing did not create racism on its own, the racism in which the field participates 'alienates us not only from others but also from ourselves and our own experiences' (1997: 200). More recently, in an interview with *The Guardian*, poet and cultural critic Claudia Rankine (2015) echoed Tatum's conclusions: 'White people feel personally responsible for racism when they should understand the problem as systemic. It is interfering as much with their lives as with the lives of people of colour.' A mainly white room – or a mainly male room, a mainly straight room, a room that is not physically accessible to all – impoverishes us all.

William Arrowsmith offers an analogy that can be helpful as we attempt move forward and create a less impoverished discipline: 'If you want to restore a Druid priesthood, you cannot do it by offering prizes for Druid-of-the-year. If you want Druids, you must grow forests' (1967: 58–59). Creative writing hasn't grown the forest well enough. We have not yet created a culture that invites, nourishes and retains a more inclusive group of individuals.

Tatum demonstrates that a variety of biases on many levels work against an inclusive community. What's striking in situations that she discusses that are akin to MFA applications and academic faculty searches is that 'the more competent the Black person is, the more likely this bias is to occur' (1997: 121), which makes long-term achievement in a field more difficult for people of color than for Whites. The higher the stakes, the greater the bias (intentional or not), so that, while a white person's accomplishments pave a smoother way, the person of color is likely to encounter as much or more racism on the higher rungs of the professional ladder. Such dynamics might explain why I was hired into a creative writing program consisting of three white male faculty, all of whom were at least 15 years older than I. Seven years later, two out of seven of us in tenure lines are women; the other woman is from Argentina, where she spent two months as a political prisoner. My students are, by and large, white; I have one person of color in my small poetry class this semester, though the Fall 2012 (latest posted demographic statistics) student population was 13% Latino, 10% Asian-American, and 2% African-American. My program, in its faculty and its students, is part of the white room that Spahr and Young investigate. As Tatum suggests, 'if making our organization a more inclusive environment is a goal, then perhaps we should have the goal reflected in our criteria so that whoever is selected can support the organization's goals' (1997: 125). Inclusivity makes for a better creative writing program and stronger literary culture and should be included in our goals.

'We like to think of ourselves as autonomous and inner-directed, that who we are and how we act is something permanently set by our genes and our temperament' (2011: 210), Malcolm Gladwell writes in *The Tipping Point*. Autonomy and individuality are deeply held American values. Originality and authorship are variations on these values; writers think of our work as integral to who we are. We tend to assume that, if we are not prejudiced as individuals, racism or sexism is not a problem in our programs or in what we write – or is a problem that will work itself out as the larger society changes rather than a problem that we can solve as individuals. Those of us with one sort of privilege or another must remember, however, as Tatum points out, one need not be to blame for prior discrimination to benefit from it anyway (1997: 9). Indeed, complacency – doing nothing to counteract systemic bias – extends impoverishment.

The NEA report on participation in the arts indicates that having a graduate degree doubles the likelihood that an individual will do creative writing (2015: 53), and more than 80% of those who had attended graduate school read a book in 2012 (2015: 68), so the composition of graduate students – across fields, not just in creative writing – tells us who is most likely to write and read. That same report also indicates that those with family incomes above $75,000 are most likely to write and those with family incomes under $20,000 are least likely to write (2015: 53). Racism, sexism and classism do affect the field of creative writing – who teaches it who studies it and who ends up writing, publishing, winning awards. That relationship between creative writing and culture works both ways. What if those of us in creative writing programs think more consciously about how the composition of our faculty, students and published writers affects the larger culture as well as the future of our discipline?

In an article in *Inside Higher Ed*, Colleen Flaherty (2014) points to the cascade effect of bias: increasing diversity of faculty is difficult without increasing diversity in graduate programs. Lack of inclusivity in our MFA and BFA/BA programs has a long-term effect on inclusivity among creative writing faculty and also who publishes and reads creative writing. In addition, Flaherty points to the tree-planting issue: 'Even trickier, experts agree, is getting more black students to stay in academe after they earn their PhDs, given climate concerns and the fact that they are also in demand elsewhere, including the much better paying corporate world. So any successful diversity plan, those experts say, will involve not only bringing more black faculty members to campus, but also address the climate issues that will influence whether they stay there.' One of the workload issues that faculty of color face (and which I've discussed with colleagues), for instance, is the heavy and often unacknowledged advising and mentorship of students of color. In addition, tools such as student evaluations – after numerous studies – are known to play into biases that include race, gender and attractiveness (for a recent general overview, see Carol Pratt's (2015) article in the *New York Times*). In other words, our focus must be on multiple aspects at once: students, faculty and the university culture.

Identity issues have long been important to me; the scholarly and creative work I've done in this area has been most focused on gender. In an article for *Legacy* in 2008, I examined gender disparity in *Poetry* magazine, major poetry awards and the Poet Laureate, and academic positions and argued that these are interrelated aspects of how gender works in creative writing. I saw the same phenomenon happening to women that Tatum outlines for Blacks, namely that sexism increases by level of achievement.

Overall, thirty-nine percent of full-time faculty are women; women hold 44.8 percent of tenure-track jobs; but only thirty-one per cent of tenured faculty are women. Male full professors outnumber female full professors across types of institutions. Doctoral institutions, more likely to house graduate creative writing programs, reveal the greatest disparity: Just nineteen percent of full professors are women. These numbers are particularly perplexing because women earn the majority of PhDs conferred, have outnumbered men in baccalaureate degrees since the early 1980s, and have consistently earned two-thirds of the English undergraduate degrees over the past forty years. (1997: 313)

Creative writing may look like a forest filled with women, but that's not quite the case.

In 2010, VIDA: Women in Literary Arts started The Count, in which volunteers 'manually, painstakingly tally the gender disparity in major literary publications and book reviews.' Focusing on prestigious venues such as the *New Yorker* and *The Paris Review*, VIDA concludes about its results, 'We were not surprised to find that men dominate the pages of venues that are known to further one's career.' VIDA's study of *The Best American* series pans out similarly, which is no surprise, since you're more likely to make it into *The Best American* if your work was published in the *New Yorker* or *The Paris Review* than in less well-funded, less well-known journals. In other words, even if women are perceived to be publishing a lot, the effect Tatum (1997) outlines exists: bias increases with achievement.

Importantly, when editors responded to VIDA's counts by saying that the publication ratio matched the submission ratio, VIDA explained why this view was problematic. In a piece called 'Why the Submissions Numbers Don't Count,' Danielle Pafunda (2015) points out that editors have control over submission guidelines and how submissions are solicited (representing an organization's goals), that women may submit at a lower rate but at higher quality because of their slower submission cycle, that male writers may benefit from socially embedded overconfidence, that no one is able to read gender blind and that every journal tends to get more good work than it can publish. Most telling, this piece suggests that blaming women for their lack of prestigious publication does not move us forward and does not contribute to a better or more vibrant literary landscape. All these assertions seem good reference points for creative writing programs and university administrators who blame the composition of the students and faculty on the applicant pool. Once again, we see that the look and vibe of the forest depends on the trees there, and the trees that thrive there depend on the environment of the forest.

Creative writing should welcome the opportunities for growth and innovation with increased inclusivity – race, gender, class, sexual identity, physical ability and so on. Where are the burgeoning English-Spanish bilingual programs that would welcome bilingual students and foster bilingual literature? If Barnes & Noble has a shelf of books in Spanish, why are some MFA students not writing in Spanish as well as in English? Some of my undergraduate students, including some Asian-American students, are studying Japanese and are interested in anime and manga, but MFA programs have been slow to respond to this form of literature and the publishing market it represents. According to the NEA report, 'Women are slightly more likely to write than men' (2015: 53). In addition, 'Women are far more likely to read books or literature than are men,' and, when men read, they are more likely to read nonfiction than are women (2015: 68). How might this information about gender help us reshape our creative writing programs to serve the current market and trends and, more importantly, create a more vibrant – larger and more wide-ranging – reading culture in the future? What if we treat diversity as a way to attract members to the community instead of a response to requests by accreditors or individuals for certain demographic compositions? What if we treat an inclusive creative writing program as part of enlarging the reading culture globally?

Gladwell's *The Tipping Point* suggests hope for a more inclusive future for creative writing. 'Look at the world around you,' he says. 'It may seem an immovable, implacable place. It is not. With the slightest push – in just the right place – it can be tipped' (2011: 211). We must find the right places to push for our efforts to make the most meaningful, swift and lasting changes. It sounds too simple to work, and possibly it is. But not pushing certainly doesn't work, and pushing without thought, focus and goals – or pushing only with a short-term or unsupported diversity quota for university faculty – is wasteful or mostly for show.

Creating group effort – instead of relying on individual good intentions – seems key to greater inclusivity. 'Once we're part of a group, we're all susceptible to peer pressure and social norms' (Gladwell, 2011: 137). This dynamic usually helps keep existing social norms in place (and limits the forest). But these influences within a group 'can play a critical role in sweeping us up in the beginnings of an epidemic' (2011: 137). Gladwell points to the preacher John Wesley as an example, but the conclusion he makes suggests a plan for creative writing: 'if you wanted to bring about a fundamental change in people's belief and behavior, a change that would persist and serve as an example to others, you needed to create a community around them, where those new beliefs could be practiced and expressed and nurtured' (2011: 137–138). That community creation sounds daunting, but he suggests, based on studies of religious movements, surprise bestselling novels and our capacity for social relationships, that 150 is the ideal number of individuals for incubating sweeping change (2011: 139). Change certainly requires more than a token hire but also far less than complete consensus to create and build momentum.

Large-scale inclusivity of creative writing requires that a social epidemic to catch on, but an epidemic starts with a group of individuals within a program and a group of programs. Because writers think of our work as integral to our individual identity and also as responding to and shaping the larger culture in which we live, it seems counter-intuitive that we are not leading the way toward greater inclusivity in our discipline, academia, publishing and society. 'Starting epidemics requires concentrating resources on a few key areas'

(Gladwell, 2011: 208). What are those keys areas in the larger discipline, in your program, in your classroom and even in your scholarly and creative work?

Creative Writing and Academia

Issues of inclusivity are not unrelated to the position of creative writing in each institution and in academia, for many of us are engaged in these discussions beyond our programs. Whether the institution really wants to do the right thing, is being pressured by its regional accrediting body or sees it as a marketing or recruiting opportunity, diversity initiatives are popping up all over academia. In 1994, the Western Association of Schools and Colleges (which we call WASC) issued a 20-page diversity statement that became part of the larger accreditation policy. The University of Southern California was one of 14 institutions that opposed the addition, arguing that WASC was overreaching its authority; it quickly instituted a diversity requirement for all students entering after 1993 'to provide undergraduate students with the background knowledge and analytical skills necessary to understand and respect differences between groups of people.' Latinos began to outnumber Whites in California in 2014; USC or my own university cannot be blind to this demographic shift, especially because the Latino median age is much younger than that of Whites. Creative writing might distinguish itself and lead the way on many campuses and in the eyes of accrediting bodies if we take inclusivity seriously in our programs – and that serves our goals for literature and culture as well.

In addition to this university-wide issue, creative writing undoubtedly will need to look closely at its place in the university and its relationship to English and the humanities, especially as our colleagues and administrators continue to talk about the so-called crisis in the humanities. Since 1970, the raw number of English majors has held relatively steady, but it has lost a lot of ground because the number of undergraduates has almost doubled, according to the National Center for Education Studies. That means that the English major is way down by percentage and, as a result, undoubtedly cut out of resources that a higher percentage of majors would garner. That's roughly the same period that undergraduate programs in creative writing proliferated from three in 1975 to 163 in 2012, according to AWP. To claim that English programs (especially in the United States) have held steady in raw numbers only because of the rise of creative writing is not a big stretch. Moreover, the annual AWP conference now draws greater attendance than the Modern Language Association conference that includes all languages, not just our literature colleagues.

It's difficult to discuss these facts with department colleagues, and, of course, literature and other courses are integral parts of creative writing curricula. There's a strong case to be made, however, that creative writing has been keeping other English programs afloat or at least ensuring that resources keep flowing into English departments. In the last seven years, while the rest of the department lost or reconfigured tenure lines, the creative writing program in which I teach increased from two to seven tenure lines (and six of us have tenure now). What does this relative strength in relation to other humanities disciplines mean for the future of creative writing? Might literary studies rethink its traditional reliance on coverage of literary periods and, instead, rebuild curricula based on conceptions of genre that align with creative writing? Might stand-alone creative writing departments become more common, for many creative writers can and do teach literature as well? If our reliance on or obligation to English departments is rethought, might interdisciplinary configurations of programs and projects – perhaps with art departments and faculty or with film schools – lead to increased strength in the academy as well as innovation in the larger culture?

If we look around at our disciplinary neighbors, we might glean some ideas to use as we shape the future of our own discipline. The visual arts offer a particularly good model for thinking about the relationship between practice and theory and between academia and creative industries. In terms of growth, however, Communication Studies offers an interesting model, with 50% more majors than English (though that depends on where journalism is housed) and an eight-fold increase since the 1970s, according to the National Center for Educational Studies. At my institution, Communication Studies has grown its major so swiftly that, despite several new tenure-line and full-time faculty, it has eliminated its minor. That's an interesting decision, one based on the knowledge that institutions often allocate resources, including tenure lines, according to distribution of majors without taking fully into account how many students a department serves in its full range of courses, including general education. To accomplish this growth, communication studies widened its scope, moving from the traditional areas of speech and debate to an array of areas relevant to careers that depend on good communication and a theoretical understanding that allows an individual to adapt to changing circumstances. While the methodology of communication studies is that of social sciences, the strategic decisions it's made to position itself in academia suggest possibilities for broader ways to define the content of creative writing, especially in the digital age and in relation to creative industries locally and globally.

All of this consideration of our discipline's place and role in the university bears on the important issue of the proliferation of MFA programs and the rise of adjuncts. Creative writing has rightly positioned the MFA as a terminal degree, which, unfortunately, leads many individuals to think that an academic teaching position is the primary goal of earning an MFA. Indeed, there exist sections of composition for many MFA-holders to teach. A report by the Modern Language Association in 2008, before we were discussing the adjunct crisis much in the United States, showed that most first-year writing courses were being taught by part-timers – 95% of sections at doctoral institutions. Even worse, these part-timers were earning lower compensation for such work than a decade earlier. The tenure-track position in creative writing is a relative rarity, especially for someone without a published book, even with an MFA.

Clearly, those of us who are concerned about the overuse of adjuncts and about the individual futures of our graduate students have an ethical responsibility to think about the role the MFA program will play in the future. Spahr and Young, in their investigations found that 6500 degrees in creative writing were awarded in 2013, up from less than a 1000 in 1985; the increase in graduate and undergraduate degrees in creative writing showed similar trajectories. If roughly 3500 individuals earn graduate degrees in creative writing each year – more graduate than undergraduate degrees in 2013 – what is the future for these new experts in our field? Since the primary goal of the MFA is writing, how do we rethink our programs in conjunction with the messages to applicants and the career possibilities for graduates? What careers, creative industries and cultural areas might our programs foster?

In addition, there are almost 3000 four-year institutions in the United States, so 163 undergraduate creative writing programs (member programs of AWP) is not a large number. Although the expansion of MFA programs may taper off, the potential for growth at the undergraduate level remains. At the same time, creative industries (also sometimes called *cultural industries*, though that term often emphasises tourism) – the term and the model that connects the arts not just with culture but with commerce that have been in place in the United Kingdom – are starting to be discussed in the United States. Founded in 1960, Americans for the Arts, for instance, has jumped on this term as part of its analysis and advocacy, and the National Endowment for the Arts is talking about creativity as a driver of the economy. Although creative writing as a field and individual creative writers may find connections to commerce and capitalism appalling, ignorance of this larger conversation does us no good. If creative writing is connected to creative industries, what risks and opportunities might our academic discipline encounter going forward? What might our undergraduate and graduate programs accomplish?

Publishing and Culture

Publishing is part of creative industries. While most of us generally agree both that one need not hold an MFA to become a published writer and also that most of our graduates will not go on to publish books, the relationship of creative writing as an academic discipline to the publishing industry cannot be denied. Faculty in creative writing are expected to publish their creative work, and, assuming that writing is the primary focus of our classes and programs, publication (and perhaps other roles in the publishing industry) is a long-term goal for many of our students, whether or not they achieve that.

In 2011, literary agent Gail Hochman gave a talk about the state of the publishing industry. I'd been a fan of Borders and sad that it had closed. But I hadn't really thought about what it meant to writers. Hochman explained that five booksellers sold more than 90% of books, and the absence of Borders left four, which wouldn't necessarily pick up the slack. She estimated that Barnes & Noble and Amazon alone sold more than 80% of midlist books that don't make it into Walmart or Target at all. In other words, a few big companies control book sales, and publishers likely produce what these outlets want to sell.

By the time I heard Hochman talk, even I had noticed that Barnes & Noble doesn't restock; if a book sells out of a store, a reader has to order a copy – and has to know to order a copy. If a book isn't on the shelf, the book lacks discoverability; like many readers, I've browsed at bookstores, then ordered from home. New books and new authors need all the discoverability they can get, but bookstores tend to support the status quo. The importance of BookScan, the Nielsen tracking system for book sales, in the way agents and publishers make decisions makes discoverability a bigger issue than in decades past. It's tough to break out as an author, and it doesn't get easier.

All this backstory is why, for instance, agents want to know what your non-existent novel is about if they like the story collection you showed them. It also goes a long way to explaining Christine Sneed's account of her own career. She published her second book in 2013 to good reviews and a cover spot on the *New York Times Book Review*. In the wake of that success and in her mid-40s, she sold her next novel and story collection to Bloomsbury, the midlist publisher of the earlier, successful book; her advance for the two-book deal was $10,000, in part because she hasn't yet earned back her larger advance on the novel that's sold more than 20,000 copies. Sneed's story is, compared with most MFA graduates, wildly successful. If her story represents success, how does knowing that shape our programs, our classes and our mentoring of students?

In addition, how might we think of our discipline as educating the agents, editors and publishers who might re-envision the publishing industry? When I finished my MFA, I landed a job as a production editor for the Entomological Society of American not because I knew meter and metaphor but because I knew the term *bluelines* from working on the student literary journal as an undergraduate. I'd learned copyediting marks in high school working on the newspaper because the newspaper was the only option for writing that was the least bit creative. I don't really know HTML, but my DOS experience as a production editor means that I understand the concept of coding, and I manage my own website using Wordpress. In fact, a writer without a website and Twitter feed is anathema to some agents and publishers, so these seemingly extraneous skills are ones our students need to be writers today as well as being transferrable to jobs not directly related to their own writing. What if we thought more seriously about the production and distribution of texts – in print and digitally – as part of creative writing in addition to the creation of texts?

The medium, in fact, is integral to the text. In her book *Writing Machines,* N. Katherine Hayles says, 'As the vibrant new field of electronic textuality flexes its muscle, it is becoming overwhelmingly clear that we can no longer afford to ignore the material basis of literary production. Materiality of the artifact can no longer be positioned as a subspecialty within literary studies [...]' (2002: 19). Though the rise of electronic texts may seem threatening to the practices of mainstream publishing and of creative writing, the book has long been a material object that we've handled, and a poetry book especially can be viewed an art object. Digital modes present opportunities for production and distribution of creative writing but also, somewhat surprisingly, re-emphasize the value of the physical book as an object.

Some creative writing programs are broadening the thinking about what constitutes creative writing to include digital modes, and that trend is likely to continue. As this new aspect of creative writing takes hold, we have the opportunity to document what we're doing and why we're doing it in a way that hasn't occurred before – to build the practice and theory together, to avoid reinventing the wheel from scratch or from lore, institution by institution. As creative writing continues to define itself, our scholarship can grow deeper and wider as well.

In many respects, the point here is that creative writing as an academic discipline feeds into literary culture more broadly. Ta-Nehisi Coates – a journalist for *The Atlantic*, a MacArthur genius grant awardee and author of *Between the World and Me* – has signed on to write the Black Panther comic books for Marvel Comics, which will likely lead to a video game and movie. Not only is this move going to garner Coates a lot of money, it also is a form of literary citizenship, a way for an acclaimed writer to shape culture. Not all of us are in a position to shape culture in large ways, but the rise of literary citizenship in our programs and classrooms is an exciting development because it works in the way Gladwell suggests an epidemic must. Literary citizenship enlarges the definition of creative writing and enlarges the influence of the discipline in and beyond the university.

Whether our students write book reviews on blogs or gather for literary readings at bookstores, their long-term habits as literary citizens will shape the larger culture in the future. Whether they write video games or read to kids at the public library, their choices going forward will have a reflexive effect on the health of our discipline. Whether or not their writing is ever published, our current students have the ability, as interconnected individuals, to cultivate the forest that is literature in years to come. What if we take this future cultivation into account as we consider our curricula now and as we assign projects in our classes and also as we consider demographics and inclusivity?

This thinking about how creative writing might shape the world may sound like disciplinary self-preservation on the one hand or full of hubris on the other. Yet art – and literature in particular because of its use of language – makes us human. Art is the demonstration of our humanity. What if we agree that, in addition to guiding our students to become better writers, we are creating a better world? What if we allow ourselves that lofty goal and make decisions about our discipline, programs, and pedagogy as if it might be achieved?

Conclusion

That these three issues – identity and inclusivity, creative writing and academia, publishing and culture – have not been adequately addressed in our scholarly work as creative writers, not in these conversation essays and not yet in other work. There's more work to be done. Let this book be an invitation for other scholars to take up where this book leaves off. Each of these three topics deserves book-length works on its own terms, and many of the conversations we've initiated or extended deserve further discussion. *What We Talk about When We Talk about Creative Writing* is designed as part of a larger conversation, one that has been emerging since creative writing became a distinct area of study in higher education, really started buzzing about 10 or so years ago and will remain boisterous many years from now. Readers, it's your responsibility to continue this discussion – in your classrooms, in your program meetings, at regional and national conferences, in the written scholarship that documents what we do and why we do it.

References

Americans for the Arts. See http://www.americansforthearts.org/by-program/reports-and-data/research-studies-publications/creative-industries (accessed 6 November 2015).
Arrowsmith, W. (1967) The future of teaching' In Calvin Bt. T. Lee (ed.) *Improving College Teaching*. Washington, DC: American Council on Education.

Association of Writers and Writing Programs (AWP) (2015) Growth in creative writing programs, 1975–2012. Association of Writers and Writing Programs. See https://www.awpwriter.org/application/public/pdf/AWP_GrowthWritingPrograms.pdf (accessed 18 October 2015).

Flaherty, C. (2014) Demanding 10 percent.' *Inside Higher Ed* 30 November. See https://www.insidehighered.com/news/2015/11/30/student-activists-want-more-black-faculty-members-how-realistic-are-some-their-goals (accessed 5 January 2016).

Gladwell, M. (2011) *The Tipping Point.* New York: Little, Brown and Company.

Hayles, N.K. (2002) *Writing Machines.* Cambridge, MA: The MIT Press.

Leahy, A. (2008) Is *Women's Poetry* Passé? A call for conversation. *Legacy* 25 (2), 311–323.

Leahy, A. (2011) Publishing: It's worse than you thought.' Facebook. 30 July 2011. See www.amleahy.com. (accessed 6 November 2015).

Modern Language Association (2008) ADE Ad Hoc Committee on Staffing. Education in the Balance: A Report on the Academic Workforce in English. New York: MLA. See https://www.mla.org/Resources/Research/Surveys-Reports-and-Other-Documents/Staffing-Salaries-and-Other-Professional-Issues/Education-in-the-Balance-A-Report-on-the-Academic-Workforce-in-English (accessed 20 July 2015).

National Center for Educational Statistics Table 322.10: Bachelor's degrees conferred by post-secondary institutions. National Center for Educational Statistics. See https://nces.ed.gov/programs/digest/d14/tables/dt14_322.10.asp (accessed 13 October 2015).

National Endowment for the Arts (2015) *A Decade of Arts Engagement.* Washington, DC: National Endowment for the Arts. See https://www.arts.gov/sites/default/files/2012-sppa-jan2015-rev.pdf (accessed 13 May 2016).

Pafunda, D. (2015) Why the submissions numbers don't matter. VIDA: Women in Literary Arts. See http://www.vidaweb.org/why-the-submissions-numbers-dont-count/ (accessed 8 November 2015).

Pratt, C. (2015) Teacher evaluations could be hurting diversity and universities. *New York Times* 16 December. See http://www.nytimes.com/roomfordebate/2015/12/16/is-it-fair-to-rate-professors-online/teacher-evaluations-could-be-hurting-faculty-diversity-at-universities (accessed 5 January 2016).

Rankine, C. (2015) Interview with Kate Kelloway. *The Guardian* 27 December. See http://www.theguardian.com/books/2015/dec/27/claudia-rankine-poet-citizen-american-lyric-feature (accessed 5 January 2016).

Sample, S.B. (1994) WASC diversity statement. *Los Angeles Times.* 9 March. See http://articles.latimes.com/1994-03-09/local/me-31709_1_higher-education-accrediting-wasc-diversity-statement (accessed 8 November 2015).

Sneed, C. (2015) Publish a book and change your life, or, well, maybe not. *The Billfold.* 24 June. See http://thebillfold.com/2015/06/publish-a-book-and-change-your-life-or-well-maybe-not/ (accessed 6 November 2015).

Spahr, J. and Young, S. The program era and the mainly white room. *Los Angeles Review of Books.* https://lareviewofbooks.org/article/the-program-era-and-the-mainly-white-room (accessed 13 May 2016).

Tatum, B.D. (1997) *'Why Are All the Black Kids Sitting Together at the Cafeteria?' and Other Conversations about Race.* New York: Basic Books.

University Profile (2012) Chapman University. See http://www.chapman.edu/about/facts-history/institutional-research/_files/info%20guides/info-guide-1213.1.pdf (accessed 5 January 2016).

VIDA: Women in Literary Arts. See http://www.vidaweb.org/the-count/ (8 November 2015).

About the Authors

Anna Leahy edited *Power and Identity in the Creative Writing Classroom: The Authority Project*, which launched the New Writing Viewpoints series, and continues to publish articles and book chapters on creative writing pedagogy and the profession. Her book *Constituents of Matter* won the Wick Poetry Prize; her most recent chapbook, *Sharp Miracles*, was published by Blue Lyra Press; and one of her essays was a Notable in the *Best American Essays 2013*. She teaches in the MFA and BFA programs at Chapman University, where she curates the Tabula Poetica reading series, edits the international journal *TAB* and directs the Office of Undergraduate Research and Creative Activity. Anna co-writes Lofty Ambitions blog. For more info, see www.amleahy.com.

James P. Blaylock is the MFA Program Director at Chapman University and has been a teacher of creative writing and composition for nearly 40 years. He is the author of 25 novels and short story collections, most recently *Beneath London* and *The Adventure of the Ring of Stones* and is one of the originators of steampunk. See www.jamespblaylock.com.

Mary Cantrell is an associate professor of English at Tulsa Community College. Her publications include 'Teaching and Evaluation: Why Bother?' in *Power and Identity in the Creative Writing Classroom*, 'Theories of Creativity and Creative Writing Pedagogy' (co-authors Mary Swander and Anna Leahy) in *The Handbook of Creative Writing* and 'Assessment as Empowerment: Grading Entry-Level Creative Writing,' in *Teaching Creative Writing*. She also contributed to the article 'Diggers in the Garden: The Habits of Mind of Creative Writers in Basic Writing Classrooms,' published in *Teaching English in the Two-Year College*.

Nicole Cooley is the author of four books, most recently *Breach* from LSU Press and *Milk Dress* from Alice James Books, and a novel. Her awards include

The Walt Whitman Award from the Academy of American Poets, A National Endowment for the Arts Fellowship and a fellowship from The American Antiquarian Society. Her work has appeared in *Poetry*, *The Paris Review* and *The Feminist Wire*, among other journals. She directs the MFA Program in Creative Writing and Literary Translation at Queens College-CUNY, where she is a professor of English.

Karen Craigo is the author of the poetry collection *No More Milk* from Sundress Publications, as well as two chapbooks. She teaches writing at Missouri State University and in the Springfield, Missouri community.

Cathy Day is the author of two books, the memoir *Comeback Season* and the story collection *The Circus in Winter*. *The Circus in Winter* was a finalist for the GLCA New Writers Award, the Great Lakes Book Award and the Story Prize and has been adapted into a musical. Cathy has been the recipient of a Beatrice, Benjamin and Richard Bader Fellowship in the Visual Arts of the Theatre from Harvard University's Houghton Library, a Tennessee Williams Scholarship from the Sewanee Writers' Conference, a Bush Artist Fellowship, a New Jersey Arts Council Grant and other university research grants. Currently, she lives in Muncie, Indiana and teaches at Ball State University, where she is Assistant Chair of Operations in the Department of English.

Douglas R. Dechow is the Digital Humanities and Sciences Librarian at Chapman University and serves as liaison to the English department. He co-authored the computer science book *SQUEAK: A Quick Trip to Objectland*, contributed to the book *Creative Writing in the Digital Age* and has presented at the Association of Writers and Writing Programs and Modern Languages Association conferences. He has held residencies at the Norman Mailer Colony, Ragdale and Dorland Mountain Arts Colony. With Anna Leahy, he co-writes Lofty Ambitions blog. His website is www.douglasdechow.com.

Dianne Donnelly is Assistant Dean of Research for the College of Arts & Sciences at the University of South Florida. She is the editor of *Does the Writing Workshop Still Work?*, author of *The Emergence of Creative Writing Studies as an Academic Discipline* and co-editor (with Graeme Harper) of *Key Issues in Creative Writing* and author of many chapters and journal articles on the subject of creative writing. She is also Associate Editor of the *New Writing Viewpoints* book series.

Sandy Feinstein has published in a variety of genres, including poetry, fiction, creative nonfiction and scholarship on medieval and early modern literature with an occasional foray into the 19th and 20th centuries. Her recent scholarship includes a co-written chapter in *Rethinking Chaucerian Beasts* and an article in *Arthuriana*. Her most recent published poem was begun while she supervised a creative writing honors thesis; she and this former student still communicate by exchanging poems in response to one another's work.

Suzanne Greenberg's novel *Lesson Plans* was chosen as a *Library Journal* Editor's Pick and was named 'One of 7 Great Books from Small Presses that are Worth Your Time' by *Reader's Digest*. Her short story collection, *Speed-Walk and Other Stories*, won the Drue Heinz Literature Prize. She's the co-author (with Lisa Glatt) of two children's novels, *Abigail Iris: The One and Only* and *Abigail Iris: The Pet Project*. Her creative work has appeared in *The Washington Post Magazine*, *Mississippi Review* and *West Branch*, among other journals. She co-wrote *Everyday Creative Writing: Panning for Gold in the Kitchen Sink*, which was published by McGraw Hill. Suzanne teaches creative writing at California State University, Long Beach, where she's a professor of English. See more at www.suzannegreenberg.com.

Kate Greenstreet is the author of *Young Tambling, The Last 4 Things* and *case sensitive*, all from Ahsahta Press. For more information, visit her site at www.kickingwind.com.

Katharine Haake's newest novel is *The Time of Quarantine*, a SPD Bestseller. She is also the author of the hybrid novel *That Water, Those Rocks* and three prior collections of short stories – the eco-fabulist *The Origin of Stars*, the *LA Times* best-selling *The Height and Depth of Everything* and the *New York Times* notable *No Reason on Earth*. Haake is a recipient of an Individual Artist's Grant from the Cultural Affairs Department of the City of Los Angeles and an Editor's Choice Award from *Cream City Review*. A regular contributor to scholarship in the theory and pedagogy of creative writing, she is the author of *What Our Speech Disrupts: Feminism and Creative Writing Studies* from NCTE and co-author, with Hans Ostrom and the late Wendy Bishop, at *Metro: Journeys in Writing Creatively*. She teaches at California State University, Northridge.

Rachel Hall's fiction and nonfiction have appeared in literary journals and anthologies such as *Crab Orchard Review*, *Water ~ Stone* and *The Bellingham Review*. She has received honors and awards from *New Letters*, *Lilith*, the Bread Loaf Writers' Conference, the Constance Saltonstall Foundation for the Arts, Ragdale and Ox-Bow. She teaches creative writing and literature at the State

University of New York at Geneseo and, in 2002, earned the Chancellor's Award for Excellence in Teaching.

Lia Halloran is a painter and photographer who has had solo exhibits in New York, Boston, Los Angeles, London and Miami. Her work is reviewed in the *New York Times*, the *New Yorker* and the *Los Angeles Times* and recently was included in the exhibition 'Haunted' at the Guggenheim in Bilbao, Spain. She is represented in New York by DCKT Contemporary and in Los Angeles by Martha Otero Gallery.

Rachel Haley Himmelheber teaches in the undergraduate Writing Department at Warren Wilson College. Her stories have appeared in journals such as *McSweeney's* and *The Lifted Brow*. Her current pedagogical projects include teaching empathy as a crucial fiction writing skill through a research-based project and teaching workshop classes that emphasize a metacognitive process so that students see workshopping as a flexible experience that they help shape.

Susan Hubbard is the author of seven books of fiction, including *The Season of Risks*; *Blue Money*, which won the Janet Heidinger Kakfa Prize; and *Walking on Ice*, which won the AWP Short Fiction Prize. Her Ethical Vampire novels from Simon & Schuster have been translated and published in more than 15 countries. Her short fiction has appeared in *TriQuarterly*, *The Mississippi Review*, *Ploughshares* and other journals. She has been a guest at Yaddo, Virginia Center for Creative Arts, Djerassi Resident Artists' Program and Cill Rialaig. Susan co-edited the anthology *100% Pure Florida Fiction*. A recipient of several teaching awards, she has taught creative writing at Syracuse University, Cornell University and Pitzer College. She served as President of the Association of Writers and Writing Programs and is a professor of English at University of Central Florida.

Tom C. Hunley is a professor of English and creative writing at Western Kentucky University, director of Steel Toe Books and lead singer and guitarist for Dr. Tom and The Cartoons. His newest books are the poetry collections *Plunk*, published by Wayne State College Press, and *The State That Springfield Is In*, from Split Lip Press. He co-edited (with Alexandria Peary) the collection *Creative Writing Pedagogies for the Twenty-First Century* from Southern Illinois University Press.

Claudine Jaenichen specializes in the relationship between design and cognition. Claudine has published in *New Writing, Parsons Journal for*

Information Mapping, Applications of Information Design, Journal of Applied Global Research, The International Journal of Interdisciplinary Social Sciences, Visual Language for Designers and *Design Principles and Practice.* Her students' work appeared in *Information Design Journal.* She is a Life Research Fellow for Communication Research Institute, Creative Director for *TAB: The Journal of Poetry and Poetics* and an executive board member of the International Institute for Information Design. See more at www.jaenichendesignstudio. com.

Nancy Kuhl is the author of *Pine to Sound, Suspend, The Wife of the Left Hand* and the chapbooks *Little Winter Theater, The Nocturnal Factory* and *In the Arbor.* She is co-editor of Phylum Press, a small poetry publisher, which has published more than 20 poetry chapbooks and pamphlets. Nancy is Curator of Poetry of the Yale Collection of American Literature at the Beinecke Rare Book and Manuscript Library at Yale University; she is the author of several exhibition catalogs, including *Intimate Circles: American Women in the Arts.* Additional information and examples of Nancy's work can be found online: www.phylumpress.com/nancykuhl.htm.

Argie Manolis is Coordinator of Community Engagement at the University of Minnesota, Morris, a small, rural, public liberal arts college where she has worked for 15 years. She teaches creative writing as a service-learning course as part of her appointment.

Tim Mayers is the author of *(Re)Writing Craft: Composition, Creative Writing, and the Future of English Studies* and numerous articles on creative writing pedagogy and theory. His novel manuscript, *Intelligence Manifesto,* won the 2007 Paradigm Prize. He is an associate professor of English at Millersville University, where he teaches courses in composition, creative writing and the disciplinary histories of English studies.

Dinty W. Moore is author of *Dear Mister Essay Writer Guy: Advice and Confessions on Writing, Love, and Cannibals* as well as the memoir *Between Panic & Desire,* a Grub Street Book Award winner. A professor of nonfiction writing at Ohio University, Moore lives in Athens, Ohio, where he also gardens.

Jan Osborn is an assistant professor in the Department of English at Chapman University, where she teaches in the Rhetoric and Writing Studies and Humanomics programs. Her book *Community Colleges and First-Generation Students: Academic Discourse in the Writing Classroom* was published by Palgrave. She has taught English in secondary public schools in Los Angeles and

Orange counties, in community colleges in Michigan and California and at State Prison Southern Michigan. She is the director of the Chapman University/Orange High School Literacies Partnership and the Orange County Literary Society Collaborative. Her scholarship focuses on discourse analysis and multilingual literacies.

Leslie Pietrzyk's collection of unconventionally linked short stories, *This Angel on My Chest*, was awarded the Drue Heinz Literature Prize and was published by University of Pittsburgh Press. She is the author of two novels, *Pears on a Willow Tree* from Avon and *A Year and a Day* from William Morrow. Her short fiction and essays have appeared in many journals and magazines, including *Gettysburg Review, Iowa Review, The Sun, Shenandoah, New England Review* and *The Washington Post Magazine*. She teaches fiction in the MA writing program at Johns Hopkins University and is a member of the core faculty of the low-residency MFA program at Converse College. See www. lesliepietrzyk.com.

Audrey Petty is the editor of *High Rise Stories: Voices from Chicago Public Housing*, published in McSweeney's Voice of Witness series. Audrey's stories and poems appear in journals such as *African American Review, Crab Orchard Review, StoryQuarterly* and *Callaloo*. Her non-fiction appears in *Saveur, ColorLines, The Southern Review, Oxford American, Cornbread Nation 4, Gravy* and the *Best Food Writing* anthology. Audrey taught at the University of Illinois and Knox College and in the Education Justice Project, Project FYSH (Foster Youth Seen and Heard) and the Continuing Studies programs at University of Wisconsin-Madison and Northwestern University. She now teaches for the Clemente Humanities Program in Chicago.

Julie Platt is a hybrid scholar who researches composition and creative writing, especially in digital contexts. Her creative work, critical work and reviews have appeared in such publications as *Computers and Composition, Kairos, Peitho, Birdfeast, Moon City Review, Barn Owl Review, Weave* and others. She is the author of the poetry chapbook *In the Kingdom of My Familiar* from Hyacinth Girl Press. She teaches writing and directs the Center for Writing and Communication at the University of Arkansas at Monticello.

Brent Royster's poems have been published in *Center: A Journal of the Literary Arts, Cimarron Review, Green Mountains Review, Iron Horse Literary Review, Mochila Review, North American Review, Quarterly West, South Carolina Review* and other notable journals. He teaches at Central Texas College.

James Ryan is a PhD candidate in composition and rhetoric at University of Wisconsin-Madison. His research interests include creative writing pedagogy, creative process, analog game design, meaningful gamification and first-year writing instruction. He is in the process of launching an online, open-access, peer-reviewed journal that will focus on creative writing theory and pedagogy.

Mary Swander taught creative writing for 35 years to everyone from kindergarteners to graduate students to senior citizens in assisted living. She is a widely published writer in poetry, nonfiction, and drama, most recently the poetry collection *Girls on the Roof*. She has contributed to collections about creative writing pedagogy and the profession.

Larissa Szporluk is the author of five books of poetry, including *Traffic with Macbeth* from Tupelo Press. Willow Springs Editions published her chapbook *Startle Pattern*. She was a recipient of a Guggenheim Fellowship and teaches at Bowling Green State University.

Stephanie Vanderslice is a writing-life blogger for *The Huffington Post*. Her numerous scholarly essays on the teaching of creative writing have been published in such publications as *College English* (which she guest-edited with Kelly Ritter in 2008), *College Composition, and Communication* and *New Writing*. She has published three books: *Can It Really Be Taught?: Resisting Lore in Creative Writing Pedagogy*; *Teaching Creative Writing to Undergraduates: A Guide and Sourcebook* (with Kelly Ritter); and *Rethinking Creative Writing*. Her fiction and nonfiction appear in many journals and online publications. In 2012, she was named CASE U.S. Professor of the Year for the state of Arkansas; in 2009, she was named ACTELA College English Teacher of the Year.

Amy Sage Webb directs the creative writing program and teaches creative writing, literature, literary editing and pedagogy at Emporia State University, where she was named Roe R. Cross Distinguished Professor. She is author of the short fiction collection, Save Your Own Life (Woodley Press, 2012). She is also a consulting pedagogy specialist for Antioch University, Los Angeles.